Managerial Fraud

I dedicate this book to my adoptive Mum, Margaret Finch. Without her love and caring I really wonder where I would be.

Managerial Fraud

Executive Impression Management, Beyond Red Flags

TERRY A. SHERIDAN

Routledge
Taylor & Francis Group
LONDON AND NEW YORK

First published 2014 by Ashgate Publishing

2 Park Square, Milton Park, Abingdon, Oxfordshire OX14 4RN
52 Vanderbilt Avenue, New York, NY 10017

Routledge is an imprint of the Taylor & Francis Group, an informa business

First issued in paperback 2020

Gower Applied Business Research
Our programme provides leaders, practitioners, scholars and researchers with thought provoking, cutting edge books that combine conceptual insights, interdisciplinary rigour and practical relevance in key areas of business and management.

British Library Cataloguing in Publication Data
A catalogue record for this book is available from the British Library

Library of Congress Cataloging-in-Publication Data
Sheridan, Terry A.
Managerial fraud : executive impression management, beyond red flags / by Terry A. Sheridan.
pages cm
Includes bibliographical references and index.
ISBN 978-1-4724-1338-3 (hardback) -- ISBN 978-1-4724-1339-0 (ebook) -- ISBN 978-1-4724-1340-6 (epub) 1. Employee crimes--Prevention. 2. Executives--Psychology. 3. Management--Moral and ethical aspects. 4. Fraud--Prevention. 5. Personnel management. I. Title.
HF5549.5.E43S53 2014
658.4'73--dc23

2014011973

ISBN 13: 978-1-4724-1338-3 (hbk)
ISBN 13: 978-0-367-66919-5 (pbk)

Contents

List of Figures

List of Tables

Preface

I have used the newly discovered Executive Impression Management typology to apply to all managers, whether executives, senior managers, junior managers or supervisors. This is because in my research and experience the role is not substantively different between levels of the management hierarchy. As the budget under direct control increases so does the number of subordinates increase and correspondingly, as does the responsibility. Management requires administration of resources both human and otherwise.

Employee roles are quite different. These are usually task-focused and lack the supervisory and husbandry component of management. At this stage it cannot be assumed that Executive Impression Management applies to all individuals in the workplace. However, my intuition leads me to believe that this may be true of other roles and also in different relationships other than work. This book concentrates on managers and their relationship with their co-workers and the foundation of their connection.

The newly found knowledge could not have emerged if the respondents had refused to be interviewed. I am enormously grateful for their courage and willingness to understand what had happened to them. Each person gave me their story, without which the investigation could not take place.

I have many people to thank for their assistance in giving me time, space and encouragement to write this book, these include Commissioning Editors Kristina Abbotts and Martin West and the publishing team at Gower. Also my family who suddenly had to manage with me not being around as much. My thanks go to my support crew in Bali, Jacky, Made, Padmi, Louise and Ross who have helped me to deal with the pressure of writing in paradise. Finally my husband who put up with my absences always encouraging me to write this book because it needs to be 'out there'.

Chapter 1

Introduction

A desperate man was sitting opposite me in a job interview. He wasn't the most attractive individual I had seen, he wasn't wearing the latest designer suit and his shoes were well worn. His smile was fleeting, his words gushed out about how he badly needed the job of locum manager and I felt he would say anything I wanted to hear in order to get a few months salary into his bank account and forestall the bank's threatened foreclosure of his home mortgage. He looked so desperate that I felt he could do anything to get his hands on some money. He was one of well over 200 managers who came to see me when I had advertised a position as a locum manager for a small business whose owner needed a break. His father was dying and he wanted to spend quality time with him before he passed away.

I quickly assessed this manager as a no-hoper. His desperation was almost annoying to me and had the air of being dangerous. What had happened was that I interviewed a far nicer individual that I had seen earlier that day. I stalled on making the decision because something about the selection I was about to make was worrying me intensely. Should I give the locum job to the desperate interviewee or the pleasant tall rather good-looking man who looked like a film star? After all, the résumé of the latter was outstanding, he lived in an expensive suburb, had many connections through his clubs and sports activities. His references were full of hyperbole about how wonderful a manager he was. Despite this, nagging away at the back of my mind was the question: 'But can I trust him?' He was almost too good to be true. I felt that the harassed-looking individual would do a reasonable assignment, his story of being retrenched was true and he was desperately trying to keep his family together and his kids at school. I also knew that the 'movie star' would normally secure any job he put his mind to. But could I trust him? And the answer to that question a few years later after my research was completed is now 'Actually no'. In fact I could not trust either of them, as both were using the device of a subtle social phenomenon called impression management to persuade me to hire them and I had not yet learned the nuances to look for.

It seldom occurs to us that a respectable senior manager could be a thief. This is because we trust such individuals to look after organisations, but how do we know that they won't run off with the money? This question led me on an interesting journey through many disciplines to find out if it was possible to detect a fraudster before they are hired. I am pleased to report that through my research I have found indicators that will work with any manager to assess if they can be trusted or not and you too can apply these indicators in the workplace.

There are two types of fraudster managers: the arrogant kind and the very different likeable ones. These two types are responsible for stealing billions of dollars from organisations around the world. Most of that money will be frittered or hidden away with only a small percentage returned. Through my research I found that these two kinds of managers ruin organisations and not only that, they wreck people's lives.

Unbelievably, these perpetrators receive softer punishments than others who steal similar amounts. That is when, if ever, they are caught. Some are quietly asked to resign due to the shame such fraud creates for their employer. Of those that come to light, some of them are even admired and do rounds of public speaking, while others will want to commit suicide. Not much research has been undertaken about the psychopathy or mental strain that underlies such harmful actions and their effect on others. The popular view is that managerial fraud is a white-collar crime and therefore is less damaging than, say, organised criminal gangs or serial murderers. Yet they wreak havoc wherever they are found.

In fact, I found that the destruction created by managerial fraud is immense with regard to the actual financial cost, and immeasurable for the psychological cost. In my research I discovered that the smaller the business, the greater the chance that the company would be put under severe financial threat by managerial fraud, in some cases to the point of liquidation. Even in larger public companies, liquidation may also be a threat. Share prices can plummet with all of the resounding effects of lowered confidence, job loss, contraction of activity and future development. Estimates have been made about the cost of this type of fraud, but as yet there is no real indicator of the true cost of managerial fraud nationally or globally.

This is partly due to the different labels applied to this crime in diverse jurisdictions and partly to the fact that managerial fraud is aggregated in job-related terms such as 'occupational fraud' or 'employee theft'. This is despite the fact that managers are more likely to steal more and are able to hide their activities longer than the average employee.[1] The whole problem seems to be ignored. It is treated like a bit of corporate bad luck. Corporations appear to want it hushed up and the academic literature virtually ignores managerial fraud. Apart from a headline or two in the media, it is soon forgotten as being no longer newsworthy.

Although I am not trained in legal or police work I was astonished at how much this problem is ignored. When I heard the stories from people who had worked with these fraudulent managers, my heart went out to them. It ruined their families, their future became bleak and some needed therapeutic counselling and even felt suicidal. What was worse was that when I started to look into this apparent lack of knowledge on the subject I found that there was virtually no scholarly work available. If those afflicted by fraud were hit by some physical disease there would be associations, back-up support and even government funding for looking at the causes and what can be done to ameliorate and prevent this scourge on society. But for managerial fraud there is nothing. There is only a large black hole of ignorance.

The closest I thought I came to being touched by managerial fraud was by a very pleasant man on a management team of which I was chair, overseeing federal government funding for local projects. He perpetrated the fraud some months after I left, but I remember distinctly the sense of shame, the guilt of having brought him in to the team and the dark discussions that went on afterwards. Looking back I can see he was one of the nice fraudsters. The amount he stole was small and if I remember rightly he served a few months in a minimum-security prison. He was a natural with people but lost his career and everything else for stealing that money. I lost touch with that organisation and don't know what happened to him or the individuals within it. From what I know now, the team must have been devastated and all trust within the teams' relationships would have been severely tested.

The other type of fraudster – the arrogant type – was a near miss for me personally, and absolutely terrible for the organisation concerned. I was on the selection panel and voted to have this applicant in a new role that was considered to be groundbreaking in its day. There is no proof of fraud, but it was alleged that he was stealing from his programme budget. He was destructive and nearly broke the organisation, yet he was never charged or ended up in jail:

1 Association of Certified Fraud Examiners. 2008. *Fraud check up*. Austin, TX: Association of Certified Fraud Examiners Inc.

he was removed from his position swiftly and quietly. However, I pity the next corporate victims on his list.

The problem with both of these types is that at the time of meeting you will be utterly convinced that they are the right person for the job. You will believe everything that they say and feel at ease knowing that at last the right person is in the role. I found that they were able to use sincerity and get me to trust them so easily that when I found out about both of them I had a horrible sense of being very gullible. Falling for two fraudsters is like Oscar Wilde's Lady Bracknell's line about losing parents: 'To lose one parent, Mr. Worthing, may be regarded as a misfortune. To lose both looks like carelessness.' Recruiting one fraudster is unfortunate, there is no doubt about it. But to come across two? I must be extremely gullible. This is not a good feeling to experience and lowers your sense of self-esteem to be hoodwinked like that.

Reaching further back into my memory the first time I ever came across such a person was when I was a young 18-year-old working as a retail assistant in a stationery and office equipment shop. A tall good-looking man came in and bought a very expensive pen. He pulled out his cheque book wrote the cheque, and presented his ID. I quickly glanced at everything, popped the cheque into the cash register and proceeded to wrap up the gold pen with his receipt. He stopped me and asked me: 'Did you check my signature?' I said yes, and being such a naive young woman blushed from head to toe and gave him the package. A few days later we heard the dreadful news that the cheque was a forgery. I owned up immediately to serving him and was informed by a rather irate employer that the purchaser had stolen the cheque book and ID cards. I can distinctly remember the shame of being duped, not only that, he went out of his way to humiliate me by forcing me to check his cleverly written forged signature – which he needn't have done. That really hurt. But it isn't anywhere as near the hurt, confusion and sense of betrayal that co-workers have when a managerial fraudster deludes them for months on end, if not years.

In order for me to talk about managerial fraud I have to deal with myths that are often said to be the mark of a fraudster. Most people will say that they can spot a fraudster. People rely on their intuition and that is what I did too. But before my discovery there was no definitive way of determining if a manager is a fraudster before being hired. Discrepancies in financial reports can be talked away, even large ones. Several noted fraudsters have in fact done this with their auditors, for instance, Nick Leeson with Barings Bank and Jeff Skilling with Enron. Current methodologies for detecting and preventing fraud are dangerous because they give a false sense of security to boards of directors and shareholders, or in the case of small businesses, their owners.

At best there are selective descriptive studies prepared by interested parties such as the Association of Certified Fraud Examiners and the 'Big Four' accountancy firms with their client companies. Usually the presentation of these summary statistics is based upon surveys or case studies from accountancy clients or from fraud investigators themselves. Neither descriptive format is helpful in understanding the possibility of fraud in an organisation nor who would be the likely perpetrators.

Aggregate summaries provide a list of characteristics such as: the perpetrator is likely to be in the 35–50 age group, male, employed with the company for a few years and so on. These characteristics can be applied to most managers. This is because we are told that almost all managers are in an older age group (apart from some notable industries such as information technology, for instance) and have been in the organisation some time to know the business enough to be promoted. Managerial fraud tends to be perpetrated by males, in part due to the fact that senior managerial hierarchies are mostly comprised of males, with women occupying lower-status managerial and supervisory positions. In fact most observers are shocked when a managerial fraudster is a woman.

This summary was totally unhelpful to me as a recruiter who needed to make an accurate selection of a manager who could be trusted enough not to defraud a business while the owner was absent. This was the task that I faced when I commenced a unique service in Australia of supplying managers to small business owners who would like, or need, to take a break from their business. Almost all of my managerial locums fit the aggregate profile and I intuitively felt that one or two of those applying for locum positions were probably 'dodgy' but apart from a gut feeling, I had no evidence to delete them from the list of candidates. I was searching for evidence that indicated a strong possibility of fraud and to weed them out as soon as possible in order to protect my clients. Upon reflection, I am surprised that no one else has bothered to do this, especially considering the enormous costly results.

Having been a small business owner myself, I knew that there were no breaks from the constant overload of work. I actually used to relish public holidays as a chance to catch up on the bookkeeping without the phone constantly ringing off the hook. Unfortunately I did not take those holidays to be with my children; they had to adjust to life with a working mother who was not there some of the time. Looking back now I regret using those holidays for work but there seemed to be no other option. We were fortunate enough to take a break for a few days in between Christmas and New Year – about a week. I could not even have that when I managed my own retail business. For years at a time I did not have a holiday, and I knew that this was endangering my health. Ideally I needed a locum to run my business while I was away.

With such experiences behind me, I knew I had to find trustworthy candidates who could be reliable enough to run a business on their own. Due to my background in social science I knew that psychometric testing relies on self-awareness, honesty and the confidence of self-disclosure by a candidate. Such qualities are missing in a liar. Even lie detector-testing gives false negatives, particularly with psychopathic individuals devoid of empathy, who have no physiological response to telling untruths.

A responsible recruiter is reduced to calling up referees provided by the candidate and perhaps a call to a previous employer. In either case, the truth may be withheld or distorted by the referee for a number of reasons such as friendship, referees who have had little to do with the candidate but look impressive to others, their own personal motives, or even retribution. Employers are after all human beings with all the foibles thereof, and therefore referee testing can be equally fallible as other tests.

Traditionally this problem from a recruitment company's perspective is usually solved with the provision of a new candidate if the selected manager turns out to be a dud within a stated period of time, say six months. Executive recruiters pride themselves on their selection practices, but the reality is that they cannot provide any more of a reassurance than a small business owner working on gut feelings as to whether the candidate is honest or not.[2] Many large companies rely on executive recruiters to find suitable candidates for their prestigious positions. The presentation and selection process is one that is revered by lower-status recruitment companies, but in fact, they make mistakes too, which is reflected in a relatively high turnover of their candidates. The recruitment industry looks at past behaviour to endorse future behaviour. But what if the past was a fabrication? And even proven past behaviour of exemplary managers does not predict the possibility of detonating aberrant fraudulent behaviour, which will be hidden from colleagues.

2 Bartram, D. 2004. Assessment in organizations. *Applied Psychology: An International Review* 53 (2): 237–259.

However, the vexing question remained. How can dishonest managerial candidates be weeded out in the selection process? This was the problem that I set about resolving in my research. The results were the development of a typology of how senior managers' impression management can provide clues to what is really going on underneath that cool 'professional' exterior that we seek in order to lead organisations.

Starting as a complete outsider, my understanding of fraud led to a long journey through criminology, psychology, sociology and even economics. Most crime research centers on two aspects of study: looking at the criminals themselves, or looking at the underlying pathology or the social causes of such crimes. Both points of view have developed their own myths. White-collar crime researchers in particular have little to go on and tend to draw on the psychological literature for explanations. While this has filled some gaps, it is not enough from a recruitment perspective to knock back an applicant. Being told that the candidate scored high in say, narcissism, would create all sorts of legal problems if denied the opportunity of employment on that basis. I suspect that my former colleagues in the recruitment industry either keep quiet or lied to a pressing but unsuccessful applicant.

My study and its results are unique because it did not rely on the fraudsters' own information, or the search for the likelihood of psychological traits and so on. Instead I focused on how could fraudster managers pull the wool over their co-workers eyes to not only steal large amounts of money but also manage to do this over some considerable amount of time. In my view, it pointed to something going wrong within the manager–organisation relationship itself, but I did not know how or why. Now I have the answers and wish to share this with the wider community. Readers are most unlikely to go to my original thesis, which is available online. However, I do not recommend it as it is long and rather boring to read. Instead I prefer to give a presentation of what I did and how, so that a professional layman can follow, and hopefully appreciate the insights that this unique study produced.

Research Techniques that Create Myths

Without any training in fraud research, I undertook an enquiry that was uncontaminated by previous theorising and teaching. As I have a fondness for using research techniques that explore human interaction I used a qualitative methodology approach, which fits in with my perspective of the world. This departure from 'normal' business research methodology is based on many years experience with quantitative research and its shortcomings. This knowledge gave me the certainty that the qualitative method would allow previously unknown insights to emerge, if there were any to draw out.

For a short time in my varied career, I actually taught master's degree students quantitative methodology and used it extensively myself. However, I later became disillusioned with its limitations for social science. Millions of studies rely upon hypothesis testing, and unless the whole population is under study, for instance all the worlds' business managers were engaged in the study, the results are in the strictest sense unusable to predict behaviour of others, say project managers. Furthermore, not all but much of the academic research in management use business students, and the study is flawed by this sample of respondents. For instance, imagine a study concludes that management's decision-making process is X,Y and Z based on the business school students' results in a laboratory setting. Then in the journal article this finding declares that this will to some degree of probability apply to all managerial decision makers. Unfortunately, despite its authoritative tone, the inference is invalid. The study only tells us the results from that particular group of business students. It cannot be said that other groups such as managers in general will behave similarly and will use such a process. Study after study is flawed but academic journals publish because the preference (some say prejudice) in business research has a bias to the quantitative. It is only in recent times, say the last decade or so, that we have seen the growth of qualitative management research, and it was this methodology that led to my discovery. I certainly would not have found this out by hypothesis testing despite the most sophisticated and complex statistical analyses that could be applied. It is a bit like throwing a drowning man lifebelts made of various materials such as stone, metal, sponge and so on. Only a certain type of lifebelt will work, one that floats, but meanwhile, many people would have died because the wrong things have been thrown to save them. If we ask the drowning man what will save him, I am sure that an immediate description will be given – something that does not sink and his safety is assured.

I recall feeling like a pioneer when I first learnt qualitative research procedures. I had to visit the health faculty at my university to learn about this methodology as it was unavailable in my business school. Sitting in classes with nurses and health workers was a brilliant introduction to one of the outstanding qualitative researchers of her day, Vera Iruita. She gave insights into how to use this novel way of approaching information. Even today there is a mass of qualitative work available in health and nursing literature, which is much larger than say those studies in leadership. Ken Parry[3] was another one of the pioneers and a student of Vera's and even though I have not met him, I have read most of his articles and felt encouraged by the application to management practice.

As with all qualitative research, I need to emphasis that my research findings are from an exploratory study, rather than a definitive testing of hypotheses. I cannot say absolutely that the rest of the population of the world's managers share the same typology of executive impression management, but I can say that it is extremely likely to be the case. I discovered a process which had been unseen before because no one has looked at the problem of managerial fraud in this manner. Because of this, I also accidentally uncovered a typology that fits with managers who do not defraud their companies, but use their organisations to service their own needs. This full typology is given further detail in another book.

THE MYTH OF RATIONALITY IN SOCIAL SCIENCE

Social science is not absolute and anyone that argues with that is being disingenuous. We can measure, infer and predict in the natural sciences, but we cannot do the same with people. Why? Because people are not rational. I give my apologies to the logical-positivists who cling to the idea that people make rational decisions. The 'science' of economics relies totally on this premise as do political science and psychology – they adapt aberrations from rationality as 'rationalised' character traits and so on.

The truth is that people do not follow strict physical laws. For example, I can say with a high degree of certainty that the sun will rise tomorrow. However, I cannot say with the same level of certainty that a particular manager will go to work tomorrow. It is likely, yes, even probable, but it is not as likely and probable as the sun rising. The sun doesn't fall sick, have accidents or become diverted or distracted by family crises into not rising at dawn. However, managers do.

I have had over 20 years experience in social science research and I can say that hypothesis testing is generally ineffective, unless using a census type of inquiry, which covers 100 per cent of the group in question. This is because the premise of all inferential statistics is that the respondents are from a truly

3 Parry, K. W. 1998. Grounded theory and social process: a new direction for leadership research. *The Leadership Quarterly* 9 (1): 85–105.

random group. It is impossible to get a random group of managers, or for that matter, fraudsters. Nonetheless we are able to say that there is good reason to believe that the findings that came out of my investigation are fairly accurate as there were certain conditions to the data analysis that were strictly adhered to, namely there was no perceived theory beforehand. Being a novice to fraud was actually a good thing. In addition, there was total reliance on the data collection and the deconstruction of the data into single units of meaning, which were then synthesised into categories, which formed the results. This methodology ensures that any other qualitative researcher will produce the same result.

I liken this process of disaggregation and reformation of data to that of bath bubbles. Everyone who has had a bubble bath knows that the bubbles never stay the same for any length of time, no matter how much bubble bath liquid is added. Each unit of meaning is a tiny bubble, and over time, due to the properties of water, surface tension and surfactants, the individual bubbles gradually join together and form larger and larger bubbles. Fortunately the qualitative process works better than a bathtub and gradually the results emerge from the units of data intact.

The recombination of these larger 'bubbles' of data has resulted in a taxonomy that experienced fraud investigators (usually police, ex-detectives, but some from legal or even accounting backgrounds) have agreed that it makes sense of what is a very messy world of occupational fraud. My company for managerial employment screening and reviewing internal promotions now uses the typology. Banks and financial institutions are particularly prone to one type of fraudster manager, small businesses to another. With the writing of this book, I hope that greater awareness and use of this typology will help ameliorate the impact of these fraudsters on vulnerable organisations and their staff.

When did Fraud Start?

The use of dishonesty to obtain goods and money has been with us since the beginning of civilisation. Many would pinpoint the beginnings of fraud with the Neolithic agrarian revolution, when growing grain crops and rearing animals replaced the hunting and gathering nomadic lifestyle. This was approximately 8,000 years ago. Ancient Mesopotamian stone tablets have been found which are mostly accounting ledgers for bushels of grain, numbers of animals and so on. And even today as people are drawn to cities to find work, they share the same purpose of their Neolithic ancestors, which is to make money for themselves by learning a craft to sell, or working for other people.

To not earn money became the road to starvation once the agrarian revolution began because it was unstoppable; people were locked in. It was impossible for many to return to their former nomadic lifestyle. It is hard for Westerners to understand that city life is actually a new and alien lifestyle to us *Homo sapiens*. Depending on where you live in the developed world our population has only been practicing it for several thousand years. Before, we lived off the land, bypassing the need for managers because the link with effort was direct to our food and shelter.

Managers only came into being when dominant individuals, for instance kings, elders and so on accumulated excess food for their needs and it needed to be supervised, gathered, distributed and sold. The plots of land under agriculture grew larger as people were dispossessed of their own land due to non-payment of debts to the local king or others. Slavery became rife. Managers were brought in and were trusted to look after their bosses' requirements and estates. Interestingly, they were not there to look after the community.

With the co-optation of managers by the ruling elites to look after their resources, the managers realised which side of their bread was buttered and became loyal servants to whomever was paying them. No doubt a few would have risked death to gather resources for their own needs, but more likely and less risky would have been making money on the side, for instance bribery and corruption, which emerged as a managerial behaviour. This 'on the side' money-making activity by managers is prevalent in the third world today. We who live in industrialised nations consider that we are above bribery and corruption. Of course the reality is that we are not, and as some managers have a predilection for obtaining more resources than otherwise possible, we have our trust in the stewardship of organisations broken time and time again. Corruption is beyond the scope of this book, but it follows that managerial fraud has been around for a very long time. Corruption can only occur when one person is considered more powerful than another. Thus managers became a prime target to appease for personal gain.

It is the installation and co-opting of managers which gives conflict theorists some substantiation of why managers get off lightly compared to other criminals: they align themselves today with powerful elites. This point we will come back to later, but it is very interesting that the first written account of managerial fraud was through the alignment of a manager with his boss.

The man concerned was Captain Xenothemis, who worked for a Greek shipping magnate who wanted to sink a ship 'full of cargo' and make a claim on his insurers. Xenothemis was obliged to sink his ship once they were out of port. This now familiar insurance scam is cited as one of the first written incidents of managerial fraud in 360BC.[4] Unfortunately for Xenothemis, who was to receive part of the proceeds of a claim for the loss of the insured cargo, there were passengers on board who got wind of the swindle. Realising that their own lives were to be risked in the scheduled sinking out at sea, they formed a civilian mutiny and seized control of the ship. They steered back to the home port and brought Xenothemis to justice. It is not known what happened to Xenothemis himself.[5] However, extorting money in this instance was viewed as theft and Xenothemis in his role of executive was deemed in breach of his office. Today this is a common comment made by judges in their sentencing of white-collar criminals.

Company fraud increased markedly upon the implementation of what is known as double ledger bookkeeping in the fifteenth century. This was possibly because the new system was not well understood by laymen. It soon became the prerogative of the accounting staff, some of whom were avaricious and saw their chance of making money for themselves by manipulating the figures. Small business owners today suffer from a similar problem of 'expert' accounting managers whom they are forced to trust: they can be hypnotised by the jargon of an unscrupulous manager. While there is a lobby of forensic accountants who wish to make business controls more and more complex, there seems to be a good argument for small business to actually keep things simple so that the owners can understand immediately their financial situation.

A good example of this is seen in a report released by the Association of Certified Fraud Examiners (ACFE)[6] stating that small businesses were vulnerable due to the lack of anti-fraud controls. While it may be true that they do not have the controls in place as with larger companies, I would argue that most small businesses do not need these expensive devices. The secret for them is to be able to understand basic financial reports.[7] There is little rocket science attached to a simple monthly profit and loss sheet with lists of debtors

4 Johnstone, P. 1998. Serious white collar fraud: historical and contemporary perspectives. *Crime Law and Social Change* 30 (2): 107–130.

5 Calhoun, G. M. 1924. The jurisprudence of the Greek city. *Columbia Law Review* 24 (2): 154–171.

6 Association of Certified Fraud Examiners. 2010. *Report to the nations on occupational fraud and abuse*. Austin TX: Association of Certified Fraud Examiners Inc.

7 Russell, Roger. 2002. Small businesses still see CPA as most trusted advisor. *Accounting Today* 16 (12): 5–7.

and creditors both paid and outstanding. Similarly a cash flow can be drawn up, and an appreciation of what remains as profit rather than money that is owed to others can be understood easily.

Unfortunately, small businesses are easy pickings for the educated manager who needs extra income by fraud. The ACFE go on to report that managers, together with owner-managers, who stole from their employer company were nine times as costly as employee frauds and found to be much more difficult to detect. In addition, they estimate a global loss of US$2.9 trillion due to company fraud. The ACFE Report also declares that in the US, their investigators said that one quarter of the reported frauds were in excess of a million dollars, with an average slow rate of detection for an alarming average of 18 months.

Recent Fraud Statistics

Using the latest reports, of which there are not many, I found that in 2003, Ernst and Young noted that there is widespread fraud across the globe. Africa had the highest incidence of fraud cases prosecuted in the world.[8] It would seem true to many who use the Internet that Africa is the home of corruption, with the scams that emanate from Nigeria being the most notorious example. However, the estimate of the extent of fraud in the business sector in the UK alone was estimated at £3.76 billion.[9] These UK costs are indicative rather than actual and there would also have to be approximately added another £1 billion to the cost of pursuing criminals and taking them to court. Fraud is estimated to have struck almost half of Australian and New Zealand businesses.[10] From their survey of 420 respondents, largely their own clients, which again would be larger organisations, the estimated cost of the surveyed frauds was over A$300 million, with an average of one-and-a-half million dollars per fraud. Disturbingly their respondents listed over 200,000 separate fraud incidents in nearly half of the reporting companies.

Fraud is not confined to the private sector. An interesting survey by BDO International reported that one-sixth of the respondent non-profit

8 Ernst and Young. 2003. *Fraud, the unmanaged risk, 8th global survey*, edited by M. Savage. Ernst and Young Johannesburg South Africa: Ernst and Young

9 Levi, M., J. Burrows, M. H. Fleming, and K. Matthews. 2007. *The nature, extent and economic impact of fraud in the UK*. London: Association of Chief Police Officers.

10 KPMG Forensic. 2009. *Fraud survey 2008*. Sydney: KPMG. www.kpmg.com.au (accessed 18 March 2009).

organisations reported fraud.[11] It was found mostly in health and social services. Cash theft and kickbacks were the most common type of fraud, and the average value was about A$50 thousand. The majority of respondents in the non-profit organisations said that they did not report the fraud to the police and interestingly one-fifth of the organisations did not actually terminate the employment of the perpetrator. In line with the private sector, nearly one-third of frauds were committed by managers and accounting staff. Tip-offs accounted for 25 per cent of the frauds being discovered in the non-profit organisations. In addition, the frauds again continue for a long time, with 14 months on average. Remarkably, the average fraud that was committed to provide funds for gambling was three-quarters larger than the average fraud for other purposes.

Fraud cost Australia alone an estimated A$3.5 billion in 2002.[12] And it hits small businesses more than employee theft of stock, armed and unarmed robberies and vandalism put together. Those authors also noted that with the increase in usage of communications and information technology, crimes of deception are becoming increasingly complicated and more difficult to discover.

What is Known About Managerial Fraud

Managers were reported to have committed just over half of the frauds in the Ernst and Young survey[13] and unfortunately for the victim organisations, nearly half of the stolen assets were not recovered. The top three areas of managerial fraud in the USA are false billing, expense reimbursement and stealing cash, with an overall median of nearly US$1 million per fraud. In their joint report the Chartered Institute of Personnel and Development and the Credit Industry Fraud Avoidance System noted that staff fraud is the most prosecuted crime in the UK, with managers named as the perpetrators of the larger frauds, making up almost half of the cases that came to court in 2004.

An interesting statistic from the KPMG report[14] is that managerial staff were able to cover up their fraud much longer than non-managerial staff. If a senior executive commits a fraud it is on average ten days short of two years duration,

11 BDO International. 2008. *BDO not-for-profit fraud survey 2008*. http://www.bdo.com.au/services/forensic-accounting/resources/not-for-profit_fraud_survey_2008 (accessed 18 March 2009)

12 Graycar, Adam, and Russell Smith. 2002. *Identifying and responding to corporate fraud*. Canberra: Australian Institute of Criminology; Johnstone, P. 1998. Serious white collar fraud: historical and contemporary perspectives. *Crime Law and Social Change* 30 (2): 107–130.

13 Ernst and Young 2003, op cit.

14 KPMG 2009 op cit.

three-and-a-half times longer than a non-management employee fraud, which averaged out as only seven months. Alarmingly, the authors found 3 per cent of detected fraudsters had a known poor track record and despite this, were still hired! Moreover, another one-fifth of the perpetrators were found to have a dishonest background after the fraud was discovered. The remaining managers had no previous convictions, yet committed 31 per cent of all frauds. Typically the managerial fraudster was employed by the organisation for a period of five-and-a-half years, with nearly four years in the position at the time of discovery; fraudster managers were very likely to be male (80 per cent) with an average age of 41 years, and their motivation was mainly greed or extravagant lifestyle.

Impact on Defrauded Organisations and Employees

Despite my own near misses with fraud, and how bad I felt, I did not realise the extent of how much others suffer due to frauds, particularly co-workers. Unfortunately, organisations suffer in many ways from the effects of fraud. According to Michael Levi[15] there may be a loss of confidence by suppliers; customers may find alternative sources and prices may have to increase to cover the loss of the fraud. Furthermore, there may be great financial and psychological harm to the remaining employees left to pick up the pieces. Peterson and Gibson found that in their case study,[16] the perpetrator was a trusted, well-liked employee. In another piece of research by Pelletier and Bligh[17] this was proved problematic because loss of trust is very high on the list of employees' emotional impacts. Resulting increased absenteeism is also noted, as are lack of commitment and loyalty and decrease in performance. Workers also expressed cynicism, anger and frustration with management, pessimism about the organisation's ability to stop further fraud and increased paranoia and fear about others in the workplace. Moreover, Johnson and Rudolph[18] found that frauds have greater impact on a small firm, which could mean loss of employment for innocent employees and also loss of pension or superannuation for owners and staff alike. Furthermore, small business owners may feel a loss of confidence to rehire and rebuild, their fraud is

15 Levi, M. 2006. The media construction of financial white-collar crimes. *The British Journal of Criminology* 46 (6): 1037–1057.

16 Peterson, B. K., and T. H. Gibson. 2003. Student health services: a case of employee fraud. *Journal of Accounting Education* 21 (1): 61–73.

17 Pelletier, K., and M. Bligh. 2008. The aftermath of organizational corruption: employee attributions and emotional reactions. *Journal of Business Ethics* 80 (4): 823–844.

18 Johnson, L. R., and H. R. Rudolph. 2008. Prevent large cash losses from small business fraud. *Journal of Corporate Accounting & Finance* 20 (1): 37–44.

comparatively larger in consequence than larger companies.[19] Considering that small businesses employ nearly half of all workers, this loss of entrepreneurial spirit will have a negative impact,[20] particularly in regional and rural areas.[21]

Despite the fact that company accountants are among the most trusted individuals in small businesses,[22] one-third of fraudsters are found in the accounting department according to the Association of Certified Fraud Examiners.[23] Colleagues of a fraudster feel betrayed if they were drawn unwittingly into the fraud,[24] therefore it is not purely financial damage that occurs, the rest of the hurt, pain and effect on people's lives remains incalculable.[25] These gruesome facts really came home to me when I started interviewing the respondents. Some were in tears about what had happened and some were angry that nothing was done by their company to help them through their trauma. They felt that no one understood the hurt and shame that they went through.

Under-reporting of Fraud

Surveys give a rough idea of how much fraud is experienced, but there are a large number of companies who do not want to attract the media limelight for any corporate wrongdoing and do not give information about their internal frauds. They often settle with the perpetrator, who is requested to leave immediately upon discovery.[26] A UK report on tackling staff fraud[27] stated that

19 Peltier-Rivest, Dominic. 2009. An analysis of the victims of occupational fraud: a Canadian perspective. *Journal of Financial Crime: A Canadian Perspective* 16 (1): 60–67.

20 Perrone, Santina. 2000. Crimes against small business in Australia: a preliminary analysis, No 184. In *Trends & Issues in Crime and Criminal Justice,* . Canberra: Australian Institute of Criminology.

21 Tinsley, Ross, and Paul A. Lynch. 2008. Differentiation and tourism destination development: small business success in a close-knit community. *Tourism and Hospitality Research* 8 (3): 161–177.

22 Smith, Russell. 1999. *Organisations as victims of fraud, and how they deal with it.* Canberra: Australian Institute of Criminology.

23 Association of Certified Fraud Examiners 2008, op cit.

24 Pelletier and Bligh 2008, op cit.

25 Levi, Michael, and John Burrows. 2008. Measuring the impact of fraud in the UK. *The British Journal of Criminology* 48 (3):293–318; also Gibeaut, J. 2007. Mortgage fund mess. *ABA Journal* 93: 50–57.

26 Australian Institute of Criminology. 2004. *Crimes against business: a review of victimisation, predictors and prevention.* Canberra: Australian Institute of Criminology; also Levi et al. 2007, op cit.

27 Credit Industry Fraud Avoidance System (CIFAS). *Employee fraud – the enemy within.* Credit Industry Fraud Avoidance System, 2004 http://www.cifas.org.uk/default.asp?edit_id=579-57 (accessed 15 July 2010).

large organisations could expect to fire 100–150 employees a year for fraud. The authors add that this is not a true indicator of the scale of fraud: the number of staff dismissals may be far higher. Also, staff about to be or being discovered may have made quick and early resignations forced by management or taken upon themselves, to ensure the fraud is not on their employment record.

Most respondents of the 2003 Ernst and Young global report[28] stated that fraud had increased against the previous year, with Europe having the lowest percentage of frauds reported and prosecuted. Considering that the number of frauds being prosecuted is estimated to be about 20 per cent of fraud committed, there remains, according to the commentators, a large amount of fraud that is undiscovered; or alternatively found out, and not prosecuted.

Lack of Prosecution

It was surprising to me to discover that about a third of companies actually do not report fraud to the police.[29] The companies felt that they were able to deal with the matter internally by warning or dismissal; a belief that the matter was not serious enough for prosecution; a fear of consumer backlash; inadequate proof and a reluctance to devote resources to the prosecution process; spending 'good money after bad' with little hope of asset recovery; sending messages out to the community about their vulnerability and encouraging more frauds.

Harm is added upon harm by not taking action because the perpetrators are free to commit similar crimes elsewhere and it weakens the deterrence effect of fraud risk-management policies.[30] Frauds that come into the public view are therefore only the tip of the iceberg. Disturbingly a UK survey found that nearly three-quarters of the respondents felt that they would commit a fraud if they knew that they could get away with it.[31]

PROSECUTION IN AUSTRALIA

Contradictory evidence in an Australian accounting firm report states that more than half of respondents reported frauds to the police and raised an internal investigation.[32] While the statistics may be contentious as applicable

28 Ernst and Young 2003, op cit.
29 Smith 1999, op cit.
30 Ibid.
31 Credit Industry Fraud Avoidance System 2004, op cit.
32 KPMG Forensic 2009, op cit.

to only their larger client organisations, the data that they draw out about the prosecution rates is intriguing. Just less than half of perpetrators were dismissed immediately, with one-fifth of companies actually allowing the fraudster to resign. Resignation has rightly been criticised because it tends to prevent further investigation, particularly in low value and or complex frauds.[33] Recovery of funds was only 11 per cent across the board for frauds in Australia and New Zealand.[34] Of this small number of fraudsters, the perpetrator returned almost all the missing funds. However, only 12 per cent of losses were paid out from insurance, which makes one wonder about the necessity of this type of insurance given the low frequency of payment. Business owners are obliged to report to the police first before making an insurance claim, which possibly explains the low payouts from insurance companies.

DIFFICULTY OF PROSECUTION

When guilt is certain, conviction should be easy but most cases are problematical, highly complex and in addition, prosecutors, the defence, juries and judges make mistakes.[35] The incidence of successfully prosecuted fraud is therefore comparatively low. If the defendant pleads not guilty, it leaves the onus on the prosecutors to put together a watertight case to secure conviction. Juries are often ignorant of company law and company accounting practice, they do not understand the differences of severity of offences, and clever lawyers can confuse them on technicalities. Together with the disparity of sentences for fraud as an offence with those for violent criminals, and the cost of prosecution and subsequent appeals, the public perception of sentencing of fraudsters is often seen as light. However, Cullen, Hartman and Jonson[36] observed that there has been a recent shift in the public's view of white-collar crime since the Enron and Worldcom cases, with an increase in social pressure to receive harsher punishment. They argue that this may be a permanent shift and not one created purely by the media's attention. A good example of the shift are the outcomes of the US President's Corporate Fraud Task Force, which had obtained 1,236 convictions within five years after the Enron collapse.

33 Chartered Institute of Personnel and Development, and Credit Industry Fraud Avoidance System. 2007. *Tackling staff fraud and dishonesty: managing and mitigating the risks.* London: Chartered Institute of Personnel and Development.

34 KPMG Forensic 2009, op cit.

35 Chang, Howard, and David S. Evans. 2008. Has the pendulum swung too far? *Regulation* 30 (4): 48–53.

36 Cullen, Francis T., Jennifer L. Hartman, and Cheryl Lero Jonson. 2009. Bad guys: why the public supports punishing white-collar offenders. *Crime Law and Social Change* 51 (1): 31–44.

Matching public awareness and expectations is only one part of the phenomenon, I found. Understanding why a senior manager would defraud an organisation is another. Most people would respond that it is greed that drives the manager and therefore the manager should be punished. This is too simplistic a framework to use when trying to understand managerial fraud, and it seemed to me that it all depends on which expert is asked.

Chapter 2

Mythological Causes of Fraud

There is no coherent thinking about fraud as a specific action perpetrated by a specific occupational group. I had to take broader theories into account but none could answer, until my own investigation, the question why do senior managers commit fraud? The answer depended on which school of thought an expert belonged to in order to have a response to the why and how.

Theoretical Hodgepodge

It turned out that many crime researchers rely on what is known as a 'hodgepodge' of theory regarding fraud in general. This in turn is seen as a subdivision of white-collar crime.[1] Dodge and Geis surmised that the study of general white-collar crime was not confined to criminology but also economic, sociological and psychological theories because this crime reflects society.[2]

Current thinking on managerial fraud is even more diverse. A sociologist will give sociological explanations; a psychologist will give personality explanations, while a police officer may give criminal justice systems explanations, such as there are not enough judges locking up criminals and throwing away the key. Unfortunately this fractured thinking creates different responses from the different approaches and further waters down the effort to nail what managerial fraud is and why it occurs.

1 Shover, Neal, and Francis T. Cullen. 2008. Studying and teaching white collar crime: populist and patrician perspectives. *Journal of Criminal Justice Education* 19 (2): 155–174.

2 Dodge, M., and G. Geis. 2009. Social and political transformations in white-collar crime scholarship: introductory notes. *Crime Law and Social Change* 51 (1): 1–3, p. 3

Auditing and Detection Theory

THE FRAUD TRIANGLE

Ask any fraud investigator about prevailing theory and they will quote the Fraud Triangle, or their own variation thereof. Probably they will not know who first thought up the idea, but it was Donald Cressey who was noted for developing the idea of white-collar crime.[3] Cressey was one of many sociologists who were interested in deviance in the 1950s and originally published his ideas as far back as 1953. The three elements that make up the fraud triangle are:

- Pressure, the motive to commit the fraud, perceived opportunity,
- Perception of being able to commit the fraud and remain undetected,
- Rationalisation, which provides a morally acceptable excuse in the mind of the fraud perpetrator to justify why the crime is not really a crime.

All three elements, Cressey hypothesised, must be present for a fraud to occur. The foundation for Cressey was a study where he interviewed convicted, imprisoned male embezzlers and found that global explanations such as greed or immorality did not fit with this group's motives. He also found that there was much more complexity in the nature of the explanations as mentioned earlier in this chapter. His conclusion was that there was a recurring theme of 'non-shareability' of the problems that the fraudsters had when they first started to commit their offences. This was related in particular to status-seeking by the offenders, and in every case he found that every prisoner was either ashamed or 'had too much false pride' [4] which prevented them from seeking help. Cressey argued it was not their immorality or their high standard of living that caused the theft, but the fact that they had no one to turn to for help to resolve their personal problems.

After Cressey's breakthrough one would have thought that instead of using prisons as a deterrence a counselling service for would-be perpetrators with problems would be the easiest and best solution to managerial fraud. But of course no-one could detect these would-be fraudsters. Later in this book

3 Cressey, D. 1973. *Other people's money: a study in the social psychology of embezzlement*. Montclair, NJ: Patterson-Smith.

4 Ibid., p. 75.

I will come back to this idea, as in some situations the Executive Impression Management corroborate Cressey's concept. The major problem with Cressey's work is that at the time it did not fit the prevailing idea of white-collar crime, where we have already been informed it was solely greed that motivated the fraudster and not 'unshareable problems'.

MOTIVES

An interesting list of causes cited by fraudulent casino gamblers (but these are not managers) was cited by Albanese.[5] These were: needing money for personal gain (18 per cent of 212 fraudster respondents); living beyond their means (14 per cent), in debt (14 per cent), temptation too great (14 per cent), greed (13 per cent), gambling, drugs and alcohol combined (9 per cent), contempt for the organisation or low pay (7 per cent,) desire to lead the wild life (4 per cent), family problems, emotional or mental illness (5 per cent), outright dishonesty, desire to blackmail the company (2 per cent) and needing a 'loan' (0.4 per cent).

There is some evidence (using descriptive statistics from reported and non-random samples of cases) from recent surveys, that lifestyle reasons were attributed to nearly 40 per cent of fraudsters.[6] For the remaining 60 per cent, it would be expected using Cressey's argument that the non-shareability of their problem that they would act alone, but 20 per cent of the KPMG group of fraudsters were acting with internal or external parties.

Nevertheless, it was argued that Cressey's work still holds true for a large percentage of fraudsters. Adapting a schema from Albanese,[7] he found two different gender responses in casino gamblers to what drives people into considering fraud: 'masculine' actions associated with status-seeking and 'feminine' actions association with protection of loved ones. Albanese is at pains to point out that Cressey emphasised that it was only the perceived insolvability that made fraud happen, but it does suggest that the masculine/feminine dichotomy results from the different 'unsolvable' situations which men and women are more likely to experience, see Figure 2.1.

5 Albanese, J. S. 2008. White collar crimes and casino gambling: looking for empirical links to forgery, embezzlement, and fraud. *Crime Law and Social Change* 49 (5): 333–347.

6 KPMG Forensic. 2009. *Fraud survey 2008*. Sydney: KPMG. www.kpmg.com.au (accessed 18 March 2009).

7 Albanese 2008, op cit.

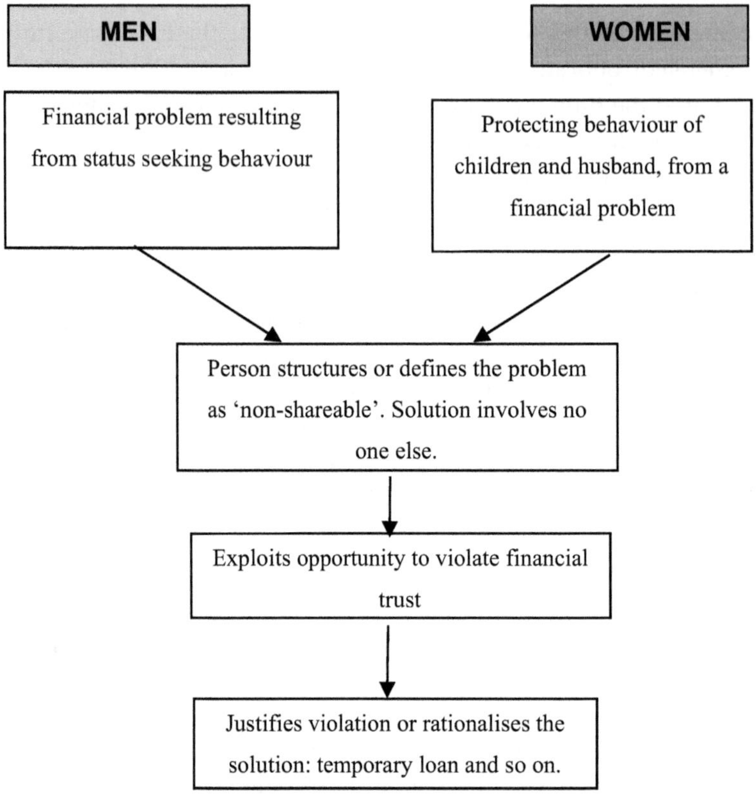

Figure 2.1 Gendered causes of embezzlement

Cressey's concept of the Fraud Triangle of motivation and opportunity has become an integral part of the fraud literature today and has also been assessed as a good tool for risk assessment.[8] Researchers have found that top management fraud (that is, senior management fraud) shares distinctive fraud triangle characteristics: there is the existence of strong financial motivations, and the involvement of individuals with opportunity who are otherwise considered respectable members of society.[9]

8 Among many others: LaSalle, Randall E. 2007. Effects of the fraud triangle on students' risk assessments. *Journal of Accounting Education* 25 (1–2): 74–87.

9 Zahra, S. A., R. L. Priem, and A. A. Rasheed. 2007. Understanding the effects of top management fraud. *Organizational Dynamics* 36 (2): 122–139.

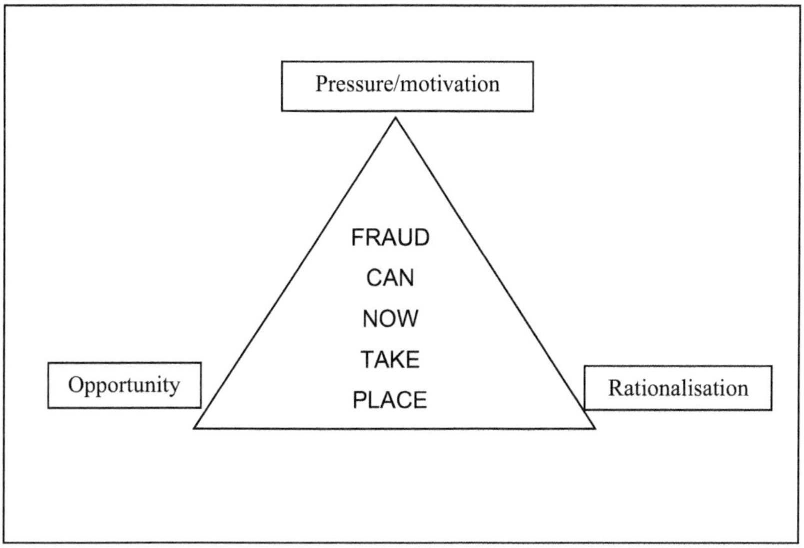

Figure 2.2 Cressey's Fraud Triangle

The Mythological Personal Red Flags of Fraud

Further work based emerging out of Cressey's Fraud Triangle, by Romney, Albrecht and Cherrington[10] saw the development of many Red Flags of fraud. The Red Flags are warning indicators in the organisations' environment, about employees and finally, the operational situation. The researchers substituted Cressey's rationalisation with honesty, as they felt that an honest person would most likely not rationalise a fraudulent act. The researchers commenced their study with a thorough literature review and with separate investigations of perpetrators and previous cases. The result was they produced a list of warning signs. Overall, they found that frustration in terms of social inequalities was a background factor, particularly if individuals felt that they were denied fair opportunities, they were liable to be dishonest. However, they did hypothesise that other factors such as size and bureaucratisation of organisations not only provide many opportunities for fraud, but lead to apathy and what they called the 'Robin Hood syndrome'. At the end of their research project, they tested 65 Red Flags retrospectively against histories of fraud and found that the Red Flags appeared in a large percentage of cases. From thereon, the Red Flags have

10 Romney, M. B., W. S. Albrecht, and D. J. Cherrington. 1980b. Red-flagging the white collar criminal; potential fraud situations have common characteristics, according to a survey of published cases, which can be used as early warning signals to prevent actual acts. *Management Accounting* 61 (9): 51–56.

dominated accountancy and auditing practice. In the USA, the Securities and Exchange Commission legislation penalises auditors for not finding or being brave enough to state that a Red Flag is observed. This legislation has come into place since the unveiling of the Enron saga and the subsequent downfall of the international Arthur Andersen accountancy firm in 2002.

RED FLAGS AND PERSONAL CHARACTERISTICS

Interestingly, some of the Red Flags consisted of personal characteristics of fraudsters, and were listed as: rationalisation of contradictory behaviour; lack of ethics; lack of stability; strong desire to beat the system; dishonesty in their background; poor credit rating and financial status.[11] When these were coupled with 'situational pressure' Red Flags of: high personal debts or financial losses; inadequate income for lifestyle; extensive stock market or other speculation; excessive gambling; undue family or company expectations; excessive use of alcohol or use of drugs; perceived inequities in the company; resentment of superiors; frustration with the job; peer group pressure or undue desire for personal gain; fraud was very likely to happen. The researchers knew that the Red Flags would be very useful for auditors and accountants to use in their work with organisational financial statements to detect fraud.[12] It is still considered the most effective approach to identifying fraud today and Red Flag recognition remains as the gold standard for detecting fraud by accountants and auditors.[13]

AUDITORS AND RED FLAGS

If you speak to auditors they will say that they use specific Red Flags to check against fraud in their auditing process. My husband, who is a fraud investigator, for several decades amusingly predicted that a company was under suspicion if the foyer had an ornate water fountain. This extraordinary observation apparently proved true many times, but I am sure that no-one would use that as a fraud indicator. However, the predictability of the numerous Red Flags was held sacrosanct by the accounting and auditing lobby. Yet external auditors are said by fraud investigation bodies to find only 1 per cent of frauds, while

---

11 Ibid.

12 Romney, M. B., W. S. Albrecht, and D. J. Cherrington. 1980a. Auditors and the detection of fraud. *Journal of Accountancy* 149 (5): 63–69.

13 Albrecht, C. C., W. S. Albrecht, and J. G. Dunn. 2001. Can auditors detect fraud: a review of the research evidence. *Journal of Forensic Accounting* 2 (1): 1–12.

employee tip-offs expose closer to a quarter of the frauds.[14] Clearly the Red Flags are not as good for detecting fraud as was first thought. Not only that, they are confusing in themselves.

I was present at an industry seminar held in Switzerland in 2007 on corporate fraud. The speaker was a European fraud investigator and the audience was comprised of mostly middle to upper management of various large Swiss companies. He read out the personal characteristics that raise the Red Flag for the auditor. He listed such attributes as: strong challenge to beat the system, wheeler-dealer attitude, high personal debt, feeling pay is not commensurate with responsibility, continual threats to quit and so on. As he paused to take breath, many occupants of the room shuffled in their seats and were obviously showing signs of discomfort. The speaker noticed this and quickly added: 'Of course, these characteristics can apply to any manager, even me!' He was correct in his observation and it clearly demonstrates the limitations of the Red Flag personal characteristics and that something more accurate is required.

The list of Red Flags started at a lengthy 65 indicators and by the year 2000 it had more than 10 pages of separate red flags.[15] However, despite the auditing profession's preference for them and a statutory requirement to look for them, only one-third of the red flags have been found to be good indicators in later work.[16] Whereas Pincus argued that they were not particularly useful,[17] Weisenborn and Norris found that the most likely indicators (out of 86 Red Flags) of fraud were: dishonest or unethical management; too much trust given to key executives and domination of the organisation by one or two individuals.[18] More recently Cohen et al.[19]argued that the Red Flags do not emphasise important personal factors of management, notably lack of ethics and personality traits, which are often overlooked by auditors. Nevertheless,

14 Association of Certified Fraud Examiners. 2008. *Fraud check up*. Austin, TX: Association of Certified Fraud Examiners.

15 Protiviti. 2000. *Fraud detection: Red Flags*. http://www.knowledgeleader.com/KnowledgeLeader/Content.nsf/Web+Content/ChecklistsGuidesFraudRedFlags!OpenDocument#Understandi ng

16 Weisenborn, D., and D. M. Norris. 1997. Red flags of management fraud. *The National Public Accountant* 42 (2): 29–35.

17 Pincus, K. 1989. The efficacy of a Red Flags questionnaire for assessing the possibility of fraud. *Accounting, Organizations and Society* 14 (1/2): 153–163.

18 Weisenborn and Norris 1997, op cit.

19 Cohen, J. R., Y. Ding, C. Lesage, and H. Stolowy. 2008. The role of manager's behaviour in corporate fraud. *Social Science Research Network* http://www.knowledgeleader.com/KnowledgeLeader/Content.nsf/Web+Content/ChecklistsGuidesFraudRedFlags!OpenDocume nt#Understanding (accessed 29 March 2009).

it should be remembered that in the interviews that Romney, Albrecht and Cherrington had were with jailed fraudsters,[20] they found that the most common cause for fraud was a financial debt or loss combined with an individual's disposition to compromise their honesty by rationalising the need for taking the money.

RED FLAGS IN OPERATION

Red Flags have been extensively utilised by the auditing and accounting professions. The KPMG Forensic report[21] found that alarmingly only 22 per cent of companies who responded to their survey ignored Red Flags. But as predicted by Cohen et al.[22] (2008) the Red Flags that were most frequently ignored were those regarding personality or indicators about the manager. The top three indicators, in order of value of fraud reported by Cohen et al., which were ignored were: signs of excessive wealth and spending, aggressive management style (possibly a version of 'wheeler-dealer personality') and provision of gifts above financial means. A disturbing trend that KPMG Forensic identified was that gambling was on the increase and speculated this would cause more people to turn to fraud.[23]

The ACFE report[24] on occupational fraud and abuse, in a survey of 959 cases, asked information about the classic behavioural Red Flags. Apart from excessive pressure from within the organisation which accounted for 23 per cent of financial misstatement cases, and being unusually close to the vendor or customer, for 35 per cent of corruption, all the factors are remarkably in line with each other no matter what type of fraud, be it asset misappropriation, corruption or financial statement fraud. The top ten variables are listed in Table 2.1. Some of the variables overlap, as several Red Flags may have been given. The percentages relate to asset misappropriation in particular, as it is the most relevant and the most frequent type of fraud committed by managers.

20 Romney, Albrecht and Cherrington 1980b, op cit.
21 KPMG Forensic 2009, op cit.
22 Cohen et al. 2008, op cit.
23 Ibid.
24 Association of Certified Fraud Examiners 2008, op cit.

Table 2.1 Top ten personal characteristic Red Flags by percentage, reported in asset misappropriation

	Red Flag	Percentage (n=850)
1.	Living beyond means	41%
2.	Financial difficulties	36%
3.	Wheeler-dealer attitude	19%
4.	Control issues, unwillingness to share duties	18%
5.	Divorce/family problems	18%
6.	Unusually close to vendors or customers	14%
7.	Irritability, suspiciousness, or defensiveness	14%
8.	Addiction problems	14%
9.	Past legal problems	9%
10.	Past employment related problems	8%

Most Effective Prevention Measures

In the ACFE 2008 report,[25] forensic accountants and fraud investigators rated internal audit best at detecting or limiting fraud. This was corroborated by separate research by Coram, Ferguson and Moroney.[26] Overall, these informed respondents rated external audit less likely to detect fraud. However, expecting external auditors to look out for the most appropriate red flags to detect fraud, argued Apostolou and Crumbley,[27] seems to be somewhat beyond their capability, as judged by their colleagues in forensic investigation. Perhaps this fact is behind the call for accounting and auditing professionals to educate themselves in other knowledge areas, such as sociology, psychology and criminology so that they can understand the problem of fraud from an enhanced perspective.[28]

25 Ibid.

26 Coram, P., C. Ferguson, and R. Moroney. 2008. Internal audit, alternative internal audit structures and the level of misappropriation of assets fraud. *Accounting & Finance* 48 (4): 543–559.

27 Apostolou, Nicholas, and Larry D. Crumbley. 2008. Auditors' responsibilities with respect to fraud: a possible shift? *The CPA Journal* 78 (2): 32–37.

28 See Krambia-Kapardis, Maria. 2002. A fraud detection model: a must for auditors. *Journal of Financial Regulation and Compliance* 10 (3): 266–279, and Ramamoorti, S. 2008. The psychology and sociology of fraud: integrating the behavioral sciences component into fraud and forensic accounting curricula. *Issues in Accounting Education* 23 (4): 521–533.

The Difficulty in Recognising Fraudsters Before Discovery

The profile of white-collar fraudsters was described in 1980 by Romney, Albrecht and Cherrington compared to other prisoners (for instance, burglars and bank robbers) as more likely to be: women, from a good family background, go to church, fewer or no prior criminal convictions, older and had a good education. The research team found that they scored higher on optimism scales, higher self-esteem and more conforming to society.

Furthermore, when the team compared to college students there were little difference. However, the jailed fraudsters did show that they more dishonest, in more emotional pain and scored higher in social deviance. The team stated that overall it is difficult identify them because 'they are very much like most other citizens',[29] thus making it impossible to forecast who will commit a fraud, as commented on 20 years later by Peterson and Gibson.[30]

Moreover, fraudsters were reported as less likely to use drugs or alcohol, and in better psychological health that other prisoners. They were more optimistic, less depressed, more motivated, had higher self-esteem, were more achievement-oriented, independent, more conforming, had more self-control, kindness and empathy than the other prisoners. This is not to say that the measures scored by the white-collar group were higher than the general population.[31]

Furthermore, many of the surveys are an accumulation of information from clients on the databases of large accounting firms[32] and can hardly be called typical of business in general. The Australian Institute of Criminology[33] has also made a similar compilation, using different data from Australia and New Zealand's criminal records, as well as the ACFE in the USA.[34] Their summary profiles are given in Table 2.2 for comparison.

29 Op cit. Romney Albrecht and Cherrington, 1980a. p.65.

30 Peterson, B. K., and T. H. Gibson. 2003. Student health services: a case of employee fraud. *Journal of Accounting Education* 21 (1): 61–73.

31 Romney, Albrecht, and Cherrington 1980b, op cit.

32 For example KPMG Forensic. 2007. *Profile of a fraudster survey*. London: KPMG Forensic. www.kpmg.co.uk/pubs/ProfileofaFraudsterSurvey(web).pdf (accessed 18 March 2011) and Ernst and Young. 2003. *Fraud, the unmanaged risk, 8th global survey*, edited by M. Savage. Johannesburg: South Africa. Ernst and Young.

33 Australian Institute of Criminology. 2004. *Crimes against business: a review of victimisation, predictors and prevention*. Canberra: Australian Institute of Criminology.

34 Association of Certified Fraud Examiners 2008, op cit.

Table 2.2 Three fraudster profiles

Characteristic	KPMG (2007)	AIC (2003)	ACFE (2008)
Age	36-55 yrs	Mid 40s	41-50yrs
Gender	Male	Male	Male
Education	Not available	Completed secondary, or have a professional qualification	High school graduate or Bachelor's degree
Occupation	Senior Manager/ manager, or CEO	Director or hired in accounting department	Manager or Executive
Company department	Finance	Accounting	Accounting
Employment record	Stable, more than two years	Stable with organisation	Never punished or terminated
Prior criminal record?	Not available	None	None
Acted independently?	Yes	Yes	Yes

All three surveys show a similar profile: male finance manager in his 40s with some years of non-problematic work history with the firm. Yet the 2007 KPMG profile remarked upon the spread of length of employment by the perpetrator, as some frauds were committed within a few months of commencement and others later. They questioned if individuals enter into the business with the full intention to defraud or if they simply saw an opportunity and took it.[35]

Surveys, via their assimilation of data, overlook possible binomial distribution. However, there is evidence in some surveys that about 3–15 per cent of fraudsters may be in a different group.[36] These would most likely be the 'habitual criminal' type that these researchers referred to. Apparently they will commit fraud as soon as they are familiar with the system, and these could include the 4 per cent of fraudsters listed in KPMG's fraudster profile[37] who were noted to have only recently joined a company prior to committing the fraud. Despite intensive psychological and modern pre-employment employment screening methods and interviewing of candidates, there has not been so far the ability to identify and reject potential fraudsters.[38]

35 KPMG 2007, p. 13, op cit.
36 Romney, Albrecht and Cherrington 1980a, op cit.
37 KPMG 2007, op cit.
38 As remarked by Guy, C. William. 2001. Eroding ethics of executive search. *Consulting to Management* 12 (3): 51–57, and Davis, Stephen Harvard. 2005. Should a 60 per cent success rate be acceptable? *Industrial and Commercial Training* 37 (6/7): 331–336, among others.

The Myths of External Versus Internal Forces

Public myths of fraudsters are summarised by Heath (2008) into two categories, character flaws (greed) and conformity in organisations that exhibit poor values (such as Enron).[39] So if you were a greedy manager and worked in Enron's finance department you would have been seen by the public as a fraudster. In the aftermath of Enron there were many innocent people including managers who did as they were told and did not steal money from the corrupt Enron. Many lost their pensions and their career as well when Enron was liquidated, families broke up, children's lives were disrupted, there were even some suicides. One example was John Clifford Baxter, an Enron executive, who was found dead in his car with a gunshot wound through the right side of his head in 2002. A gun was found in his car and a suicide note was left in his wife's car at their home. He left a wife and two children. His reputation was that he was a 'good guy' and he was about to testify before Congress about his role in Enron.[40]

Making Some Sense of the Hodgepodge

It is important to be aware of one's own bias about how we think about crime. Our worldview will dictate how we perceive managerial fraudsters, and this perception may interfere with what is truly going on. Keeping an open mind to all theoretical propositions is therefore a good thing so that we are not blind to the usefulness of that theory.

One way I found useful to classify the various psychological and sociological theories on fraud was by contrasting those that emphasise intrinsic factors with those that focus on external pressures. In this context, external factors are outside the person's control and the behaviour is shaped by society and so on. Intrinsic factors refer to a variety of theories, which see the motivation and production of the crime as a product of forces within the individual. There are many disparate theories that have been advanced over the years to explain this type of crime and Table 2.3 summarises some of the more popular thinking with their proponent authors.

39 Heath, Joseph. 2008. Business ethics and moral motivation: a criminological perspective. *Journal of Business Ethics* 83 (4): 595–614.

40 BBC World News. Sunday 27 January, 2002. *Enron's J Clifford Baxter: A profile* http://news.bbc.co.uk/2/hi/business/1784945.stm (accessed 22 December 2013).

Table 2.3 Theories applied to studies of white-collar crime, which can be applied to managerial fraud

External Forces	Internal Forces
Class and the corrupting influence of organisations – known as Differential Association (Sutherland 1940)	Control Theory (Hirschi and Gottfredson 2000)
Social Structures and faulty socialisation (Merton, 1938) functionalism. The Maximiser (Murphy and Robinson 2008) Choo (2007) on executives and the American Dream	Control Balance Theory (Tittle 2004)
Neutralisation theory (Sykes and Matza 1957)	Personality traits: Psychology, social psychology. (Higgs 2009. Paulhus and Williams 2002, and many others) • Fear of falling from high status, need for success • Lack of integrity • Lack of social conscience • Egocentrism • Narcissism • Omniscience • Omnipotence • Invulnerability
Social Exchange (Hansen 2009) general social theory	Corporate psychopaths (Babiak and Hare 2007)
Social/Industry/Organisations (Zahra et al. 2005)	Addiction, particularly gambling (Australian Institute of Criminology, and PriceWaterhouseCoopers 2003)
The leadership role itself (Bucy et al. 2008)	Immorality (Brinkmann 2001)
Rational Choice Theory – competition and fear of failure. Competition, excessive pay; excessive pressure to perform (Sayles 2006)	
Critical criminology (Tombs and Whyte 2002. Friedrichs 2004. Russell 2002. Wozniak's peacemaking 2009)	

External forces

As an ex-social worker with a first degree in Social Administration I was familiar with the social conditions that push the individual into committing crime, and of course crime would include fraud. Leading this approach is differential association theory, which includes Sutherland,[41] espousing that the criminal behaviour of white-collar workers was due to contamination from corrupt organisations. As a direct result of employment with these

41 Sutherland, E. H. 1940. White collar criminality. *American Sociological Review* 5 (1): 1–12.

organisations, the individual becomes co-opted into deviant behaviour. Naturally this depends on the length of time of the exposure, the frequency and the intensity of the underlying messages, as Tittle, Burke and Jackson pointed out later.[42] The researchers found evidence in the light of conflicting results from previous studies that differential association contributed to perpetrators' criminal motivation but not to the overall attitude of criminal respondents. This corruption approach explains what happened to employees of Enron who were co-opted and joined in with the deviant culture of the company, which upon detailed examination was described later as a cult by Tourish and Vatcha.[43]

More generalised theory states that the social structure of society itself is a consensus-based perspective and this in turn dominates thinking about criminology. It is argued that it is faulty socialisation that is said to be the cause of crimes. This stemmed from Robert K. Merton's earlier social structure theory[44] and explains how deviant subcultures have their own norms and values that spring from poor social conditions such as slum housing and so on. This theory hardly explains crimes from those of low socio-economic groups but does not explain a Harvard graduate going on to milk a corporation as in Jeff Skilling's example with Enron.

Interestingly, when applying consensus theory to corporate executives, it has been said that business schools produce unethical graduates due to the emphasis on the pursuit of profit in their course work.[45] Ghosal has been particularly critical of what is taught in business schools, and there is certainly the difficulty that in the US where the MBA in particular is deemed to be the right qualification to be recruited into large companies. A recent example was described a test to verify the Fraud Triangle theory found that business students have a propensity to cheat.[46] To me this is a warning bell about the moral integrity of that group of people. Putting ethical considerations of non-

42 Tittle, Charles R., Mary J Burke, Elton F. Jackson. 1986. Modeling Sutherland's theory of differential association: towards an empirical clarification. *Social Forces* 65 (2): 405–432.

43 Tourish, D., and N. Vatcha. 2005. Charismatic leadership and corporate cultism at Enron: the elimination of dissent, the promotion of conformity and organizational collapse. *Leadership* 1 (4): 455–480.

44 Merton, Robert K. 1938. Social structure and anomie. *American Sociological Review* 3 (5): 672–682.

45 Coleman, James William. 1987. Toward an integrated theory of white-collar crime. *The American Journal of Sociology* 93 (2): 406–439. In addition, Ghoshal, Sumantra. 2005. Bad management theories are destroying good management practices. *Academy of Management Learning and Education* 4 (1): 75–91.

46 Becker, D'Arcy, Janice Connolly, Paula Lentz, and Joline Morrison. 2006. Using the business fraud triangle to predict academic dishonesty among business students. *Academy of Educational Leadership* 10 (1): 37–54.

identification of subjects aside, why were 'the propensity to cheat' students allowed to graduate with this finding? It is rather like breeding dogs for show purposes, they may have the right colour, shape and so on, but the breeder does not address the fundamental problem of character, and the breed may be anti-social and bites children. Our social outrage at this propensity would demand that breeders would change and 'breed out' this type of temperament. However, in our business schools very few appear to care about the anti-sociability and avarice of the graduates about to be unleashed on an unsuspecting public.

Some business schools have developed units on business ethics and ethical governance, however these as yet are mostly electives and none are seen to be mandatory.[47] It suggests that if ethics are meant to be absorbed through purely living in society, being raised in a social environment like our civilisation, somehow morality should permeate the brain. Unfortunately this is clearly not the case, and other thoughts and factors have to be taken into consideration.

Recently Murphy and Robinson describe a 'maximiser' type of manager.[48] This theory proposes that an individual's desire for high status, coupled with constrained educational and career opportunities, creates the pressure for fraud. Pressure to perform builds up as these individuals progress through life. Choo and Tan[49] took this further and found evidence that fraudster corporate executives felt a 'broken trust' by shareholders and boards. This is derived from agency theory, and therefore they 'rightfully' take retribution by fraud, which is meant to complement the gaps in the American Dream of a high-status city home with country cottage, designer wardrobe, trophy wife, status cars and equally commensurate children's education and so on.

One fascinating insight is neutralisation theory as expounded by Cressey,[50] who realised that criminals do not conform to expectations of society yet they actually think that they do. I found this paradox intriguing as apparently this occurs through a neutralisation process or watering-down in their thinking which produces a softer non-deviant image that they can live with. For example a fraudster might say that he was merely 'borrowing' from the company and the loan would be repaid as soon as possible. This is said to form an integral part of the deviance, that fraudsters see themselves as normal human beings.

47 I am hoping that by the time this book is published there will be evidence to the contrary.

48 Murphy, Daniel S., and Mathew B. Robinson. 2008. The maximiser: clarifying Merton's theories of anomie and strain. *Theoretical Criminology* 12 (4): 501–521.

49 Choo, Freddie, and Kim Tan. 2007. An 'American Dream' theory of corporate executive fraud. *Accounting Forum (Adelaide)* 31 (2): 203–215.

50 Cressey 1973, op cit.

This was also one of the reasons that I did not want to interview the fraudsters themselves: I felt that they would try to persuade me that they were in the right, despite a lengthy trial and enough evidence to produce a verdict beyond all reasonable doubt. It seemed obvious to me that their colleagues would have a more balanced view.

Applying the neutralisation process to white-collar crime, which is where Sykes and Matza actually began their work comparing middle-class bankers' norms with those of juvenile delinquents.[51] Both groups saw themselves as part of society, and as ethical and moral human beings. And so it has been argued that white-collar criminals see themselves as being part of society, certainly not outside it, which gives rise to, as Heath pointed out, the paradoxical behaviour of stealing in a society which condemns such an act.[52]

Readers maybe familiar with such notable social theorists as Durkheim and Marx who thought that crime was an inevitable result of social causes. With my social work and social policy background, this seemed highly plausible that Durkheim's anomie and Marx's alienation theories suggesting an abnormal separation of people from important and integral aspects of human nature such as shelter and enough food, being connected with their family group and so on, which leads to deviant behaviour. Alienation, said Marx, occurs when people are deprived of their rightful self-determined economic means of production. In comparison, the theory of anomie developed from the nineteenth-century social theorist Emile Durkheim, focuses on a loss of social norms in certain individuals which would lead to suicide: 'Man is the more vulnerable to self-destruction the more he is detached from any collectivity, that is to say, the more he lives as an egoist.'[53] From these two concepts from Marx and Durkheim, C. Wright Mills proposed that two classes were highly susceptible to alienation.[54] Interestingly, he says that it is not only street criminals but also corporate managers who are equally alienated by capitalism to operate socially acceptable exploitation. This would particularly affect the middle to senior managers because society rewards those who take advantage without conscience and disparages those who do not make money. Such a society 'will produce the sharp operator and the shady deal'.[55]

51 Sykes, Gresham M., and David Matza. 1957. Techniques of neutralization: a theory of delinquency. *American Sociological Review* 22 (6): 664–670.

52 Heath 2008, op cit.

53 Giddens, Anthony. 1972. *Emile Durkheim: selected writings*. London: Cambridge University Press, p. 113, excerpt from Durkheim's Moral Education.

54 Mills, C. Wright. 1959. *The power elite*. New York: Oxford University Press.

55 Ibid. p. 347.

Consequently, it is proposed, the growth of alienation and anomie as a result of industrialisation and its attendant force of capitalism, with its drive to accumulate money, will naturally produce white-collar crime among corporate managers. It would seem to me that if this is the case most managers would be fraudulent, but I knew from my corporate experience that they are the exception rather than the rule.

However, I still needed an explanation that covers the rich kids who had everything in their childhood. Hansen uses social exchange theory to understand fraud within the elites of corporations.[56] This is useful, explains Hansen, because social exchange theory originates from economic theory and places the motivation squarely on money rather than psychological factors. This is because she sees corporate elites as reciprocating social networks and if there is one fraudster there will be others implicated or involved. The emphasis therefore is on a dishonest organisational culture corrupting others. This mutual exchange certainly explains what happened with Enron's board and its top management team, as described by Tourish and Vatcha,[57] but it fails to explain fraud that is solitary and kept secret from colleagues.

In desperation I suspect, some scholars offer a concoction of theories. For example, with many apologies to Zahra, Priem and Rasheed[58] who combined external and internal theories of criminal deviance: societal, industry and organisational, with a moderating variable of the individual characteristics of the fraudster. Applying the team's causal hypothesis, there are outside structural causes, with intervening variables of the individual's characteristics. In the case of managerial fraudsters, these characteristics would include intelligence, social status as well as an ability to 'pull off' the deceit. Despite this cocktail of theory we are still left without a succinct understanding of what is going on.

I found that critical criminological theory stemming from Marxist thought[59] would predict that society would produce criminals as a natural outcome of the process of capitalism. If everyone were co-operative and sharing the means of production, there would be no need for fraud. Indeed if anyone upset the

56 Hansen, Laura L. 2009. Corporate financial crime: social diagnosis and treatment. *Journal of Financial Crime* 16 (1): 28–40.

57 Tourish and Vatcha 2005, op cit, also Friedrichs, D. 2004. Enron et al.: paradigmatic white collar crime cases for the new century. *Critical Criminology* 12 (2): 113–132.

58 Zahra, Priem, and Rasheed 2007, op cit.

59 Such as Russell, Stuart. 2002. The continuing relevance of Marxism to critical criminology. *Critical Criminology* 11 (2): 113–135; Tombs, S., and D. Whyte. 2002. Unmasking the crimes of the powerful. *Critical Criminology* 11 (3): 217–236.

balance by committing fraud then they would be punished accordingly, as they are being purely selfish. This would be the very thing that radical theorists abhor, that is being selfish (land and property ownership) to the detriment of others (you and me).

A postmodern critical criminologist, Wozniak uses a surprising variation on the theme of radical theory insofar as he accepts the radical view of conflict of society, and dominance of the power elite, but he refers to a new reaction to criminal acts as 'peacemaking'.[60] This is based on everyone being connected to each other, even those who commit serious crimes. Wozniak sees the connectedness of social structures, crimes, social harm, the law enforcement and corrections systems and peacemaking alternatives. These must be seen together as an integral system for any real reforms to take place. Peacemaking proposals would include reconciliation, conflict resolution and restorative justice. In Wozniak's view, these are alternatives to the power elites' social controls of existing harsh non-rehabilitative penal institutions and the perpetuation of crime and poverty. Normative as this thinking is, to me it sounded like a good prescription for reforming the suffering caused by these highly paid fraudsters.

Wozniak is not alone, in many ways his views would be similar to those who believe in non-violence as the only solution. In Hindu Bali, there is an understanding that good must confront evil and accept the interlocking challenge. The day after the special holy day of Nyepi rejoices in good overcoming all evil acts through the intervention of holy spirits. An individual who has caused injury to another, even accidentally, must make peace with the victim. If they fail to do so, then the bad luck (karma) that they have created stays with them into future reincarnations. Christian, Jewish and Muslim faiths all have repentance as a core concept for sins that have been committed. Even though many in the western industrialised world have disconnected with their cultural religions, millions around the world still believe that crime is wrong and hold repentance as a key part of restitution. I will return to this theme later on how to deal with the fraudster in the organisation. However, crime grows and is with us in abundance today, including such variations as managerial fraud.

60 Wozniak, J. F. 2009. C. Wright Mills and higher immorality: implications for corporate crime, ethics and peacemaking criminology. *Crime Law and Social Change* 51 (1): 189–203.

The Myth of Internal Forces

Putting this section together I focused briefly on the thinking regarding internal factors that predispose a person to crime. One popular internal force concept is Control Theory, which is based on lack of self-control that causes impulsive behaviour and therefore criminal activity.[61] Self-control is an interesting factor because it is a counteracting control mechanism, through morals and ethics to free will. Being impulsive or out of control is therefore against the fundamental mores of a democratic-based society. However, I suspect that this is more likely to happen to adolescents than to middle-aged executives, who attract lighter sentencing and less harsh punishments than 'street offences'. Control theory was hoped by its authors to be the one grand unifying theory that explained all criminal behaviour.

However, critics argued that there is a tautological problem about control theory, insofar as low self-control in people who normally adhere to the social mores and values of society (which is the causal explanation for white-collar crime) may not be as criminal or as aggressive as implied.[62] Secondly, questions exist about the stability of self-control over a criminal person's lifetime; for example, does lack of self-control decline with age? Control theory also ignores the effect of peer group pressure on adolescents[63] and corporate pressure on white-collar criminals as Sutherland proposed much earlier. Piquero and Piquero[64] found that corporate offending propensity and behavioural indicators of low self-control were unrelated, a result inconsistent with the general theory.

To continue further, Tittle developed a modified version of control theory, known as Control Balance Theory,[65] in which to account for motivation of

61 Hirschi, Travis, and Michael R. Gottfredson. 2000. In defense of self-control. *Theoretical Criminology* 4 (1): 55–69.

62 Among others, Geis, Gilbert. 2000. On the absence of self-control as the basis for a general theory of crime: a critique. *Theoretical Criminology* 4 (1): 35–53; and also Smith, Tony R. 2004. Low self-control, staged opportunity, and subsequent fraudulent behavior. *Criminal Justice and Behaviour* 31 (5): 542–565.

63 Heaven, Patrick C. L., and Michael Virgen. 2001. Personality, perceptions of family and peer influences, and males' self-reported delinquency. *Personality and Individual Differences* 30 (2): 321–331.

64 Piquero, Nicole Leeper, and Alex Piquero. 2006. Control balance theory and exploitative crime. *Criminology* 44 (2): 397–430.

65 Tittle, Charles R. 1995. *Control balance: toward a general theory of deviance.* Boulder, CO: Westview; and Tittle, Charles R. 2004. Refining control balance theory. *Theoretical Criminology* 8 (4): 395–428.

criminal behaviour, particularly among corporate elites. He explains that this fills the gap in current theory, which fails to account for such high-level crime.[66]

Tittle argues that the type of deviance will be explained at the point where motivation intersects 'with the magnitude of one's control ratio [how much control an individual has, as compared to the control exerted on that person], opportunity, constraint and self-control'.[67] However, as Tittle himself asserts, this is a hypothetical model which therefore has limitations in the real world in terms of predictive power, but it is useful for dealing with criticisms of control theory.

From a completely opposite theoretical position I found there were Rational Choice theorists.[68] They paradoxically agree with Sutherland's view (even though they come from opposite ends of the theoretical spectrum) that fraud comes out of opportunities that become open to the perpetrator in corrupting organisations. Decision-making is said to occur before the crime is committed and a mental calculation is made as to the possibility of being caught and how much risk is involved, compared to the amount of money that can be seized.[69] However, even with these constraints, an individual can weigh up a decision to commit a criminal act on the balance of probability of being caught, and the likely penalties for being caught against the prospect of securing gain from the employing organisation. Thus if penalties are high, and the likelihood of being caught is great, the potential perpetrator is said to be deterred from crime.[70] Criticism levelled was that in reality, it did not produce any greater insights than already gained through other previous empirical research.[71] In addition, it leans on maximising utility as a leading factor for our behaviour, which could result in mass fraud by people maximising their utility. From what little I knew about fraud there were some cases where it seemed that the fraudster almost subconsciously wanted to get caught.

66 Tittle 2004, p. 396.
67 Ibid., p. 423.
68 Sayles, Leonard R. 2006. The tipping point: how good executives go bad. *Corporate Finance Review* 11 (1): 18–26.
69 Shover and Cullen 2008. Op cit.
70 McCarthy, D., S. M. Puffer, R. C. May, D. E. Ledgerwood, and W. H. Stewart. 2008. Overcoming resistance to change in Russian organizations: the legacy of transactional leadership. *Organizational Dynamics* 37 (3): 221–235.
71 Akers, Ronald L. 1990. Rational choice, deterrence and social learning theory in criminology: the path not taken. *The Journal of Criminal Law and Criminology* 81 (3): 653–676.

Of more interest to me was the work performed by Bucy et al.[72] They asked 45 experts in white-collar crime, 'Why do white collar workers commit these offences?' Money, financial gain and greed were the most often ascribed reason for managers engaging in criminal acts. Some respondents reported that the perpetrators operated from a fear of failure or of losing status or lifestyle. Most described the typical Type 'A' personality – clever, risk-taking, arrogant, greedy, aggressive, and self-centred – as frequently being the type of person that they had to deal with in fraud. 'Interestingly, less than 5% of the study participants expressed the view that white collar criminals commit crimes because they are "amoral" or evil.'[73] Again, this reflects the view that purely stealing money from a corporation is a lighter crime than the results of organised crime.

Personality Traits

Reviewing personality traits is a necessity in criminological research. It is impossible to ignore, yet in many ways seems to be impossible to believe. There is no criminal personality, per se. At best there are only traits that appear to indicate the potential of crime. The Bucy team identified eight personality traits that 'fuel' white-collar criminality, and these are outlined in the list below.

- **Need for control** – so they aspire to leadership positions. These individuals are assertive, decisive and active and naturally climb to the top of the corporate ladder. They can also be likened to gamblers who are hooked on their need to control the next bet.[74]

- **Bullying** – behaviours are seen in individuals who are ambitious and aggressive, so as to enhance personal gain. People become afraid to question the bullies and live in a culture of fear.[75]

- **Charisma** – these types of leaders are not necessarily operating out of the good of the corporation, Enron demonstrated a remarkable

72 Bucy, P. H., E. P. Formby, M. S. Raspanti, and K. E. Rooney. 2008. Why do they do it? *St John's Law Review* 82 (2): 401–571.

73 Ibid., p. 407.

74 Burger, Jerry M., and Harris M. Cooper. 1979. The desirability of control. *Motivation and Emotion* 3 (4): 381–393.

75 Einarsen, S., M. S. Aasland, and A. Skogstad. 2007. Destructive leadership behaviour: a definition and conceptual model. *The Leadership Quarterly* 18 (3): 207–216.

set of charismatic leaders that determined the culture of the organisation.[76]

- **Fear of falling** – fear of losing what the person has gained, when such a loss is perceived as highly possible. Perpetrators of fraud, due to this factor, were viewed as short-term, that as soon as they have enough in the bank account they can stop.[77] The existence of long-term fraudsters somewhat counteracts this idea.

- **Overwhelming need for company success** – to increase shareholder value, or it can be tied to personal ambition. It is fuelled by greed and the need to be successful.[78]

- **Lack of integrity** – lack of moral compass, which therefore allows them to commit fraud.[79]

- **Narcissism** – their sense of superiority spurs activity that makes the fraud an entitlement, or a special privilege. This is often seen in negative leaders, as observed by House and Howell and Higgs.[80]

- **Lack of social conscientiousness** – individuals who have a propensity for fraud do not show prosocial values or activity.[81]

There is a vast personality literature in the psychological body of empirical work about the reasons for criminal behaviour which is impossible to include in this book, but suffice to say most of the major trends are covered in the above list. There is one exception and that is Machiavellianism, which is treated separately below.

Machiavellianism receives its name from the writer in fifteenth-century Florence, Niccolo Machiavelli, who wrote the treatise *The Prince* on the art of

76 Tourish and Vatcha 2005, op cit.

77 Kets de Vries, Manfred F. R. 1989. Leaders who self-destruct: the causes and cures. *Organizational Dynamics* 17 (4): 5–17.

78 Brottman, Mikita. 2009. The company man: a case of white-collar crime. *American Journal of Psychoanalysis* 69 (2): 121–135.

79 Brinkmann, Johannes. 2001. On business ethics and moralism. *Business Ethics: A European Review* 10 (4): 311–319.

80 House, Robert J., and Jane M. Howell. 1992. Personality and charismatic leadership. *The Leadership Quarterly* 3 (2): 81–108; also Higgs, Malcolm. 2009. The good, the bad and the ugly: leadership and narcissism. *Journal of Change Management* 9 (2):165.

81 Collins, Judith M., and Frank L. Schmidt. 1993. Personality, integrity, and white collar crime: a construct validity study. *Personnel Psychology* 46 (2): 295–311.

manipulation to achieve and retain power. Individuals said to be Machiavellian are viewed with suspicion because they will manipulate whoever is in their way to achieve power. High-scoring 'Machiavellians' conform less to norms and values of society and where the risk was low, would steal more often in a laboratory experiment posed by Harrell and Hartnagel.[82] Interestingly, high scorers could only be trusted with close supervision. Machiavellianism is also seen as one personality trait of the Dark Triad,[83] which in turn is linked with fraudulent behaviour.

Fear of failure from intense competition comes from the social choice, rational choice theory embedded in consensus consensus-based free free-market thinking, developed from the works of Adam Smith and earlier. The basic tenet is that every individual is free to choose to work, and free to choose to excel, thereby a sense of competition is generated. In the world of work, competition is fierce and a strong motivator for deviance as suggested by Coleman,[84] as few would want to be a failure in the eyes of the family, company, or society.[85]

Particular personality traits of executives, who commit 'corporate malfeasance' as theorised by Richard Sternberg,[86] were found to be different in some ways to the already mentioned personality traits. These are egocentrism, omniscience, omnipotence and invulnerability. The use of the name corporate refers to the type of personality trait of corporate individuals. There are four corporate traits: egocentrism, where risky decisions are made in the individual's own interests; and omniscience, when executives believe that they know everything. Being widely perceived as being a financial authority makes them blind to their ignorance in other areas. This also creates unrealistic beliefs about themselves.[87] Omnipotence is the third factor, where an individual considers that the rules do not apply to them. Finally, and somewhat not surprisingly, there is a sense of invulnerability where the executives believe themselves so powerful that they can get away with anything. The delusion is that they

82 Harrell, W. Andrew, and Timothy Hartnagel. 1976. The impact of Machiavellianism and the trustfulness of the victim on laboratory theft. *Sociometry* 39 (2): 157–165.

83 Paulhus, Delroy L., and Kevin M. WIlliams. 2002. The Dark Triad of personality: narcissism, Machiavllianism and psychopathy. *Journal of Research in Personality* 36 (6): 556–563.

84 Coleman 1987, op cit.

85 Riordan, Catherine A., Marsha K. James, and Michael J. Runzi. 1989. Explaining failures at work: an accounter's dilemma. *Journal of General Psychology* 116 (2): 197-205.

86 Summarised in Hochhauser, Mark. 2004. Smart executives, dumb decisions. *Risk Management* 51 (9): 64–65.

87 Greener, I. 2006. Nick Leeson and the collapse of Barings Bank: socio-technical networks and the 'rogue trader'. *Organization* 13 (3): 421–442.

believe that they will have total support from boards and shareholders, or will get by on their own quick thinking.[88]

Another characteristic that relates to our possible managerial fraudsters, rather than a theory, is that quite a few fraud offences occur because the perpetrator has a clear addiction problem, most commonly gambling, and needs access to money to fund their habit.[89] However, it is not a common feature of all fraudsters, and we do know that not all gamblers are fraudsters. In the sample[90] of serious fraud offences (serious was classified as frauds in excess of A$100,000) in 1998–99 in Australia and New Zealand, only 14.5 per cent of offenders committed fraud because of gambling. This statistic varies with the non-inferential statistical report by KPMG,[91] where the motivation of gambling was cited for 44 per cent of the offenders.

Gambler fraudsters in the KPMG Forensic survey[92] were presented as different from non-gamblers in terms of gender, with more female offenders represented than non-gambler offenders; and age. The males tended to be younger by a few years, while the females were a few years older. The gambler fraudsters committed more cheque fraud, misappropriated funds, and obtained more goods and services by deception than other fraudsters. Most gamblers used almost all of the stolen money on their addiction and the rest on living expenses. This is in contrast to the non-gambling fraudsters who tended to use the proceeds for a luxurious lifestyle. Notably gamblers tended to take smaller amounts compared to other fraudsters, and of interest to the workplace, half of the gambling offenders committed their fraud against their employers.[93] Conflictingly, the KPMG Forensic survey in 2009 attributed 44 per cent of fraud motivation to gambling, and 37 per cent to lifestyle, 22 per cent of all perpetrators were managerial staff and most acted alone.

There is a psychiatric disorder of pathological gambling as described by the American Psychiatric Association,[94] which features a list of behaviours

---

88 Hochhauser 2004, op cit.

89 Sakurai, Yuka, and Russell G. Smith. 2003. Gambling as a motivation for the commission of financial crime. In *Trends and issues in crime and criminal justice no 256*. Canberra: Australian Institute of Criminology.

90 Australian Institute of Criminology and PriceWaterhouseCoopers. 2003. *Serious fraud in Australia and New Zealand*. Canberra: Australian Institute of Criminology.

91 KPMG Forensic 2009, op cit.

92 Ibid.

93 Australian Institute of Criminology and PriceWaterhouseCoopers 2003, op cit.

94 American Psychiatric Association. 2013. *Diagnostic and statistical manual of mental disorders*, 5th edn. Arlington, VA: American Psychiatric Publishing.

for the clinician to diagnose: preoccupation with gambling; need to gamble with increasing amounts of money in order to achieve the desired excitement; repeated unsuccessful efforts to control gambling; is restless or irritable when attempting to cut down or stop gambling; gambles to escape; after losing money often returns to get even ('chasing one's losses'); lies to family members, therapist, or others, to conceal the extent of involvement with gambling; has committed illegal acts such as forgery, fraud, theft, or embezzlement to finance gambling; has jeopardised or lost a significant relationship, job, or educational or career opportunity because of gambling, and relies on others to provide money to relieve a desperate financial situation caused by gambling. Interestingly, this diagnosis belongs to the impulse-control disorder group, and may lend support for the control theory, with its low impulse-control mechanism. So control theory may be able to explain more than I first thought.

The Australian Institute of Criminology[95] quoted that an estimated quarter of a billion dollars was lost in 528 gambling-related cases heard in the Australian courts in the previous ten years. The Institute concludes that gambling is seen as an explanation of fraud, but not the motivation, with punitive sentences handed out by the Australian courts rather than accepting it as a pathological mental disorder and ordering counselling and treatment programmes.

The Myth of Psychological Factors for Fraud

Unfortunately, despite the impulsive group, there is no single valid or reliable marker in a person's make-up that indicates a fraudster.[96] The psychological factors most linked with fraud, as listed by Duffield and Grabosky, are: dishonesty, lack of integrity and untrustworthiness. A common element to fraud is the financial strain felt by the perpetrator; another element for business people could be loss of power, material wealth and pride. Poor lifestyle choices could contribute to fraud, for example, gambling, relationship breakdown and addictive illicit drugs. This is known colloquially as 'the hypothesis of the 3Bs – babes, booze and bets'.[97]

95 Australian Institute of Criminology. 2008. Gambling motivated fraud in Australia: who, why and how. In *AIC Crime Reduction Matters*, No. 72, 19 September 2008 Canberra: Australian Institute of Criminology.

96 Duffield, Grace, and Peter Grabosky. 2001. The psychology of fraud. In *Trends and issues in crime and criminal justice*, . Canberra: Australian Government, Australian Institute of Criminology.

97 Ibid., p. 2.

Some fraud offenders feel that they have to have power over others, and take pleasure in deceiving others and humiliating them through their gullibility. They also demonstrate a misanthropic view of human nature coupled with disrespect for their victims. Honest people are viewed as tremendously naive for not taking advantage of what is on offer. Fraud committed by executives and managers, according to Duffield and Grabosky, appears to be perpetrated by overly ambitious individuals who are narcissistic; surrounding themselves with 'yes men' and able to take extraordinary risks in the face of no sensible opposition. They tend to overwork others, are likely to respond angrily to criticism, and they have a sense of superiority. The rate of narcissism is estimated to be 1 per cent of the population, but considered to be far higher in the fraudster group. Feeling as though they have been treated unfairly is considered to be another characteristic, along with a sense of territoriality about their office, computer or department.

Psychopathy

Interestingly, fraud committed against companies can also be seen to be the prerogative of the psychopath. Psychopathy is a personality disorder, not a mental illness: it is noted as a dimensional construct with a range and degree of characteristics and not a finite, discrete category of behaviour.[98] The psychopath's main difference from others is lack of empathy together with lack of affection or remorse and a seemingly arrogant indifference.[99] The disorder is estimated to affect 1–3 per cent of the population, and Duffield and Grabosky speculate that this type may be over-represented in fraud cases.[100] They hypothesised that situational pressures on fraudsters may vary regardless of psychological factors, and as they move from one environment to another, more controls may be operating which inhibits the possibility of fraud. There is a lack of research about such personality types and more has to be produced to achieve a definitive set of characteristics, rather than the anecdotal ones reported in surveys. Also they paradoxically note that some factors such as ambition may be highly desirable in executives, and not necessarily denote a propensity to fraudulent activity.

98 Walters, Glen D., Chad A. Brinkley, Philip R. Magaletta, and Pamela M. Diamond. 2008. Taxometric analysis of the Levenson Self-Report Psychopathy Scale. *Journal of Personality Assessment* 90 (5): 491–498.

99 Babiak, Paul, and Robert D. Hare. 2007. *Snakes in suits*. New York: Harper Collins.

100 Duffield and Grabosky 2001, op cit.

Some of the leading researchers of the 'Dark Triad' of personality factors[101] found there was perhaps an overlap between narcissism, Machiavellianism and psychopathy. However, these are very separate personality constructs, despite other research stating the contrary.

Because lower status employees are not much use to corporate psychopaths in their climbing up the corporate ladder to gain power, 'the psychopath's mask will often come off in front of staff, and employees will pick up on the psychopath's game before management does'.[102] This indicated to me that subordinate co-workers would be able to see through managerial psychopaths, and including subordinate co-workers in the study was therefore paramount.

Corporate Criminal Psychopaths

Clarke estimated that in Australia 2 per cent of male managers and 0.5 per cent of female managers were corporate psychopaths.[103] He developed three subtypes of the workplace psychopath. The 'occupational psychopath' uses his occupation as means for power and control, for example being a corrupt policeman. The 'organisational psychopath' needs to get to the top, no matter what or whom gets in their way, and lastly the 'corporate criminal psychopath' who shows more long-range planning, and secures trust from corporate victims over a period of time. Of these subtypes, the corporate criminal is the most likely to commit fraud, because money is viewed by this type of perpetrator as giving access to power over an extended period of time. While the other types are capable of fraud, they tend to use more aggressive means to fulfil their power needs and produce a quicker pay-off. Apparently female psychopaths are just as likely to commit corporate fraud as males in this subtype.

Finally, in an interesting study of the psychopaths' self-concept, Tamayo and Raymond[104] found that the psychopath's sense of self was actually very negative, with low self-worth making them self-centred. Despite being fully aware of the results of their actions and their understanding of the norms and values of society, they still commit crimes. This inconsistency is believed by the authors to be due to a paucity of fantasy life, leading ultimately to an

101 Paulhus and Williams 2002, op cit.

102 Morse, Gardiner. 2004. Executive psychopaths. *Harvard Business Review* 82 (10): 20–22.

103 Clarke, John. 2005. *Working with monsters: how to identify and protect yourself from the workplace psychopath*. Sydney: Random House.

104 Tamayo, Alvaro, and Felix Raymond. 1977. Self-concept of psychopaths. *Journal of Psychology* 97 (1): 71–78.

underdevelopment of a moral self. Related to this lack of moral self, other researchers[105] have found that subclinical psychopaths can have a dismissive attachment pattern, whereby a child grows up with little or no moral compass.

Attachment Theory

When looking at attachment theory, which I have used in screening individuals for managerial positions, the world is divided into three or four (depending on the author) possible types of maternal attachment. Attachment theory comes from the maternal deprivation work of John Bowlby in the early 1950s.[106] Basically infants who are deprived of their mothers can engage in very disturbing behaviour later in life. This is why adoption of babies is not encouraged by Save the Children Fund and many other child welfare agencies outside of the USA. There is overwhelming evidence that to remove a child from its mother is to give the baby a life sentence of poor outcomes. Adoptees are known to be over-represented in prison populations, the mental health system, and physical health systems. They are also prone to suicide and lifelong depression. I should know, I am an adoptee myself and researched extensively in the late 1990s the available research on the effects of adoption on children. It is not the adoption per se but the cutting of the maternal bond that Bowlby described.

Steve Jobs of Apple Inc. was an adoptee and exhibited a drive that was admired for being so creative. There was a dark side to his drive however, and he never stopped working all his life. Dave Thomas was another hard-driven adoptee who founded the Wendy's International hamburger chain in the US. In 2002 there were over 6,000 Wendy's outlets at the time of his death, which is testimony again to this overwhelming drive to succeed. What people do not understand is that the basis of the drive is to overcome the rejection that is felt by the infant by the mother permanently leaving. There are countless business men and women who are adoptees who didn't succeed; all trying to do the same thing, prove that their mothers were wrong to reject them.

So for me, when screening, having a managerial candidate adoptee rang warning bells. I would then carefully interview to evaluate if the adoptee had become aware of their dark motivation and if so, how successful were they

105 Williams, Kevin M., Alicia Spidel, and Delroy L. Paulhus. 2005. Sex, lies, and more lies: exploring the intimate relationships of subclinical psychopaths. In *First Conference of the Society for the Scientific Study of Psychopathy*. Vancouver, BC: University of British Columbia. Available from: *www2.psych.ubc.ca (accessed 23 March 2010)*

106 Bowlby, J. 1979. *The making and breaking of affectional bonds*. London: Tavistock.

on dealing with it. This may sound discriminatory, as a small business owner may prefer to have a Steve Jobs be a temporary manager while hospitalised for an emergency appendectomy. However, people who work with such driven bosses know the pressures that they work under and how much they drive other people. Maternal deprivation and poor maternal attachment therefore are not good indicators, unless the individual manages it competently and a recovery process is engaged.

Being an ex-social worker and community mental health worker I knew the importance of a secure family attachment and asked all respondents in the interviews if they knew of the fraudster manager's family background. None did. Certainly by reviewing the cases of known fraudsters since the completion of the research, it is quite clear that an unsupportive family to the child can lead to impulsive behaviour and therefore fraud later on in life: however, it is not the primary drive and does not explain what is going on.

Miscellaneous Myths

Finally, there are many practitioners in the field who develop their own sources of motivations and classifications. Lori Richard[107] a Security and Exchange Commission Director in the US, classified peoples' fraud motivations into the following subsets: the 'grifter' who sets out to steal money and plans it in advance, taking care to select their victims. The 'borrower' is merely intending to borrow the money as a short-term loan that they plan to repay, this category also includes the manager who lies about financial performance results always hoping that with the next statement, the business will right itself. The 'opportunist' is the one that sees a way of taking cash easily out of the business and does so, without really reflecting on the outcomes. Another type is the 'crowd follower' who feels as though they are doing what everyone else is doing, and if that is fraud, so be it. Lastly, there are the 'minimisers' who justify their actions by saying that the fraud has little or no impact on the organisation concerned; their fraud is a drop in the ocean compared to annual revenue.

107 Richards, Lori. 2008. Why does fraud occur and what can deter or prevent it? In *Southwest Securities Enforcement Conference*. Fort Worth, TX: U.S. Securities and Exchange Commission. Available online at http://www.sec.gov/news/speech/2008/spch090908lar.htm (Accessed 10 March 2009)

Michael Levi,[108] a well-respected criminology scholar, put together a similar interim framework, by classifying pre-planned fraudsters, from 'intermediate planned' fraudsters (those who started out their employment with honest aims) and 'slippery slope' fraudsters who trade recklessly and resort to fraud to right the wrongs that have happened. Some would argue[109] that these are categories of description of how the fraud occurs are excuses and not the real motivation, and once again there is no clear picture of fraud motivation and types of behaviour even with the criminology practitioners.

Need for more Scholarly Work

In my view there is an appalling lack of scholarly work on white-collar crime, corporate crime and corporate fraud, which was a conclusion reached before me by Shichor[110] after analysing citations and references used in academic publications. He concludes that this is due to the fact that most researchers view this area as a subfield rather than a subject in its own right. However, he is more hopeful than I that more researchers will be attracted to the field in the future as I found investigatory research very difficult to implement.

This optimism is not shared by Shover and Cullen[111] who contend that disunity reigns. This adds unnecessary complexity for researchers with their different perspectives and it actually discourages scholarly work. What makes matters worse is that fraud issues are not taught in business schools, and there is little or no content in accounting courses about fraud.[112] Other commentators such as Apostolou and Crumbley[113] felt that increased awareness of fraud was of the maximum importance as well as the need for increased financial controls. Therefore it is necessary for fraud to be on the curriculum for managers to be trained properly. Choo and Tan[114] go on to say that fraud would be difficult and complex to teach due to the lack of consistent theory. However, at the moment

108 Levi, Michael. 1988. The prevention of fraud. In *Crime Prevention Unit: Paper 17*, edited by K. Heal. London: Home Office Crime Prevention Unit. Available online at: http://collection.europarchive.org/tna/20080205132101/homeoffice.gov.uk/rds/prgpdfs/fcpu17.pdf (Accessed 14 July 2009)

109 Konovsky, M. A., and F. Jaster. 1989. 'Blaming the victim' and other ways business men and women account for questionable behaviour. *Journal of Business Ethics* 8 (5): 391–398.

110 Shichor, David. 2009. 'Scholarly influence' and white-collar crime scholarship. *Crime, Law and Social Change* 51 (1): 175–187.

111 Shover and Cullen 2008, op cit.

112 Choo and Tan 2007, op cit.

113 Apostolou and Crumbley 2008, op cit.

114 Choo and Tan 2007, op cit.

'Most business school graduates would not recognize a Fraud if it hit them between the eyes.'[115]

Some scholars contend that the right theoretical approach has not even been made yet. For instance, Shapiro[116] argues that the focus is in the wrong direction altogether and that researchers should concentrate on the breach of trust that occurs in organisations due to white-collar crime, not the crime itself. This remark demonstrates the lack of coherence in the research effort. Finally, academic researchers in the past have been heavily criticised for not focusing on fraud either theoretically or empirically.[117]

Such is the criticism of a theory of fraud or the lack of it. Even on a practical basis there is criticism of data collection by governmental agencies as well as academics in Australia.[118] What is required are consistent offence categories, consistent data-recording practices in the various jurisdictions, improving detection and reporting and improving the quantification of monetary loss. In his concluding remarks Smith recommends: 'there exists a need for ongoing monitoring of data collection, recording and reporting practices concerning fraud throughout Australia. Only then, will Australia be well-placed to understand the full extent of this, its most costly form of crime.'[119] Perhaps Sutherland was right in his assertion that corporate power elites control the regulation of white-collar crime. In addition, Yeager's comments about obstructions that academic crime research face ring true. These forces include general impediments regarding the pursuit of the truth of 'corporate wrongdoings' and barriers to operationalise research including the blocking of academic careers and research funding.[120]

115 Albrecht, W. Steve, Conan C. Albrecht, and Chad O. Albrecht. 2004. Fraud and corporate executives: agency, stewardship and broken trust. *Journal of Forensic Accounting* 5 (1): 109–124, p. 124.

116 Shapiro, Susan. 1990. Collaring the crime, not the criminal: reconsidering the concept of white-collar crime. *American Sociological Review* 55 (3): 346–365.

117 Some critics include Baucus, Melissa S. 1994. Pressure, opportunity and predisposition: a multivariate model of corporate of corporate illegality. *Journal of Management* 20 (4): 699–721, and Hayes, H., and T. Prenzler. 2003. *Profiling fraudsters: a Queensland case study in fraudster crime. Final report to Crime Prevention Queensland.* Brisbane: Griffith University.

118 Smith, Russell G. 1997. Measuring the extent of fraud in Australia. In *Trends and issues in crime and criminal justice.* No. 74 Canberra: Australian Institute of Criminology. Available online at: http://aic.gov.au/documents/2/F/9/%7B2F915E58-E75E-4E30-A428-0215B2AFA36E%7Dti74.pdf (Accessed 27 November 2009)

119 Ibid., p. 6.

120 Yeager, P. C. 2009. Science, values and politics: An insider's reflections on corporate crime research. *Crime Law and Social Change* 51 (1): 5–30, p. 7.

All this has created a vacuum. We have had to contend with the understanding that it will never be gained as long as interested parties, that is, the power elite, wish to thwart the regulatory process for their own ends.[121]That is, until I created my own research agenda, coming at the subject from a completely neutral point of view. I am not a criminology student, neither am I a fraud investigator. I received no research funds from any institution or assistance. My business school funded a data-collection trip, but other than that, there was no cash or kind payments to prompt me to look at the world from a perspective other than my own. This was due to the fact that I have a solid research background and comprehensive grounding in the social sciences with my first and second degrees. My lack of training in fraud saved me from believing that the Red Flags and the Fraud Triangle or any other theory was the holy grail and that all I needed to do was test it.

Why has Fraud not Decreased?

Surprisingly, the example of courageous whistle-blowers, like Sherron Watkins at Enron, has not stopped the overall increase in fraud. Yet the Association of Fraud Examiners (ACFE) Executive Summary[122] stated unequivocally that their data proves that hotlines for whistle-blowers are highly effective (44 per cent more) in detecting million dollar frauds and far better than auditing.[123]

This ACFE report found that less than half of the banks in the survey had installed hotlines, and this was five years after Enron filed for bankruptcy protection and the massive corporate fraud was exposed. However, in the same survey, nearly half (48 per cent) of the identified executive/owner frauds were exposed through tip-offs from informants, both inside and outside the company.

Tip-offs Work

Tips therefore are regarded as the most important tool to detect and deter executive fraud. Generally, tips came from a variety of sources. From the ACFE's sample of tips: 64 per cent were identified from employees, 18 per cent were

121 Cooper, Kathie, and Henmant Deo. 2005. Recurring cycle of Australian corporate reforms: 'a never ending story'. *Journal of American Academy of Business, Cambridge* 7 (2): 156–163.

122 Association of Certified Fraud Examiners. 2006. *Report to the nation on occupational fraud and abuse*. Austin, TX: Association of Certified Fraud Examiners Inc.

123 Ibid., p. 4.

given anonymously, 11 per cent from customers and 7 per cent from suppliers. Extrapolating this figure to all executive/owner frauds (somewhat tenuous but they are the only data available) implies that the tip-off rate from employees was 31 per cent. The remaining 17 per cent were from outside the company or anonymously, the latter of course could still include company employees. As the ACFE reports[124] maintain, tip-off rates for executives/owners are higher as these fraudsters have more power in the company and can override the normal controls of internal and external audits. Therefore, company informants appear a much more powerful means of exposure of executive/owner fraud than traditional forensic accounting methods.

If there is a good number of tip-offs coming from employees about managerial fraud, why then is the rate of discovery not higher? Attitudes towards hotlines are generally positive;[125] with accountants more in favour compared with other groups. They reportedly say that the cost of the hotline installation and maintenance is a way to offset the losses that can occur.[126] Information about fraud would most probably come from a person who is connected with the fraudster. It is proposed that this person will be close and has a developed sense of moral reasoning.[127] Apparently, informants are more likely to be more altruistic than others, prosocial in their outlook and able to resist organisational retaliation.[128] Hooks et al. use Rest's Four Component model for moral behaviour and action: the whistle-blower must be sensitive to the wrong-doing, that is, to see the fraud for what it is; apply moral reasoning to which behaviour to utilise; to use their own values in making a decision, and finally and the most difficult component of all to apply, have the moral strength to carry out the informing process.

Immorality or Blindness?

Thus moral sensitivity is the foundation to whistle-blowing behaviour; co-workers have to see the fraud for what it is and commence to make ethical decisions about it. Given that whistle-blowing is the best way to stop executive fraud, it is obvious that this sensitivity should be encouraged. However,

124 Association of Certified Fraud Examiners. op cit., this includes both 2006 and 2008 reports.

125 Childers, D. 2009. Tapping into tips. *The Internal Auditor* 66 (6): 29–32.

126 Flesher, D. L. 1999. Attitudes toward whistle-blowing hotlines. *National Forum* 79 (2): 5–7.

127 Hooks, K. L., S. E. Kaplan, J. J. Schultz, and L. A. Ponemon. 1994. Enhancing communication to assist in fraud prevention and detection; comment: whistle-blowing as an internal control mechanism: individual and organizational considerations. *Auditing* 13 (2): 86–131.

128 Dozier, J. B., and M. P. Miceli. 1985. Potential predictors of whistle-blowing: a prosocial behaviour perspective. *Academy of Management Review* 10 (4): 823–836.

what about the people who do not report the fraud who are still close to the fraudster? Do they see the fraud reflected in behaviour, but not mention it, or are they really blind to it? If they are blind to it then the next question should be: Why is this so? It is the same conundrum that faced the listener to the fairy tale of the Emperor's new clothes. That hoax was based on an illusion. Is this what happens with workers who work closely with fraudster executives?

Dishonesty as an Illusion

One of the basic issues in organisations is honesty in communication.[129] Honesty has been seen as a virtue of social consequences, it is about reality and telling it as it is, despite the pain that truthfulness may cause to the listener.[130] Broughton warns us that those who tell lies are weaving an illusion,[131] which results in confusion about what the reality is. Others are duped, says Grover, to take in the illusion and it proves harmful to them because it is a distortion of reality. In addition, Smith argues that creating illusions is ultimately self-destructive because success in life actually depends on reality.[132] And there is a twist in who can be honest and who cannot in the face of a liar: 'At the deepest level he is counting on everyone else not to fake reality so that he can get away with faking it – in other words, he wants other people make his unreality real.'[133]

Some commentators argue that the use of honesty is the crux of social interaction to be real. To use Rand's words, 'Honesty is not a social duty, not a sacrifice for the sake of others, but the most profoundly selfish virtue man can practice: his refusal to sacrifice the reality of his own existence to the deluded consciousness of others.'[134] Sissela Bok outlined a *Principle of Veracity*,[135] which makes the moral assumption that lying is wrong because if the world is composed of lies the individual cannot trust any social interaction, therefore everyone benefits if lies are not told. Furthermore, honesty has to be reciprocal. Dishonesty exploits others and finally does not change the facts – reality. Smith

129 Williams, K. C., E. H. Hernandez, A. R. Petrosky, and R. A. Page. 2009. The business of lying. *Journal of Leadership, Accountability and Ethics* Winter: 1–20.
130 Grover, S. L. 1993. Lying, deceit, and subterfuge: a model of dishonesty in the workplace. *Organization Science* 4 (3): 478–495.
131 Broughton, T. A. 1995. Some notes on the art of lying. In *The best writing on writing*, ed. J. Heffron, 1–14. New York: Story Press.
132 Smith, T. 2003. The metaphysical case for honesty. *Journal of Value Inquiry* 37 (4): 517–531.
133 Locke, E. A., and J. Woiceshyn. 1995. Why businessmen should be honest: the argument from rational egoism. *Journal of Organizational Behavior* 16 (5): 405–414, p. 143.
134 Rand, A. 1957. *Atlas shrugged*, p. 495. New York: Random House.
135 Bok, Sissela. 1978. *Lying: moral choice in public and private life*. New York: Vintage Books.

writes that a liar, no matter how hard he tries, simply cannot create reality. In conclusion she says: 'The need for honesty stems from our self-interested need to respect the law of identity … Since the reason to be honest is self-interested and the facts necessitating honesty are inescapable, we have a compelling motivation for honesty.'[136] That being the case, and this motivation exists for all, then honesty would be the best policy in managerial social interaction. Indeed, to be found to tell a lie in a résumé or CV is the best way to sabotage job prospects. It creates amazement within me whenever this occurs. How on earth does a candidate feel that they can deceive the employer and get away with it? There are mandatory regulations in the finance industry in the US and the UK which are slowly being adopted elsewhere, for pre-screening all applicants for positions within the financial industry. Yet we still see attempts to inflate or even make up a university degree or two and embellishment here and there as to duties of the previous roles. Some say that business people have to use these little devices in order to get along in this highly competitive world – are they sanctifying an illusion?

Deception

An illusion is actually deception and has been seen as a necessary part of business and that executives have to have a 'special ethical outlook'.[137] Carr went on to say that anyone in a managerial capacity faces the practical realities of telling lies. In fact, if you do not you are giving your competitors the market edge. It is a fact of life that you need to 'bluff', which means omission of information, lies or exaggeration, to keep the business going.[138]

The potential of today's management practice can therefore encompass a degree of cunning, lying, deceit and acts of omission to gain power over competitors.[139] An explanation from Livingstone Smith gave reasons for how lying and deception became part of the human psyche, evolving for millennia to assist in everyday living.[140] Essentially lies are not tolerated within the tribe but are used outside the tribe. This explanation would cover lying to outsiders, presumably for strategic reasons, however, as Smith argued there are no

136 Smith, T. 2003 Op cit, p. 531.

137 Carr, A. Z. 1968. Is business bluffing unethical? *Harvard Business Review* 46 (1): 143–153.

138 Ibid., p. 172.

139 Takala, T., and J. Urpilainen. 1999. Managerial work and lying: a conceptual framework and an explorative case study. *Journal of Business Ethics* 20 (3): 181–195.

140 Livingstone Smith, D. 2007. *Why we lie: the evolutionary roots of deception and the unconscious mind*. New York: St Martin's Griffin.

differences in lying (apart from severity, she claimed) as all lies are dishonest, disregard reality, and harm the listeners in the short run, and the perpetrators in the long run.[141]

We know that some managerial fraudulent behaviour carries on over years. Organisations are a theatre for some business owners and executives to create fraudulent activities for their own gain. Other explanations of greed and exploitation are required. The adage that 'power corrupts' is often quoted in the political sphere, but it is also very applicable in businesses and its management.[142] We must accept the lies and deceit? Whatever happened to ethics? I remember teaching business ethics at Curtin University, Australia, it was only for a semester or two, but it was a very useful exercise for me to witness the differences in culture with business students. The class was split in gender about 50–50, but their country of origin was very different, I had Indonesian students, Singaporean, and I believe some of the first Chinese students. The 'western guys' were outnumbered by about four to one. And there I was, teaching western ethics to Asian students. I realised that going through the standard texts was not going to help. How could most of the class get the idea of ethics if I am talking to them about obscure philosophers and religions that most have never heard of? At one point I abandoned the curriculum and asked them how they would deal with the problem of theft perpetrated by a family member. Almost all of the Asian students replied that they wouldn't blow the whistle on them or report them to the police. Whereas the Australian students, including some new British migrants, tended to say 'the right thing': that they would report the family member. This caused some disbelief by the Asian business students, who were horrified that westerners would betray their family members. It was pointed out to me by one brave student that to be disloyal to their family member was impossible. This didn't quite come home to me until I was leading some training in Singapore when I realised that for the participants, the sense of community was paramount. All were helping each other, particularly if a family member is involved: it was the number one thing to do, the group was beyond self. One could not sleep doing otherwise.

When I brought up the problem of business corruption in eastern societies to my class, the response was varied. It is sensible to thank the person who brought you business; but it was not reasonable to have gangs demanding

141 Smith 2003, op cit.

142 Ashforth, B. E., and V. Anand. 2003. The normalization of corruption in organizations. *Research in Organizational Behavior* 25: 1–52.

protection money. Not for the first time, this researcher learnt much from her students. From this experience I was introduced to the fact that all cultures adhere to the Golden Rule: Do unto others as you would have done to you, or variations on that theme.

With my recent research into primitive villages in Bali, I have found that this assumption predicates everything, the community and family are together as one. Without family and community a person would be in a living hell. Discrepancies like fraud would be judged by the whole Banjar – sort of a town hall-type meeting of the village. Redress would have to take place and making peace must be done – but not at all costs. Genuine redress has to exist, similar to the radical critical theorist Mr Wozniak, referred to earlier.[143] When I asked about such anti-social acts a villager told me that he could not remember in his whole life (he was about 55 years old) any such incident happening. It was just not on the horizon for a villager to do this to others. And I may add, this applies to the administrator of the desa (village) who is a functionary of the Indonesian government democratically elected by the Banjar every two years and whose responsibilities include collecting taxes and ensure that all duties are paid. These villagers managed to do this without an MBA or even formal schooling. They learnt this over many generations spanning thousands of years. It really seems a sad story when we look at our own society and see the frauds perpetrated by people who are trusted but are totally without ethics, and devoid of a sense of harmony and community.

Business Ethics

Business ethics as a field grew in the 1970s with the concern of lack of morality in business practices.[144] Several decades later, Mintzberg[145] and Drucker,[146] two management gurus, were equally concerned about management practice being unethical and immoral. They sought to raise management's game regarding organisational control and the environment. Thus business ethics can be classified on several levels: the personal, the institutional and the macro level.[147]

143 Wozniak 2009, op cit.

144 For example Lacroix, W. L. 1976. *Principles for ethics in business*. Lanham, Maryland: University Press of America. Also Brinkmann 2001, op cit.

145 Mintzberg, H. 2004. *Managers not MBAs: a hard look at the soft practice of managing and management development*. San Francisco, CA: Berrett-Koehler.

146 Drucker, P. F. 1999. *Management challenges for the 21st century*. Oxford: Butterworth-Heinemann.

147 Zimmerli, W. C., and M. S. Asslander. 2007. Business ethics as applied ethics. In *Corporate ethics and corporate governance*, ed. W. C. Zimmerli, K. Richter and M. Holzinger, 37–54. Berlin and

Focusing therefore on the area most relevant to my investigation, ethical leadership, I found that it is in itself is not a single construct. There is much debate over what it is and how it can be learned.[148] Similarly, Gini[149] contends it is in a mix of the person, the job and the context as well as the goals that are to be achieved and that all have to be taken into account. There are many writers in this area, and some use religion as a basis of a value system for moral leadership, for example Ryan uses Islam as his normative value system.[150]

Ethics is a largely normative discipline in approach aimed at improving management practice.[151] However, there is a growing body of empirical work to support ethical leadership[152] and to explain that when unethical managers produce unscrupulous work practices that these undesirable practices could spread to other workers in the organisation.[153] But as Weymes noted, notwithstanding this knowledge the pressure to make profit drives managerial performance and the environment and social responsibility is given little attention.[154]

Other critics of modern management have come forward in the last few years,[155] who describe despotic coercive management practices that are incompetent and inefficient as well as highly destructive to workers.

New York: Springer.

148 Brown, M. E., L. K. Treviño, and D. A. Harrison. 2005. Ethical leadership: a social learning perspective for construct development and testing. *Organizational Behavior and Human Decision Processes* 97 (2): 117–134.

149 Gini, A. 1997. Moral leadership: an overview. *Journal of Business Ethics* 16 (3): 323–336.

150 Ryan, L. V. 2000. Moral aspects of executive leadership. *International Journal of Value-based Management* 13: 109–122.

151 See Moore, G. 2008. Re-imagining the morality of management: a modern virtue ethics approach. *Business Ethics Quarterly* 18 (4): 483–511; also Price, T. L. 2003. The ethics of authentic transformational leadership. *Leadership Quarterly* 14 (1): 67–82; and Pelletier, K., and M. Bligh. 2008. The aftermath of organizational corruption: Employee attributions and emotional reactions. *Journal of Business Ethics* 80 (4): 823–844; and finally Trevino, L. K., and S. A. Youngblood. 1990. Bad apples in bad barrels: a causal analysis in ethical decision-making behaviour. *Journal of Applied Psychology* 75 (4): 378–385.

152 De Hoogh, A. H. B., and D. N. D. Hartog. 2008. Ethical and despotic leadership, relationships with leader's social responsibility, top management team effectiveness and subordinates' optimism: a multi-method study. *The Leadership Quarterly* 19 (3): 297–311.

153 For example Fleming, P., and S. Zyglidopoulos. 2008. The escalation of deception in organizations. *Journal of Business Ethics* 81 (4): 837–850; and Ghosh, D. 2008. Corporate values, workplace decisions and ethical standards of employees. *Journal of Management Issues* 20 (1): 68–87.

154 Weymes, E. 2004. Management theory: balancing individual freedom with organizational needs. *The Journal of Corporate Citizenship* Winter (16): 85–99, p. 88.

155 For example Conger, J. A. 1990. The dark side of leadership. *Organizational Dynamics* 19 (2): 44–56; Hooks et al. 1994, op cit. and Konovsky and Jaster 1989, op cit.

Over the last three decades there has been a development of a new construct of transformational leadership.[156] This is seen as the emergence of a new style of manager, empathetic, visionary, ethical and emotionally aware. This concept was opposed to transactional leaders who are generally considered to be old-style, authoritarian and coercive.[157] In addition, transformational management is seen as a moral approach to business practice.[158] However, criticism of managerial morality continues unabated, with immoral or even amoral management seen at the top of business organisations and dishonesty and lying appearing to be rife inside and outside organisations.[159]

The Trickster Within Us

The Trickster is one of the archetypes that Carl Jung theorised as part of the collective unconscious of humankind.[160] He noted that the Trickster appears in many cultures and surmised that these archetypes are within our evolutionary structure, or in today's terms, genetically transferred from parents to child.

The archetypes have a function and that is to form rites of passage to the development of our psyche. Jung refers to archetypes of the Spirit, the Mother, the Hero, the Child, and interestingly, includes the Trickster. It is important to realise that we are not talking about images, these archetypes are more a part of our spirituality and each is part of our journey through life. Jung theorised that the goal of each of us is to become individuated. This is a state of acceptance of all of that which is in us. No one side should dominate our thinking or decisions. If we fail to reach this goal we will stay stuck and repeat behaviour that is self-destructive, less than positive and unharmonious to our psyche and relationships with others. This is not a religious state nor a state of Enlightenment, it is purely psychic growth. However it is normative, that is something to strive towards, as it puts us in equilibrium with the archetypes. If you like, individuation gives us happiness. So each archetype forms a necessary role for us to absorb and accept.

156 Burns, J. M. 1978. *Leadership*. New York: Harper and Row.
157 McCarthy et al. 2008, op cit.
158 Turner, N., J. Barling, O. Epitropaki, V. Butcher, and C. Milner. 2002. Transformational leadership and moral reasoning. *Journal of Applied Psychology* 87 (2): 304–311.
159 Williams et al. 2009, op cit.
160 Jung, Carl Gustav. 2009. *Liber Novus (The New Book)*. Translated by J. P. Mark Kyburz and Sonu Shamdasani. Philemon Foundation and W.W. Norton & Co.

Despite different cultures the Trickster tends to be male. Also the Trickster can be in the form of an animal, for instance the wily fox, or even changing from a man to a God and back again. The Trickster can be cathartic so as to protect us from our own delusions. For instance, a clown makes us laugh as he slips on a banana skin. What we are witnessing is an act that is reminiscent of us being foolish. We know deep down we are capable of doing very foolish things. However, we do not like to be reminded we are foolish because it clashes with our sense of perfection. Jung knew that the drive to be perfect was nonsense. We are mere mortals and we must accept all of the parts of ourselves, including the parts of us that make us do foolish things.

Let me use an example. Most children seem to go through a phase of stealing small things. In my childhood it was mostly pilfering sweets from a local shop. I remember the self-righteousness felt by myself as a 7-year-old when some local children got caught and the police were called in to admonish the culprits. They received their lesson early in life and did not have to deal with far more serious consequences later. Imagine a similar event committed for the first time at the later age of say, 30 years and the theft is a bottle of whisky. Many people would think that the individual must be mad, and others may press for charges to be laid. Either way it is considered strange behaviour. Those who follow Jung's archetypes will understand that this is not madness nor is it criminal, the individual was tricked into doing it as a way of solving craving for alcohol. If reminded of what they have done, the person feels foolish, and it is this emotion of foolishness which indicates that the Trickster within the dark side of each and every one of us is at play.

We all are prone to the Trickster element. We can be tricked at times to do something wrong. But as with many Tricksters, self-awareness through acknowledgement cuts through the delusion of perfection and with that experience we grow, but only on the condition that we realise that it is a lesson to learn. The banana-slipping clown makes us laugh, as there but for the grace of God, as they say, go I.

Given the right concoction of circumstances we may all be given to thievery. Leave me alone in the Louvre with no guards or security and I might be prone to stealing the Mona Lisa, if I had an irresistible urge to own it. This is the trickery that my psyche could conjure. Fortunately I have no desire to own it. Furthermore, it will be very unlikely that the circumstances would occur and I can chuckle at my own example. Something that I am doing through laughing at myself is accepting this part of me. What I have found with years of experience and thought about the human condition is that many people do not wish to acknowledge their faults, and their Trickster within them is deluding them with the illusion of perfection.

Our different cultures across the globe have the archetype of the Trickster. In Judeo-Christian and Islamic religions the Trickster is the Devil or Satan, or the fallen angel Lucifer. The archetype is not confined to religion, it is present in our literature and our songs, and is represented everywhere. It is ubiquitous and pervades our advertising, our falsified image of ourselves, our sense of beauty and so on.

Walking around with long unwashed straggly hair does not bode well for us in Western culture, and soon we are despised by most people for looking like that. Perhaps you have witnessed, as I have, that people sporting long greasy-looking dreadlocks tend to be given extra scrutiny when going through Customs at an airport. Yet when we are under tremendous stress, one of the things that can happen is that we do not look after ourselves as we should and the unkempt appearance is a signal of our real selves. In this state we are not bothered with keeping up the pretence of perfection. One of the most amazing aspects of the stress is that in this condition, as the Shadow takes over, we are able to flatly deny, even by looking in a mirror, that we sport such a dishevelled appearance.

Denial

I have prepared many long-term unemployed and unkempt managerial clients for employment interviews. Some of them have not taken my gently given advice to have a haircut easily. Most are taken aback by my effrontery. After some persuasion they often change their minds as they learn that they are indeed very stressed and anybody in their shoes with that amount of stress will 'forget' to get their hair cut. Using this model they can understand what happens to them in their distress. I used to feel that haircuts were very difficult topics to cover in my line of work, but now I have the courage even with the most difficult of clients to talk about this social taboo.

I know that the Trickster is only part of us, but it is not *all* of us. And therein lies a truth. No matter how much the dark side or Shadow takes over, somewhere deep inside is the good that remains of our humanity. Jung never implied that there were evil people to be hated, he wanted us to know that this is merely a part of our human condition and that the sooner we realise this dark part of ourselves the better, because it is at this point that we will change and become happier within ourselves.

Self-knowledge is an important issue: I know that I can steal but I choose not to. Therefore being responsible for billions of dollars in one of Australia's superannuation (pension) funds and holding the master key to every office in the tallest office tower in Perth did not tempt me. The tools were all there: the knowledge of access passwords, how the financial system worked and so on. At that time I had circumstances that could easily have caused me to steal hundreds of thousands of dollars. I had recently divorced and was left with mortgage payments that were too high for me to service. I was a single parent with one child in an expensive private school, the other at university and equally dependent on me. I could have cracked under that financial strain and taken a 'loan' from my employers' funds.

Thankfully, I did not do it. The reason being is that what I had found out in my healing process from the lifelong effects of post-traumatic stress disorder that money is nothing, it is human relationships that matter. To steal would not have bought me happy lasting relationships, it would have only served to buy me some time before the banks were after me again for the mortgage payments. Naturally, before long I would have had to 'borrow another loan'.

It was this knowledge about what is important in my life that prevented me from stealing. Relationships are formed on respect, appreciation of the other person's natural gifts and ultimately on trust of the other person. With no trust there is no relationship. Therefore, when my CEO ordered a secret check on my company credit cards I knew that he did not trust me, that the purported relationship we had was non-existent. My health at that time deteriorated considerably under the stress from his bullying, and I was hospitalised twice being unable to breathe from a complex respiratory disorder. When my finance manager told me privately when I was in hospital the second time that he was ordered to do the credit card check in my absence, I knew that I could no longer stay in that job and from that point on with what little energy that I had, I brokered a deal to leave the pension fund director's position.

Looking back I am pleased with my performance. The previous finance director was impugned by gossip from the CEO that he was pilfering. I have no evidence of that and probably it was untrue, but it demonstrates the damage that can be done to a reputation if fraud is implied against a senior manager. I suspect the same happened to me as I was unable to find another position in a two-year job search. Certainly I have evidence that this CEO put in writing that

I was unable to perform in my job, so why not a hint or two regarding fraud as well? The irony of course is that the very same CEO was hauled over the coals for his own credit card expenditures – a hot topic with public administrators in any country. He claimed innocence of this charge, but nevertheless was forced to repay certain items for international conference and travel expenses.

Accusing someone of fraud is therefore a very difficult matter, and there are many points to consider. What evidence is there of this? Is it true or just a disgruntled employer annoyed with a subordinate leaving? Proving guilt takes a long and costly investigation to find irrefutable evidence that the crime has been committed. Otherwise it is merely character assassination.

It is also far better to deal with the propensity to defraud at entry stage into the organisation, than after the fact. Less harm is committed and the organisation is protected. But the huge question remains: how can we decide who has a predisposition to defraud and who does not?

For an organisation to come to terms with the possibility of fraud is in itself a big step. It is acknowledging that this can happen, and risks must be mitigated and handled appropriately. However, ordinary reference checking will not screen for this propensity, neither does psychometric testing or the myths of personality, red flags, psychology theories. Something else has to be used to get at the truth of whether a managerial candidate has this predisposition.

If the Trickster is in all of us, how can we screen if the person has properly 'dealt' with this issue? Certainly it would feel improper to ask if a job applicant stole candy as a child. This is part of our private self, not the public persona that we have put together for our transactions within society as a manager. We would not like to be asked such questions and furthermore we may not want to tell the truth – particularly if individuation, accepting all the bad parts of ourselves, has not occurred.

There is one way that circumvents denial and can give us an accurate observation in finding out the true state of self: asking others who work with the individual in question. Talking to co-workers is a very valuable tool, and many will recognise this as the 360-degree performance evaluation used in some companies. The feedback has to be understood against this test of validity: if most respond with the same issue, then likely as not, there is a problem. If the responses are varied then the opposite conclusion must be drawn. Taking the opportunity to receive feedback from those all around you is a courageous act. Being self-aware was one of the aspects that was noticed by the participants in the study of the benign managers. The malevolent managers, however, were never cited as being self-aware. In addition, I remember when engaged in a conversation with a fraudster psychopath about the lack of feelings that was shared by individuals with this pathology. The answer came back in a rage: 'How dare you say that I have no feelings! You have no idea how much hurt I received from Mr A all those years ago, and I *still* feel it!'

Of course, what I was referring to is empathetic feelings, not the 'feeling' of being slighted or wronged. The mere fact that this outraged person had misunderstood my observation suggests the psychopathic condition. The anger was meant to stop any further discussion, and I must say it was quite effective. When rage storms through the office, you can be sure that the Trickster is at work.

The Trickster therefore is something that we all have to have to come to terms with in our own personality traits. It is also something that must be dealt with in the organisation. The labels that the 'Trickster management process' is given always fascinate me. Risk management is one label, fraud investigation another; there is also internal auditing, security, forensic accounting, human resource functions and so on.

Sadly, the smaller the organisation the less attention is given to the function of fraud deterrence. Small and medium-sized businesses (SMEs) usually do not have anyone assigned to checking and regulating the purchasing, payroll and financial accounting functions. Aberrations are dealt with on an as-needs basis. If figures do not add up some clerk is given the task to find the error because no fraud is expected, only a clerical error with data input.

A Working Definition of Management Fraud

As the reader can now appreciate, there is no coherent theory on management fraud and I had to construct a working definition for senior management fraud myself. I was surprised to find this was necessary, but after using several authoritative sources I defined it with the following precepts:

- premeditation[161]

161 American Institute of Certified Public Accountants Inc. 2002. *Appendix to SAS No. 99, fraud risk factors* American Institute of Certified Public Accountants, Inc. Available from the American Institute of Certified Public Accountants Inc. website: http://fvs.aicpa.org

- use of deceit, trickery or cunning[162]
- to gain corporate property for personal gain using complex fraud to simple embezzlement[163]
- by dishonest means, through the abuse of power[164]
- by a manager in an organisation whose job it is to make major decisions[165]
- the conduit for which is the established position of trust and stewardship in an organisation.[166]

Therefore it does not include financial statement fraud, but refers only to assets such as cash that are secreted away. These six aspects are important to keep in mind when reviewing the cases, all of which were for direct personal gain and not manipulation of financial accounts to drive up the share price, for instance.

Equally, the managerial fraudster cases had to be those who were sentenced to jail, so that there was no issue about innocence or guilt as far as the judicial system was concerned. The frauds had to be perpetrated over a reasonable period of interaction with co-workers, the minimum was set at six months. In addition the fraudsters had to have stolen in excess of A$1 million (approximately over £670,000). Most stole much more than that. The largest amount was over A$19 million. One fraud was carried out over eight years, and it is an extraordinary feat to keep that amount quiet and away from the eyes of your staff or board. Which leads us to the question how on earth did the managerial fraudsters managed to pull the wool over the eyes of everyone in the organisation? Everyone here includes Red Flagging auditors, internal auditors and company accountants.

Other explanations must be found instead of using the ongoing myths of the fraud investigation lobby. Granted that these fraudsters by being managers must be clever and have a higher IQ perhaps than most people, so must investigators. Yes, they have control of their workplace. But to work

162 Ramamoorti 2008, op cit.
163 Association of Certified Fraud Examiners 2006, op cit.
164 Sutherland 1940, op cit; also Johnson, L. R., and H. R. Rudolph. 2008. Prevent large cash losses from small business fraud. *Journal of Corporate Accounting & Finance* 20 (1): 37–44.
165 Zahra et al. 2005, op cit.
166 Association of Certified Fraud Examiners 2006, op cit.

with someone on a day-to-day basis and it turns out years later that he has been robbing the firm of millions, there must be an explanation somewhere, yet there is no hint that something is wrong. Are these individuals clever at weaving delusions or illusions? Trickery or witchcraft? Gullibility or magic? It was time to get serious to understand what is going on. Myths are useful to explain behaviour but not that great in predicting it. There are probably many senior managers who are psychopathic, narcissistic, Machiavellian, alienated working class, wheeler-dealer or adoptees out there who do not defraud their organisations. So what on earth is going on here? The next part of the book talks about the discovery of managerial fraudsters, who they really are, what they do and why.

Chapter 3
Impression Management

Goffman's Breakthrough

The questions posed demonstrate that in my view it is vital to understand the social interaction process between the fraudster managers and their co-workers. My viewpoint though was not a complete *tabula rasa*, I needed to find a way to determine if the manager sitting in front of me wanting a locum job was in fact the person he said he was. Another recruitment manager happened to say over coffee one day that what people do in interviews is 'impression management' to get the job. I had no idea what impression management was, and afterwards tracked down the originator of the term, Erving Goffman, and I read his book *The Presentation of Self in Every Day Life*.[1] I was very interested, and read his other works where he looked at different areas, like mental asylums and references to gangsters. Ironically, terms that I had used in my earlier work as a mental health professional such as stigma and labelling theory, stemmed from him. At last I had found something that had a ring of truth about it. I was intrigued and studied more about Goffman and his theory of impression management. No theory or empirical research so far has given a satisfactory understanding of how fraudsters can maintain the delusion of honesty with their colleagues. Their excessive lifestyle and greed does not seem to be noticed by anyone, let alone staff inside the organisation, and the question remains as to why and how this illusion works.

The Theory of Impression Management

Goffman argued that everyday social interaction is to be viewed almost like a theatrical production between an actor and an audience. The actor performs to persuade the listeners that the role that he is playing is legitimate. The audience, by their usually passive act of paying attention, support that role accordingly through their belief that the actor is who he says he is. When things go wrong

1 Goffman, E. 1959. *The presentation of self in everyday life*. New York: Anchor Books, Doubleday.

for the actor, the audience, to assist the flow of the social process, uses tact and other embarrassment reduction techniques. Goffman believed that this dramaturgical approach is an integral component in all daily interaction, which of course includes management and employees within an organisation.

POWER AND CONTROL

Consensus-view academics liked impression management, as it is obviously mutual consent that is the basis of the interaction. Interestingly though, diametrically opposed to consensus theorists, conflict theorists, those who believe that society is not consensual at all and is marked by conflict between individuals and groups, have been equally attracted to impression management and its dramaturgical context, because it explains power relationships within social interaction. In the concept of impression management, Goffman explicitly states that impression management is actually a method of control, and that a priest just as much as a con man will try to control his target audience's perception of him. However, Goffman was wise to the counterbalancing power of the audience: if people detect any omission, interruption or contradictory signs, disbelief will reign. Once that happens it is almost impossible for the actor to regain those individuals' trust.

Impression management theory was chosen for the backbone of the investigation because it offers a different and interesting perspective of allowing for an illusion mechanism and its influence on its recipients. To use Goffman's dramaturgical phraseology, the illusion is daily social life, full of symbols and shared understandings. In the context of fraudster managers, the stage is the organisation, with the actors (fraudsters) and audiences (co-workers) playing their respective roles. It is by using this construct that the subtleties and nuances of the interactions of fraudster and non-fraudster managers and their employees can be studied. Being a senior manager in an organisation requires the individual to be in a certain role, they must be seen to be acting out that role according to the expectations of others. It is also a tightrope of balancing expectations from different groups who may make their own claims on the manager, for instance customers, suppliers, and so on. This results in behaviour where the same executive has to play variations of his role to different audiences, for instance, shareholders would be talked to differently than subordinates, to meet their separate expectations. Being 'all things to all men' is a difficult task indeed, as I found out once for myself by seeing the Dean of a business faculty in a supermarket being dragged along by his wife to do the shopping. It was such a shock to see him out of context that I only managed to burble a few inane sentences and quickly left the scene.

It is to be expected that within the context of the organisation, power and authority impose restrictions on normal impression management processes. The following quotation illustrates this well: 'Even the frankest and bravest of subordinates do not talk with their boss the same way that they talk with colleagues.'[2] There is often a tacit agreement regarding lack of information between middle management and their aggressive mobile top executives who really do not care about the future of the organisation. This is the 'need to know' situation, which has let down many a manager when they find out that the opposite was occurring. Equally in government departments managers ensure that their minister does not know everything that is going on: the minister is part of the political system and not necessarily in agreement with the executive function of government.

Goffman's work was to introduce the idea of performance in everyday life, but his critics argue that he left the empirical component to others.[3] However, there is no doubt that impression management applied research has proliferated, including in the field of management, since his death.[4] Unfortunately there has been little application to the field of fraud. However, it has been used as the basis of many studies, primarily in the social psychology arena, to explain why people lie and deceive in experiments as well as in real life.[5]

Relevant Key Elements of Impression Management Theory in Today's Organisation

At this point it is as well to draw attention to the various components of impression management theory that are relevant to the study of managerial fraudsters. This section outlines the dramaturgical interplay of the actor and

2 Robert Greenleaf, cited in Rosenfeld and Giacalone 1991, in *Applied impression management*, ed. R. A. Giacalone and P. Rosenfeld. Newbury Park, CA: Sage, p. 7.

3 Manning, P. 1992. *Erving Goffman and modern sociology*. Stanford, CA: Stanford University Press.

4 For instance Jayakody, J. A. S. K. 2008. Charisma as a cognitive-affective phenomenon: a follower-centric approach. *Management Decision* 46 (6): 832–845, Mangham, I. 1990. Managing as a performing art. *British Journal of Management* 1 (2): 105–115; Wood, R. E., and T. R. Mitchell. 1981. Manager behavior in a social context: The impact of impression management on attributions and disciplinary actions. *Organizational Behavior and Human Performance* 28 (3): 356–378.

5 For example Gardner, W. L., and M. J. Martinko. 1988. Impression management: an observational study linking audience characteristics with verbal self-presentations. *Academy of Management Journal* 31 (1): 42–65; Leary, M. R., and R. M. Kowalski. 1990. Impression management: a literature review and two-component model. *Psychological Bulletin* 107 (1): 34–47; Rozell, E. J., and D. E. Gundersen. 2003. The effects of leader impression management on group perceptions of cohesion, consensus, and communication. *Small Group Research* 34 (2): 197–223.

the audience, the importance of authenticity for the actor and the reciprocation process of the audience in organisations.

DRAMATURGICAL FOCUS

Goffman expanded on an existing perspective that human beings act like actors on a large theatrical stage.[6] The basis of human beings playing out their own dramas came 20 years earlier from a theatre critic. It must have occurred to the critic that just as we see a play enacted that there is a corollary process of theatrical stance taken by social organisations and the people within them. Goffman however arrived at his own conclusions from his Ph.D. work in the Shetland Isles of Scotland some 30 years later. The theatre model was extended and elaborated into a radical and innovative way of looking at the world. Goffman's ingenuity was to transfer the worldview of sociologists into the personal sphere, from the macro, as it were, into the micro. His ideas popularised a relatively unknown concept from 'the extreme into the mainstream' attracting researchers from sociology and later, social psychology and psychology.[7]

Many mistakenly believe that Goffman was taking a literal stance, but in fact he was using a metaphorical, approach. It was Burke, who was literal, who used the Shakespearean quotation: 'All the world's a stage, and all the men and women merely players. They have their exits and their entrances; and one man in his time plays many parts, his acts being seven Ages'[8] to exemplify his adherence to drama. Goffman however, transferred from the theatre and applied it directly into ordinary lives.[9] The following points raise two fundamental differences in Goffman's theorising, in his definitions and the methodology he used.

GOFFMAN'S DEFINITIONS

Goffman states his definitions in the introductory words to his seminal work *The Presentation of Self in Everyday Life*. He defines that a performance is an activity that is aimed at influencing the audience: each part of the performance

6 Watson, C. 1982. The presentation of self and the new institutional inmate: an analysis of prisoners' responses to assessment for release. *Symbolic Interaction* 5 (2): 243–259.

7 Giacalone, Robert A., and Paul Rosenfeld, eds. 1991. *Applied impression management: how image-making affects managerial decisions*. Newbury Park, CA: Sage.

8 Young, T. R. 1990. *The drama of social life: essays in critical dramaturgy*. Piscataway, NJ: Transaction Publishers, p. 10.

9 Sinha, P. N., and B. Jackson. 2006. A Burkean inquiry into leader–follower identification motives. *Culture and Organization* 12 (3): 233–247.

is a routine and when this is played over and over again it forms a relationship with the audience.

It is quite clear then that Goffman took the dramaturgical idea and extended it further as a symbol to understand daily life within its social context. Thus impression management was involved with social interactions that incorporate actors and audiences, in a reiterative process of understanding and shared values.

MICRO OBSERVATIONS

Goffman pioneered the field of close observation, without audio or video recordings. He closely studied micro aspects of ordinary social life, not previously done before – apart from his social anthropologist mentor, Lloyd Warner.[10] This was in the days before qualitative methodology in business and organisational concepts were rarely used. Goffman's legacy includes many concepts. Stigma, labelling theory, and institutionalism are still current, decades after their publication. Goffman's work has been found to be robust theoretically and offers contributions to the understanding of social concepts such as identities, interaction rituals, social power, culture, language, and emotions as well as deviance.[11] Goffman's theories are still actively taught in sociology classes and have influenced thought concerning social action for nearly 50 years. But what he is renowned for today, and which is of increasing and lasting interest among social researchers, is the concept of impression management.

After his initial influence from social anthropology, Goffman started to work and write on his own. *The Presentation of Self in Everyday Life* was first published in the 1950s. His argument was that people are actors in their everyday lives. Individuals put on a show to their audience, whoever that audience may be, for instance their family, workplace or community. This was far beyond merely taking on social roles and role-playing. These were the very minutiae of day-to-day activity. Like theatre, he saw the audience had an effect upon the actors, who were in part controlled by the audience reaction, but Goffman's investigation took the idea much further. This needs to be discussed further In order to understand the power of impression management we need to examine this in detail.

10 Collins, R. 1986. The passing of intellectual generations: reflections on the death of Erving Goffman. *Sociological Theory* 4 (1): 106–113.

11 Brown, D. K. 2003. Goffman's dramaturgical sociology: developing a meaningful theoretical context and exercise involving 'embarrassment and social organization'. *Teaching Sociology* 31 (3): 288–299.

RECIPROCATING AUDIENCE

In his opening remarks to *The Presentation of Self in Everyday Life* the reciprocal nature of the audience is firmly established, there is a process of gathering information about the actor. In this way, the audience can establish reciprocity with him.[12] The classic example of how this happens without any acknowledgement from either side is the accent of English people. Our English ears are tuned in to accents so that we could determine where the person was from, not only geography but which social strata did the person emanates from – upper, middle or working class.

I was brought up by a Canadian mother who was mistaken for an American by the English most of her life, she unhappily suffered from the innate prejudice against America in the Second World War. Even working in a military uniform factory did not win her brownie points with her English workmates and she was ostracised by the ignorance of others. This example is replicated time and time again with which district an English person was born in and the social status of parents. Regional accents did not used to be tolerated in any management position apart from the local factory that they managed. To get on in their careers people had to drop their dialect and speak with a BBC television accent. To oversimplify, snobbery lived in each class, looking up to others and down on the rest as demonstrated by John Cleese, Ronnie Barker and Ronnie Corbert in the *Frost Report* 1966 in their take on the English class system. Being imprisoned by class and region meant that only certain outcomes could be achieved. The working class were condemned to borderline poverty, middle-class tradesmen clung to a bourgeois way of life, while the upper class played games in their country houses and conducted wars based on jealousy and envy.

A good example of this class prejudice was Margaret Thatcher, Prime Minister of Britain in the 1980s, who was mocked as being a grocer's daughter by many members of Parliament in her party which in turn was mostly controlled by the upper class. By being a grocer's daughter she was framed as someone with lesser intelligence and fortitude than others. The gender issue of course condemned her further. Margaret Thatcher established a persona that was the opposite of what was expected of her, being highly intelligent, hard working and with political nous, her reputation was such that she was called The Iron Lady. This persona was used continually despite the many deleterious effects of her governance on ordinary British people who elected her into power.

12 Goffman 1959 op cit., p. 1.

This persona, however, is different from the inner self. The inner self is not exposed, there are only signs of its existence. Goffman felt that only under psychotherapy or by examining dreams could the true inner self be drawn out for the individual to see. From awakening in the morning until going to sleep at night, the individual carries out performances in front of others. These performances are expected and accepted and are far beyond merely acting.

Goffman classified each role as having expectations which must be met in order for the audience to receive it a successful performance. Individuals and audiences are so expert in this daily interplay that we are almost blind to what they do in the theatre of everyday life. In fact, Goffman states that it is only when there is some disruption that the theatrical elements become exposed and recognised. The person and the audience then openly fix the disruption, the individual can be embarrassed, and use devices such as jokes, apologies, talking about other instances, to smooth over the inconsistency. Goffman defines these as 'defensive strategies'. The audience, however, uses 'protective practices' to preserve the social situation. Tact is seen as first and foremost the strategy that is used by an audience. Whenever I present a talk on managerial fraud and I am at the point of explaining impression management I often insert a completely inappropriate slide in my presentation. When it is showing I continue talking as if nothing is wrong. Very slowly my audience becomes aware of the awful gaffe I have made. But they don't know what to do next. Usually after some minutes while I talk about this slide some brave person puts up their hand and politely tells me that the image on the screen makes no sense in relation to what I am saying. Everyone looks aghast at my apparent idiocy, but all are relieved to learn that I deliberately put that slide in the presentation so that they can feel for themselves the embarrassment felt when a role is not played to expectations. It is this feeling that has to be developed more among employees to make them aware of possible fraud. Goffman cleverly observes:

> *It should be added that while we may be ready to see that no fostered impression would survive if defensive practices were not employed, we are less ready perhaps to see that few impressions could survive if those who received the impression did not exert tact in their reception of it.*[13]

And here I believe lies the answer to our question, but it requires further digging to see it in all its glory and understand how these managers who defraud large amounts of money get away with it for such an extensive period of time.

---

13 Goffman 1959 op cit., p. 14.

DRAMATIC REALISATION BETWEEN AUDIENCE AND ACTOR IN THE CORPORATE SETTING

For managerial fraudsters there would be an overlay of an added element of activity in their dramatic realisation. Goffman saw this as a problem for many people in their work activities who are outside the public eye. Whereas policemen, ambulance personnel and firefighters work in public space, an accountant for instance has little or no public activity apart from presenting reports of financial data.[13] This means such performers are left with the conundrum of spending time to communicate their act, so that the audience will actually recognise it, or remain ignored. A sort of calculation takes place and performers may resort to expressing their public drama. They may be using their clothes, or actions, or who they circulate with, what they talk about, or the way they talk to enact their drama. Goffman notes that social climbers in particular (compared with career climbers), are ripe for examining the idealisation that takes place. The upwardly mobile tend to espouse what is seen as the best of the next social rung upwards and this is reflected in their homes, their possessions, even clothing. Does this happen to the managerial fraudsters who desire money to create the next social rung for themselves? As we have seen many fraudsters do have a lavish lifestyle.

Idealisation of the act is a two-edged sword with executives. Goffman makes specific reference to the fact that many executives are unaware of their physical appearance. The audience (employers) want 'to see "Hollywood" types, good looking, tall, not smoking or drinking too much in the course of the interview'.[14] This reminds me of the appealing candidate that was a possible choice of the locum management position. However, the executives appear to carry out their performance very well once *in situ*: 'executives often project an air of competency and general grasp of the situation, blinding themselves and others to the fact that they hold their jobs partly because they look like executives, not because they work like executives.'[15] And this is the point of impression management, not only do actors play the part; the illusory process is entrenched in our daily life. Remembering the Emperor and his new clothes, the Emperor wanted to look the part of the successful leader and therefore was vulnerable to the tailors who understood this social device implicitly, and duped him into buying the magical cloth to make a new set of clothes. As we know, the storyline is that a little boy who was not part of the trick shouted out

14 White, R., and D. Hanson. 2002. Corporate self, corporate reputation and corporate annual reports: re-enrolling Goffman. *Scandinavian Journal of Management* 18 (3): 285–301.

the fact that the Emperor was walking around with no clothes on which ended the delusion.

THE IMPORTANCE OF THE AUDIENCE

Impression management at first appears to be a one-way manipulative process, but in fact it is a two-way process. The audience is the final critic and judge of what the actor is trying to convey. Impression management lives or dies on audiences' reactions. For instance, Clark and Salaman[15] used the impression management approach to gain a better understanding of the executive recruiter's role in selection processes.

They found that shortlisted candidates were coached on the client's vacant position but usually without any clues being given as to the identity of the organisation. The coaching process sometimes took several meetings, and could involve videoing, giving feedback to the candidate and advising on grooming, personal manner and so on. By the time the preferred candidate was put before the audience, the employer had been groomed by the backstage manager of the executive recruitment company on the candidate's positive attributes. The interview takes place and the candidate is able to field all possible questions, because the questions that were likely to be asked were known in advance. The stage is likely to be the recruiter's office, usually boardroom-like in appearance. If the audience, that is the employer, appreciated the show then the candidate is offered the job. And if it is otherwise, the employer is later persuaded to take the same candidate, being told that this one, out of many others who have been interviewed, is the only one both suitable and available.

This happened to me some time ago when I was looking for an executive position. I was brought in several times for a particular position and got to know the headhunters quite well. The *pièce de résistance* was after my interview, when the manager of the headhunting company told me sternly while escorting me to the back door 'Do not stuff up if you get the job!' Clearly I was not the preferred candidate but they still wanted to take the money if the foolhardy employer chose me. Happily for everyone, I did not get the job, although I was anxious to win it at the time. Many years later, when I recruited locums I hoped to be far more fair and honest with candidates.

15 Clark, T., and G. Salaman. 1998. Creating the 'right' impression: towards a dramaturgy of management consultancy. *The Service Industries Journal* 18 (1): 18–38.

However, the above examples illustrate beautifully the dramaturgy of every day events and the reciprocal nature of the performance. Each player is undertaking impression management for others to view and therefore they act accordingly. Here are several actors: the executive recruiter, the candidate and the hiring employer. Each party wishes to convey the 'right' impression of themselves. The executive recruiter wants to suggest the image of professionalism: as the fount of knowledge of all things regarding recruitment, of being polished and slick, ready to handle and steer any concerns of the audience with a steady hand, like a coxswain in a racing rowing boat. The primary objective of his activity is to obtain a fee for the service rendered. The secondary objective is to have repeat business, either from the client audience immediately or longer-term business from the candidate once he is *in situ* and wants to hire new staff. The show ends with a satisfied client receiving the 'best' candidate for the position, and the recruiter receives a fee and the prospect of further business. And so the wheel turns once more in the impression management process.

ACTING IN TRUTH

'Acting in truth' may seem a bit too far-fetched, given that Goffman says that people are continuously acting, but as he was at pains to point out, this is done almost subconsciously. Furthermore, for most people, there is no malicious strategic intent. Honest people may be doing an honest day's work, going home to honest families and relaxing because they know that they have been true to themselves and their integrity is intact. The only way to ascertain the actor's true attitudes, Goffman says, is indirectly from the performance. It is the indirect nature of what is truly going on that shows impression management in a negative way. Many individuals can put on an act with the intention to deceive or manipulate, and at first glance the performance is believable. The audience, says Goffman,

> *will be forced to accept some events as conventional or natural signs of something that is not directly available to the senses … the individual will have to act so that he intentionally or unintentionally* expresses *himself, and the others will in turn have to be* impressed *in some way by him.*[16]

Goffman goes on to explain that there are two different sign activities, the expression that the actor *gives*, and the expression that the actor *gives off*. If

16 Goffman 1959 op cit., p. 2, author's emphasis.

the two are in harmony, the audience accepts the performance. If there is a discrepancy, the actor is viewed with suspicion, even though there may not be any tangible evidence to support this view. Thus the executive recruitment example outlined above can only work if there is no discrepancy or divergence in what is given and what is given off by the three parties. What we are getting to here is that the giving off component is the assurance of honesty that we intuitively pick up. For this to be received the audience must be reassured intuitively on the issue, which is the underlying condition of impression management, the authenticity of performance.

GIVING OFF AUTHENTICITY

Goffman did not fully explain fully the giving off process, but he argues that audiences are expert enough in daily transactions to identify when a person is inauthentic, implying that authenticity must be the foundation of the social interaction. Being inauthentic may be intuitively sensed perhaps through a detail that is seen to be not quite right or an uncomfortable feeling, but nothing more tangible than that. I have already demonstrated in my introduction that with the two managers before me for the locum position, only the dishevelled manager looked and seemed out of place. The tall handsome one appeared to be the best fit. But was I wrong in my liking the Hollywood star or was I having misgivings to reject the desperate manager?

The audience can only make inferences about the actor's behaviour based on their own past evidence. No amount of past evidence however, will be continually be held in any one person's mind, so the judgement process has to rely on the most recent part that the actor has performed. The audience therefore has to either judge on actual behavioural discrepancies or intuitively grasp signs that things are not as they should be. The actor therefore is driven to seek to control the conduct of his audience:

> *This control is achieved largely by influencing the definition of a situation which the others come to formulate, and he can influence this definition by expressing himself in such a way as to give them the kind of impression that will lead to act voluntarily in accordance of his own plan.*[17]

The actor implicitly requests belief from the audience, as much as the audience wants to believe the actor. As Goffman says:

17 Goffman 1959 op cit., p. 15.

> *They are asked to believe that the character they see actually possesses the attributes he appears to possess, that the task he performs will have the consequences that are implicitly claimed for it, and that in general, matters are what the appear to be.*[18]

There are two extremes to this reciprocal arrangement perpetrated by the actor. The first is that he himself believes totally in the 'real reality', and this sincerity convinces all but the most cynical of audiences. The other position is that the actor may, rather cynically, not believe his own performance and regard it as an insincere show. This is a bit like being faced with a friend's ugly baby. Do you continue with the cooing? Of course we do. We cannot be rude and say how ugly the baby looks but we know that we are being insincere at that moment.

Goffman takes pains to excuse our insincerity by pointing out that that these performers may not be doing this for purposes of self-interest or gain, but because it is demanded by the situation. He gives the example of a doctor resignedly giving placebos to hypochondriacs to illustrate this point. There is a push–pull with the performer to be sincere or be keeping up with appearances, depending on the circumstances. He explains further that this will happen despite the fact it may not exactly hold true.[19]

The checks and balances to inauthenticity are present in the form of the actor's sense of shame, guilt or fear of being found out. Goffman thought that these would offset and prevent many performers from misrepresenting the facts. The ugly baby may not receive as many cooing responses as a pretty bonny infant. However, clucking noises about how he will grow into being a fine young man and so on are our way of dealing with the misrepresentation of our authenticity.

However, there will be times when intentional misrepresentation will occur. Audiences are alerted to this, and look for clues that are not readily manipulated by the performer. Often these will be non-verbal signs in the actor's appearance: the giving off process, as previously mentioned. However, here lies the conundrum: because audiences tend to believe that no person in their right mind would try to act a lie, with the immediate prospect of being humiliated when the truth inevitably comes out, they are actually laying themselves wide open to such manipulation. The basis of the interaction is that the actor has a moral right to play the part. If it turns out that the actor is

18 Goffman 1959 op cit., p. 17.
19 Goffman 1959 op cit., p. 21.

an imposter, the audience declares that he has no right to that performance. Goffman explained that if the audience is persuaded that the actor is genuine in his role they undergo a questioning of what is real and what is not.

Feeling duped is not a pleasant thing for any audience, and it breaks all the social rules of the reciprocity of social interaction. It also takes away trust, which is one of the unspoken foundations of impression management. Interestingly, white lies are not viewed as violations of trust, particularly if they are used to save the face of an audience member, according to Goffman. Deliberate lies, however, are not excused, because they immediately erode trust. Moreover, it may only take one lie to be found out and the rest of the performance is put under question and not believed, even if it is the truth. Authenticity and trust therefore go hand in hand and underscore the audience reciprocity that Goffman envisaged with impression management.

However, misrepresentation is not a mask that an individual puts on to do impression management. In fact, it is quite the opposite. It is intrinsically part of our social behaviour and reflects the social reality around us:

> *Goffman's position is that there is nothing inherently unreal about the scripts and parts we play, that they in fact reflect real aspects of our complex selves. Roles are real and authentic parts of who we are, not false masks that cover up some deeper self.*[20]

Audiences acknowledge that they cannot perceive all that is going on underneath, but if there is anything that is remotely suspicious, the inauthentic activity acts like a magnet for disbelief and further scrutiny. And that's the thing that makes inauthentic actions stand out Goffman says. Authentic actions are unnoticed, because they are part of the person. Goffman emphasises this authenticity and implicitly with it trust, in daily actions is the crux of what is *not* noticed. He attributes no malicious intent to daily impression management, but the intellectual problem with his thinking is that impression management ordinarily is not seen and therefore receives minimal attention from social researchers, or anyone for that matter.

By using the constructs of dramaturgy and impression management, the student of social life potentially holds a unique way of organising material and analysing action. Later Goffman points out that: 'To say that he [the

20 Johnson, A. 1995. *The Blackwell dictionary of sociology: a user's guide to sociological language.* Cambridge, MA: Blackwell, pp. 87–88.

performer] assumes a role and presents himself through it is already a bias in the direction of wholeness and authenticity. What he does is to present a one-man show.'[21]

Goffman observes that when a person enters the presence of others there is an instant appraisal that takes place. This is predicated on the audience's own experience of this 'type' and expectations of this type's role. But there is an underlying test of authenticity that occurs:

> *Many crucial facts lie beyond the time and place of interaction or lie concealed within it. For example, the 'true' or 'real' attitudes, beliefs, and emotions of the individual can be ascertained only indirectly, through his avowals or through what appears to be involuntarily expressive behaviour.*[22]

AUTHENTICITY IN TIMES OF CRISIS

Finally, Goffman talks about specific situations, life crises that reveal the true self to all who are there to observe. He discusses how our capabilities are learnt and put in place almost out of habit and form the concept of character from the actors' associated qualities. These form a mask, which is put on by the actor in every interaction. Because the mask is learned behaviour, there is no doubt that under certain situations it will slip. He goes on to say that when the individual is under acute pressure, suddenly there are 'fateful consequences'. There is a risk of the mask slipping, and this is the time observations can be made about the 'secondary' qualities of the character. As Goffman said: 'in the heat and haste of the moment, naked self interest may obtrude'.[23]

Goffman predicted that the matter of task performance at this crucial time would cause an individual's primary characteristics to fail him. The impending adrenaline-fuelled situation may make him nervous, run away or freeze him into inaction. Alternatively, if the person is a strong, true character, it can create a huge step forward in performance and the audience will be very persuaded of the integrity of this individual. Goffman ascertains three types of characters: (i) Weak: 'evidence of incapacity to behave effectively and correctly under

21 Goffman, E. 1974. *Frame analysis, an essay on the organization of experience*, p. 547. Boston, MA: University Press of New England. Original edition, 1974.

22 Goffman, 1959, op cit., pp. 13–14.

23 Goffman, E. 1967. *Interaction ritual: essays on face-to-face behavior*. New York: Pantheon Books. Original edition, 1967, p. 216.

stress of fatefulness is a sign of weak character'.[24] (ii) Strong: 'evidence of marked capacity to maintain full self control when the chips are down is a sign of strong character'.[25] The actor keeps on regardless of the pressure. (iii) Average: they are not judged – the performance is as expected by the audience.

Goffman is at pains to point out that primary properties of an individual can be delivered any time, once the behaviour is learnt, in any situation that is not a crisis, but once the situation changes to having meaningful consequences for him, then the secondary qualities, that of the 'character' are judged. One may approve or disapprove of primary qualities, but this is of no consequence, Goffman says. Qualities of character, however, are paramount, and always judged on a moral basis. And it is this evidence that gives the individual his individual 'flavouring': 'a single expression tends to be taken as an adequate basis for judgement'.[26]

The individual properties of character according to Goffman[27] are displayed in Table 3.1.

Audiences do not tolerate discomposure; they become ill at ease and feel uncomfortable with what is going on with the actor, because it makes the actor's character less appealing. Certainly in my PowerPoint presentation when the inappropriate slide pops up, I am open to a severe critique of my intelligence. Some have said that the wrong slide confirmed for them my lack of understanding about such a complex theory! Furthermore, they were annoyed that I didn't seem to be perturbed by the fact it was the wrong slide

Table 3.1 Goffman's properties of character

Property	Description
Courage	Ability to face great risk.
Gameness	Achieving goals no matter the setbacks.
Integrity	Being able to resist temptation, particularly when faced with great gains and little impunity e.g., fraud. Self-discipline reinforces integrity.
Gallantry	Continuing a performance even at cost to self.
Composure	Calmness in a great crisis. Anger shows loss of control. It requires: presence of mind, capacity to think despite what is going on, dignity and stage confidence – not showing any stress.

24 Ibid., p. 217.
25 Ibid., p. 217.
26 Ibid., p. 218.
27 Ibid.

as I kept up my performance. In fact, Goffman thought that the nature of character was based on individuals having to keep up the social interaction that they are involved in and not show any signs of stress, however slight. The most miniscule sign of stress will lead to degeneration of his character in the eyes of the audience. Fortunately my audiences were relieved that they were not wasting their time by watching an altered photograph of a kangaroo with a pint of beer at the table and that I was truly who I said I was, a social researcher, and I had completed my experiment to teach them what happened when they are the audience using me as the 'actor'. Not only could there be aberrant details, there could also be physical and even facial signs such as tiny muscles constricting on the actor's face. All of this will uncover him.

Audiences can be even more sceptical, as we have seen in job interviews, and therefore start to screen the participant from what he is *giving off*. As discussed earlier, this is largely ungovernable by the actor. Despite the audience checking on validity as soon as the actor starts performing, the very clever actor will then plant seeds of the ungovernable aspects of his performance to convince the audience of the authenticity of his behaviour. Audiences can sense that the actor is doing this, and therefore make judgements which once again occur out of his control, thus symmetry, a social ebb and flow, happens between actor and audience.

For the first time we are being told that in the actor's accounts of self there is fusion of what is predictable to what is not. Similarly there is tension that flows internally within a manager when he consciously conducts an impression management exercise to improve his standing with an organisation. Even tried and tested strategies may fail the manager if the audience detects something untoward.

This balance of observation and detection is seen in small business owners, who when recruiting staff, cite honesty as the most preferred trait in an employee.[28] The small business owner when meeting the candidate evaluates this virtue. If the applicant fails to convince then nothing else will get them the job. The applicant cannot get past first base, to use a baseball analogy. Business owners cannot afford the services of a recruiter and will rely on their time-tested audience role of detecting any discrepancy intuitively and verifying authenticity of the performance. This is not as unsophisticated as it may seem. Peeters and

28 Bartram, D. 2004. Assessment in organizations. *Applied Psychology: An International Review* 53 (2): 237–259.

Lievens[29] investigated how structured interview formats influenced the use and effectiveness of verbal and non-verbal impression management. Results demonstrated that the interview format affected the kind of tactics used by job seekers, which in turn positively influenced interviewer evaluations. This is exactly the type of reaction that would be anticipated in dramaturgy, that the audience participates and influences the situation or drama outcome. The finding that candidates can favourably influence interviewers is corroborated by a host of other researchers in different settings.[30]

However, for larger organisations the incoming manager may sit a barrage of tests and as discussed earlier have a staged interview, but it is afterwards when the individual commences work that the audiences of colleagues and subordinate employees begin an intensive screening of authenticity, albeit informally. It is at this point that the foundation of authenticity, that is trust, is established and the audience begins to feel comfortable, or not, with their new manager. More research is required to understand this process as on the whole, authenticity of managers is still largely unexplored.

NEGATIVITY

There is a negative side to an individual openly manipulating audiences. Goffman recognised this when he later stated that people try to manipulate not only themselves but also the situations in which they interact. A case in point is his discussion of fabrications, where people are led to believe that a particular situation exists, when in fact it does not.[31] This brings us back to authenticity and the motives of the actor, which are internal processes unseen by the audience and relating to the self. Actions as presented in Goffman's earlier work are mere projections of the self, but what the self is, positive or negative, that drives these actions, remains unclear.[32] This question of what

29 Peeters, H., and F. Lievens. 2006. Verbal and nonverbal impression management tactics in behavior description and situational interviews. *International Journal of Selection and Assessment* 14 (3): 206–222.

30 Among many others, Gilmore, D. C., and G. R. Ferris. 1989. The effects of applicant impression management tactics on interviewer judgments. *Journal of Management* 15 (4): 557–564; Silvester, J., F. M. Anderson-Gough, N. R. Anderson, and A. R. Mohamed. 2002. Locus of control, attributions and impression management in the selection interview. *Journal of Occupational and Organizational Psychology* 75 (1): 59–77; Stevens, C. K., and A. L. Kristof. 1995. Making the right impression: a field study of applicant impression management during job interviews. *Journal of Applied Psychology* 80 (5): 587–607.

31 Goffman 1974, op cit.

32 Travers, A. 1997. 'Erving Goffman and modern sociology' by Philip Manning (a review). *Reviewing Sociology* (1) (electronic article) http://www.rdg.ac.uk/RevSoc/archive/volume10/number1/10-1e.htm (accessed 28 June 2010).

is the self will be returned to later in this chapter. I will discuss this further because the self remains unknown yet we assume we know the self in others and indeed ourselves.

Use of Impression Management as a Research Tool

Goffman proposed that impression management is continual and present in every social interaction, even the most mundane. For example two people meeting: 'Good morning.' The 'good morning' offered in reply will contain much assurance for the actor that all is fine with his audience. Tonal inflections of speech – even an executioner can use the same salutation to the condemned man, and the same reply can be made, carries out the same social interaction in total. These two different contexts demonstrate the vast range from the mundane to the extraordinary in a social exchange. The complexity of impression management however, is remarkable.

As the process of impression management is unremitting and out of sight, how can we note it as present? Goffman's surprising but brilliant approach is to focus on those events where impression management is disrupted or fails. His first book contained chapters on discrepancies and communications that are out of character. Additionally, in later writing, *Interaction Ritual* and *Frame Analysis*, he focuses mostly on disruptions to illustrate the pervasiveness of impression management in social action. If you wish to understand the impression management process you should study disruptions and discrepancies in line with Goffman's own original approach. Managerial fraud is one such disruption to impression management because the audience – co-workers – failed to pick up or respond to discrepancies with their fraudster manager.

SETTING UP THE INVESTIGATION

That meant I had a working theory that could be used for the investigation as well as a working definition of executive fraud, which relies on notions of intentional deceit by trusted stewards of organisations. This in itself is an interactive process between two or more parties: the organisations' owners, employees and the fraudster. The application of theory centred on the fraudsters' motivation, whether intrinsic or external, does little to explain the social dynamics between fraudsters and their colleagues. However, if misrepresentation or breach of trust is crucial to the definition of managerial fraud then a relevant theory needs to address the dynamics of representation.

This is the gap that impression management addressed in its appreciation of the depictive process in everyday life that forms around every actor.[33]

FINDING THE CO-WORKERS

The investigation was set to go, all that had to be done was prepare an interview guide and find some co-workers of fraudster managers. Probably the most challenging part of the research was to find the people who worked with a fraudster manager. In order to start the theoretical sampling, a fraudster manager had first to be identified, next the organisation had to be found (not often reported in the media) and finally the co-workers were to be contacted. I sent letters explaining the research and was very surprised at the lack of co-operation by banks and financial institutions to participate. They cited various reasons why they could not pass my request to interview on to co-workers, and all of the excuses were frankly rubbish. By the time of the thirtieth or more refusal, I was facing a dire collapse of the research. I also came to the conclusion that big business hid behind supposed legal reasons. At one time I had contacted a director of a national bank responsible for internal fraud and she gave me her full backing. Later this was stalled by their legal department so that I could not use that fraud case.

As I felt a singular case study was far from revealing, I had to press on using many channels to locate a fraud. Even Court of Criminal Appeals' judgments were used to find cases. 'Regular' cases, that is, those that are not appealed, do not have published outcomes, so it was impossible to trace individual cases or find a particular type of case. Furthermore, none of the court officers who were contacted wished to spend their time searching for cases. They were busy enough as it is. Police fraud squads declined to assist in finding cases, because their resources had to focus on active frauds.

At one stage, 24 fraud cases were compiled from Internet media sites, of which only 8 fraudsters satisfied the selection criteria. The companies listed were researched and I approached an appropriate contact. Usually this was a HR manager but in some cases could be the CEO or a board director. This person was telephoned or contacted by email, and a formal invitation was sent by email to that person to forward on to employees who worked with the fraudster.

33 Goffman 1967, op cit., p. 5.

Data collection from most of the larger enterprises that suffered major loss from managerial fraud was prevented by the refusal of companies to forward the request for interviews to the co-workers of the fraudster managers. This was said to be on the grounds of privacy. Typically financial institutions' response ran along the lines of:

> *Regretfully [the corporation] cannot assist in providing the information you seek. The [corporation] is bound by the Federal Privacy Act, and specifically the National Privacy Principles in relation to the disclosure of 'personal information'. While employment records are in exempt [sic] from the privacy legislation if the act or use of the information is directly related to the employment relationship, the use of the personal information regarding current or former [corporation] employees requested by you does not fall within this exemption.*

I had no interest in the name of the respondent, this was made clear from the outset and in my replies to each organisation reiterating that there would not be any trespassing of privacy guidelines. However, the invitation was usually ignored. This was not particular to this study, Lee and Renzetti note that 'powerful gatekeepers can impose restrictions on researchers in ways that constrain their capacity to produce or report on findings that threaten the interests of the powerful.'[34] It was very hard to not fall into this line of thinking as I kept on getting knocked back.

It was through this process of locked gates guarded by obsessive wardens that I then fully understood the concerns of Yeager[35] and especially Dodge and Geis,[36] who appreciated the problems of scholarship related to aspects of white-collar crime: 'The work demands creativity in the collection of data, often zealously guarded by powerful forces. It encourages in-depth case studies and challenges those involved to shift paradigms to account for changing and complex methods of law-breaking.'[37] This was somewhat alarming and was beginning to seem true.

34 Lee, R. M., and C. M. Renzetti. 1990. The problems of researching sensitive topics: an overview and introduction. *American Behavioral Scientist* 33 (5): 510–528, p. 514.

35 Yeager, P. C. 2009. Science, values and politics: an insider's reflections on corporate crime research. *Crime Law and Social Change* 51 (1): 5–30.

36 Dodge, Mary, and Gilbert Geis. 2009. Social and political transformations in white-collar crime scholarship: introductory notes. *Crime Law and Social Change* 51 (1): 1–3.

37 Ibid., p. 3.

I then contacted management and business associations but they would not oblige either. Finally I sent out an appeal to co-workers on local radio, and I was able to interview some very interesting cases indeed. The public therefore, unlike the financial institutions, are interested in fraud research. Perhaps it was this exposure that the larger institutions wanted to avoid, to unearth evidence that would be problematic for them. Whatever prevented them, it was very short-sighted on their part.

This reminds me of when I was being considered as a consultant by a fairly large concern to pinpoint areas of employee theft and bribery. I stated that I felt confident on dealing with this and turn their culture around. I will always remember the business owner saying to me 'Oh I know that you will find theft all right!' but I didn't win the contract because it was an obvious possibility regarding bad publicity in this case, that she did not want to uncover it. It tells you much about a company that is managed like that, and at one point earlier the company suffered a A$2 million fraud and the CEO fired the accounts manager, because he was the senior manager responsible for the thieving employee. Today I feel very sorry for that accounts manager, he did not see a fraud that was hidden by deceit and cunning, nevertheless he lost his job and reputation in the process.

Finally, all of the co-workers satisfied the criteria of working with the fraudster manager at the time of the fraudulent activities and had regular if not daily interaction with the manager. All fraudsters were convicted and received prison sentences and almost all satisfied the monetary value: the lowest amount was just over A$950,000, the highest nearly A$20 million.

PREPARING FOR THE INTERVIEW BEFORE SELECTING THE CO-WORKERS

For qualitative methodology to work, one of the most important principles is to allow the interviewee freedom to express whatever they want to say. This could have been a plethora of loosely connected items or a planned speech prepared by the interviewee, it does not really matter in terms of the data being collected. The format is purely a framework in which the interviewee is able to talk about their experience. All I had to do was start the ball rolling with: 'Tell me what happened.'

Everything that was said was recorded. In this unstructured part there were times that an interesting point came up and the co-worker was asked to expand on it. Usually it was an open 'In what way?' Freefall interviewing seems simple, but in fact it is not. Restraint must be used to avoid asking leading questions and jumping to conclusions, and also to avoid the use of closed questions which the respondent would oblige with a simple yes or no.

SENSITIVITY TO THOSE WHO HAVE WORKED WITH A FRAUDSTER

Certain factors have to be borne in mind at such an interview. This is not for the faint-hearted. Some interviewees had threats made to them by the fraudster or their families, and a few of those appeared to have organised crime connections, although not in the instance of the fraud itself. Experienced researchers find that just dealing with deviance is in itself an emotionally charged issue[38] and there may be some 'I should have's' and 'I ought to have done that's.' which come out. These must be treated with great respect, as we do not yet have a guide on how to work with a fraudster manager. Self-flagellation is not pleasant to record, but it does happen, especially if the co-worker felt responsible in some way.

Painful subject matter needs time to come out as the interviewee remembers the past experience and relives it. Most interviews were about an hour but some stretched to two hours. It was also possible that the co-worker never had a formal debriefing, especially if they left the organisation soon after the fraud. Sometimes the interview became the first account to an outside observer. This type of interview is very similar to a therapeutic relationship, particularly if warmth, responsiveness and a genuine interest in what the person has to say is present.[39] All I can say is that the bravery of the co-workers was immense. It was particularly arduous if the person concerned liked the manager and trusted him. The sense of betrayal and hurt was present throughout the interview and they battled on to tell what they had seen. I think this is similar to debriefing a victim of a car accident or some other great trauma, the shell-shock is still etched on their faces years afterwards.

Great care was exercised in regard to the venue, and I ensured that the co-worker was at ease and ready to participate. I had no idea what would be said in the interviews. However, I knew that with my previous interviewing in therapeutic settings as a social worker, mental health worker and management counselling that I could manage successfully to take on the interviewer role no matter how difficult.

---

38 Lee and Renzetti 1990, op cit.

39 Cannell, C. F., and R. L. Kahn. 1953. The collection of data by interviewing. In *Research methods in the behavioral sciences*, ed. L. Festinger and D. Katz, 327–380. New York: Dryden Press.

Never knowing what could be said was enough to be apprehensive about. I suddenly had an ethical dilemma when it struck me that the interviewee conducted her own fraud while the spotlight was on the other manager. When I mentioned this to someone, I was laughed at and I am quite sure it made a good story around the water cooler at the office. I could not give corroborating evidence, otherwise I would have had gone directly to the police. This situation however proves how complex crime research is. The interview has not the same vows of silence as the confessional in the Catholic Church, and the interviewer has to be aware the whole time that further criminal activity could come to light.

A second part of the interview was answering questions from a previously constructed interview guide from impression management theory and the hodgepodge of possible factors. It took the form of a semi-structured checklist asking true/false statements on the characteristics of the interaction between the fraudster and the co-worker. This was to ensure all aspects of the possible characteristics of fraudsters that was reviewed were covered (see Table 3.2). Interestingly enough, some co-workers talked at length in this part of the interview more than the initial part. It was almost as if the informal part warmed them up. Their true/false statement was recorded and many went on to give much more insight and pages of data.

Table 3.2 Topics covered in the question component of the interview.

Theoretical Context	Topics
Impression management	Immorality or amorality; dishonesty; moral behaviour and views
	Authenticity; being a good actor; masking behaviour
Red Flags	Greed
	Financial stress
	Marital difficulties
	Dominating personality; 'yes men'
	Work long hours, no holidays
Red Flag and neutralisation theory	Rationalisation behaviour
Social Psychology	Depression
	Social monitoring
	Machiavellian
	Addictive behaviour; gambling
Psychopath - general	Superiority; low view of humanity; lack of empathy
Psychopath - organisational	Dominating personality
Psychopath – corporate criminal	Conscientiousness

The questions were formed to force a choice between positive and negative answers to avoid 'fence sitting'. This was not a survey, only an attempt to see if recipients had noted aspects that were seen as 'traditional' fraud personal characteristics.

Table 3.2 shows that there was a collection of factors for fraud. Items were also added to see if the participant held high self-esteem, and gullibility towards the fraudster, as well as any critical incident cited by Goffman as noted earlier, where the real character could be seen. Finally, the recipient was asked if there were any further ideas or comments about their interaction.

The constructs developed from the various aspects were randomly put together on the checklist, so that one question did not lead into another. This meant that returning to a particular issue in a later question often refocused the recipient to bring out further information.

THE NON-FRAUDSTER SAMPLE

Thinking that the non-fraudster sample would be much easier to achieve, I was surprised at how difficult this too proved to be. Many managerial associations were contacted along with graduate schools of management, all in vain. Finally managers were contacted through Internet sites that specialised in sharing contact information about managers and professionals who had voluntarily put up their own details for networking purposes, for example LinkedIn.com. This was supplemented by personal contacts who knew others and the process slowly produced a satisfactory sample of non-fraudster senior manager co-workers who were willing to be interviewed.

HOW TO WORK WITH BUBBLES

I will briefly describe the constant comparison methodology to demonstrate how the data were analysed, as it may be new to many. Altogether I gathered 16 hours and 20 minutes of interviews. The audio recordings were each transcribed directly word for word, contiguous with the actual audio recording, ready for analysis. These were grouped into items of meaning which could be merely one word if it was expressive enough to a paragraph or two if the meaning was all the same. This generated 3,859 separate units of meaning, and when grouped together coalesced into 2,029 separate nodes or what I prefer to call them, bubbles.

Coding was separated into two parts according to where the utterances were in relation to the interview. All of the first part of the interview was unstructured and free-flow and grouped under 'Their Stories', whereas the second part of the interview was highly structured with two separate sections as described earlier under 'Question Data'. Somewhat surprisingly, the second part produced more data than the first for some respondents, but these data were still kept separate and grouped together under Question Data. The fraudster data were coded first.

All the utterances were coded as free codes, just like bubbles in a bath. In this way, there was no forcing of the data into preconceived tree-form hierarchies. Due to my previous experience that the constant comparison method worked, I was able to gather together groups of data. The bubbles began to form. These groupings were open coded and great care was taken to reflect the coalesced meaning. References to the Macquarie Dictionary, Roget's Thesaurus and online dictionaries and thesaurus were made to match the intent with the words uttered. Sometimes this would take several hours of checking and re-checking that the bubble name was a good reflection of the meaning.

The groups of data gradually formed into their own associations. As I had the voice of the recipient at my fingertips, it felt very much like a natural process with constant verification of what the words were intended to mean by the recipient. Hearing the inflection of the tone of voice directly with the written word as subtitles is a wonderful way to recall and understand the meaning as it was said. Video recordings would have been similar with body language also to be coded, but as this was such a sensitive issue it was decided to make audio recordings only. I worked with the co-workers of fraudster managers first and a number of larger bubbles or categories emerged. By the end of the constant comparison process with these categories, I felt highly confident regarding the strength of the data. These categories of meaning formed constructs, which in turn formed overarching themes – equivalent to Glaser and Strauss' core category.

I covered a blank wall with pieces of paper and stood back to synthesise these categories. There are computer programs for this, but to my mind nothing beats a blank wall and many bits of paper to move around. I found that I used the computer for the detail, but the wall was better for the overall themes. This assisted the emergence process to keep me in the detail plus overview mode of the process. Categories of meanings were inspected and disassembled and re-categorised as necessary. At all times I was aware of my own bias as much as possible, and tried to keep the effect of value judgements to a minimum and bracket internal thoughts about possibilities about the data. Another source of possible contamination was that some co-workers were likeable, others less so, and it took some self-discipline to not allow this to interfere with the coding. Constraining outside and internal distortion was a foremost concern in all of my analytical work as it can unravel with less than the utmost effort.

Overall it took about two weeks for the coded fraudster data to emerge into a theme. Glaser and Strauss, the masters of grounded theory, note this quickness as a normal process in the emergence of categories and core processes. Similar concepts emerged from each set and the Question Data produced its own verification. The development of constructs assisted in the formation of the themes after much deconstruction and reconstruction. This was somewhat cumbersome at times, but greatly assisted me in focusing on what was represented in the concept.

After the fraudster data were coded, I turned to the co-workers of non-fraudster senior managers and repeated the process. Once that was concluded, using the same constant comparison process with reinforcement from the recipients' voices, large bubbles of meaning emerged which formed into constructs and overarching themes. There was a distinct similarity between their Stories concepts and those from the Question Data.

Chapter 4

The Makings of the Fraudster Manager Typology

Again, I wish to say that I did not have preconceived ideas of what the data would 'bubble up'. As I built the model my fraud investigator husband was amazed at how the bubble process worked as I added pieces of paper of the different constructs that were emerging on my office wall. He would argue certain points occasionally, but I stuck to the methodology of constant comparison, and then saw what the data were indicating. These he accepted with very good grace, especially when he saw the outcomes emerging as a new piece of theory. To have an expert on my doorstep was a good thing in many ways, but I didn't want to have his worldview impressed upon the data. This process had to be pure and uncontaminated. Having used this methodology before,[1] I knew that the data had to 'find their own voice'.

The core process, or if you like, the new bit of theory that materialised, I labelled Executive Impression Management. This covers in my mind managers in general as well. To call the new core process as Manager Impression Management was too confusing, so Executive Impression Management it was.

From this it was found that the co-workers of fraudster and non-fraudster managers' Executive Impression Management, perceive that:

- Managers use five different types of impression management.
- Fraudster managers use two of these types of impression management.
- Non-fraudster managers use the remaining three types of impression management.

1 Sheridan, T.A., 2005. *Voicing women managers' unemployment experience in Australia: the hidden toll.* Perth: Women Chiefs of Enterprises International (Australia) August.

I have labelled each type according to what the co-workers had to say about the type of manager who used their Executive Impression Management.

There are two types Executive Impression Management that fraudster managers used:

- The Arrogant Fraudster
- The Likeable Fraudster.

The other Executive Impression Management that the non-fraudster senior managers used were:

- The Respectful
- The Tyrant
- The Mediocre.

The latter three types are discussed at length in another book.

Previously the extent of knowledge about white-collar criminals, let alone managerial fraudsters, has not changed much since Romney, Albrecht and Cherrington wrote in 1980 when they found out that this is not a easy task because they look the same as 'normal' people.[2]

Using the findings of this investigation, a step forward has been made because managerial fraudsters use different forms of impression management than the rest of us. This is the missing piece of the puzzle that has perplexed us for so long. Outwardly the fraudster managers look normal. Nevertheless underneath the mask is a crook. It is the mask that fooled all of us including such great minds as Romney, Albrecht and Cherrington, the founders of the Red Flags. Previous quantitative investigations could never single out this difference. It was the qualitative application to the fraudster managers' co-workers that supplied the answers, and not only that the information they gave was rich in insight and gives us clues as to what to detect in aspiring managers to prevent fraud in organisations.

2 Romney, M. B., W. S. Albrecht, and D. J. Cherrington. 1980a. Auditors and the detection of fraud. *Journal of Accountancy* 149 (5): 63–69, p. 65.

The Arrogant Fraudster

The name for this type of Executive Impression Management, which exudes from those managers who defraud organisations comes from their superior attitude to the workplace, and as co-workers witnessed, to the rest of their world, family, friends and so on.

This feature was composed of arrogance, maintaining a successful appearance and the co-workers feeling of whatever was said 'was all about him'. All who worked with what was later to become identified as an Arrogant Fraudster reported this feeling of superiority imposed upon them.

Co-workers also noted particular behaviours such as being egotistical, grandiose or narcissistic, which they tie to the arrogance of this type of fraudster.

In relation to a question on self-awareness:

> *Researcher: Did [the fraudster] ever understand his strengths and weaknesses as far as you saw?*
>
> *Co-worker: No, he thought he was the best at everything. Soccer ... with women, yeah.*

Egotistical behaviour ranged from wanting to be the centre of attention, to grandiose thinking, to being aloof. Clashes over wanting more pay more than what the manager was worth is another strategy to fulfil their narcissism. A co-worker reminisced that:

> *I remember over the time more than five or six times and he'd always tell [me] about how he had been in the bosses office, and 'I said to [the boss], listen ... I just told them and they just said yes because they wouldn't say no to me because I'm so great' and that kind of thing.*

The Arrogant Fraudster demands respect rather than earning it from subordinates. This came out a number of times, especially if for some reason they felt unsure of their power over others. Seeking leadership positions was seen as a deliberate way to have power over people. And in a more esoteric form of leadership, doing acts of kindness that were later seen as nothing more than a means to gain superiority.

> *He sponsored two Ph.D. students from India, and the local Graduate School of Business named a research room after him, because of his donations and support to the students undertaking their Ph.D. .... Masterful.*

Finally, the use of power plays was evident in the fraudsters preference for younger staff when hiring the 'right' people; thus providing a context where colleagues were considerably less experienced and skilled.

All the co-workers were made to feel inferior to the Arrogant Fraudster and this was maintained all the way through their employment. This is not confined to subordinates but also to upline superiors and even boards of management. This superiority was based on observation of egocentricity, appearing to be successful and pure unadulterated arrogance. Egocentricity is also a form of narcissism and co-workers observed that the Arrogant Fraudster had a compulsion of wanting to draw attention to themselves. In some cases this was done through showing off and posing as the good guy. In contrast, other fraudsters tended to have a particular need to be liked by colleagues or their boss.

Having a successful appearance includes a range of data relevant to the Arrogant Fraudsters' community roles, professional image and reputation, qualifications and education as well as status symbols. Having the appearance of having a well-recognised reputation, qualifications and education appeared to be another area of appearing successful, as part of the ruse.

From a different perspective, a recipient remarked about the fraudster after he was caught that the fraudster wanted to be regarded as a great man:

> *I mean, his ego, yeah he hurt himself as much as he hurt other people. His ego didn't handle being caught too well and yeah, I couldn't imagine it would. And with his friends, how he would have dealt with his friends and his family? That part of the family too, I think, I always thought that that would have been hard for him just because he's always been about impressions and being so great. So the fact, okay here's one piece of proof he isn't so great. Cold hard facts. To wonder what, he was doing his friends' tax and all this kind of stuff. I think, would he have ripped off his mates? It wouldn't surprise me, nothing would now, I mean for what he did to be able to front those guys every day you know.*

In other cases, superiority was demonstrated through some level of arrogance. Data in this category contained comments relevant to behaviours such as being grandiose or showing bravado.

DISGUISE

Falseness is a key component to the way the fraudster's impression management was received and reported in the interviews by the Arrogant Fraudster's co-workers. As the interview data was of reminiscence the co-workers talked about data that bubbled up into the categories of dishonesty that they saw; how the fraudster fooled everyone; was seen as harmless; their hiding behaviour; the long time it took to keep up the charade and interestingly from an impression management point of view that the Arrogant Fraudsters wore a mask.

Dishonesty was a category comprised of relatively large amounts of data. From how they abused their friendship, to being a very good liar:

> *and he is good at it because he could look you in the eye and be your friend and lie to you. He could keep that up. Well he kept it up for years.*

There were no warnings of the manager being fraudulent, which was remarked upon by the co-workers in their interviews. This is very important for people to be aware of, that the strength of the Arrogant Fraudster is overwhelmingly convincing.

> *But in essence, no warning bells, no-one that I spoke to gave really any indication of 'You need to be careful', or anything of that nature.*

> *In reality, there was nothing then, or later that really made me think, 'Oh wait a minute. This person has a propensity to be dishonest' on those lines.*

Another feature was that the Arrogant Fraudster would demonstrate that they were in total control of their work. This could be signalled through an obsessively tidy desk or the opposite, a complete mess of paperwork, which would look intimidating to an outsider.

Co-workers also discussed the Arrogant Fraudster's hiding behaviour. This would happen in a number of ways. They noted the fraudster managers' ability to throw off suspicions by various means, including balancing the books if necessary:

the [department] needed some money and there was a loan there of A$1,800 paid to the [organisation] – we knew nothing about. Funnily enough, [the department] actually paid that money back too, but it never came back here. I don't know where it went, somewhere else. But some of the A$58,000, [the fraudster] used that to paid that A$1,800 loan. So the books were ok.

They also tried to correct some of the fraudulent transfers even after they were about to be found out. Hiding behaviour appeared to be all about avoiding discovery at any cost. They were desperate to hide what they have done.

Data demonstrated that Arrogant Fraudsters would do all sorts of tricks to avoid detection, even little things like closing down the computer screen when anyone came near their desk, or changing the conversation.

The co-workers also referred to how Arrogant Fraudsters hid the money and assets. This information became known after the discovery but is relevant as one component of the fraudsters' behaviour before their fraudulent activities were discovered. They wished to cover their tracks just in case things went against them. This protective behaviour was demonstrated in an illuminating exchange between myself and a co-worker about the hiding behaviour:

Researcher: [Referring to notes]He was a gambler wasn't he?

Co-worker: Well we didn't know that.

Researcher: Afterwards. That's the reason why he was stealing.

Co-worker: Apparently. [said with disbelief]

Researcher: You don't believe it then?

Co-worker: No. He's still got the money.

Researcher: Has he?

Co-worker: I firmly believe it's locked up in his father's safety deposit box, because we had him followed before he went to jail. We've got video evidence of him marching in and out of the bank in town depositing money and we've learnt enough to find out that the deposit box is in his father's name. The coppers [police] told us that. Because we went to the coppers and they said we can't touch it because it's not in his name it's in his father's name. So yes you are right he has been using the safety deposit box and it is in that bank but it's not in his name. And we know he had a very good safe in his house at home, so he was just emptying his safe before he went to jail and that's where he stuck it. We also know that because the police told us that the records they got from the casino indicated he actually took more out of the casino than went in there. So he laundered it. So as far as we're concerned he has still got the money.

Another common approach was to hide their stolen assets by putting houses in other people's names, usually compliant relatives and friends, and to leave a minimal paper trail. The tactic of a fraudster registering assets in another person's name was unfortunately not only linked to housing. Tracing assets caused great frustration for the business owners.

We know that he had other motor vehicles in his sister's name. I said to the administrators he had up to four vehicles … and I don't think any of them vehicles were registered in his name. So when we tried to track down where they went, they couldn't, they weren't in his name. Nothing to do with him. He paid cash for them and put them in his sister's name.

Some of the data demonstrated issues relevant to the prolonged period in which participants were exposed to the Arrogant Fraudster's behaviours. Commonly it was between three and four years, the longest was eight years. The data in this category showed that co-workers perceived behaviours such as a building-up of stress, which demonstrated itself in comments about fraudsters becoming careless, or through a comparison of first impressions with behaviours over length of time.

STRESS BUILDING UP

One interview participant described a fraudster who tried to release his anxiety in other ways with obsessive behaviours such as hand washing and excessive nail biting. Getting angry was another way to reduce anxiety, one fraudster had an extreme reaction to a missing briefcase:

he always had his briefcase with him and he lost it once or someone stole it. And I can remember him being crazy about that so I don't know whether there was cash involved in that or a cheque or reasons that he should have been worried but yeah I mean and I know I'm pretty laid back and I lost something I'd go 'Damn you!' and ring up and cancel my cards and get over it. But he was raging over it. I remember him being really overly upset about it.

The weight of the strain and becoming careless was demonstrated in several ways: becoming disinterested in work, casual delegation of tasks, a lack of focus on specific work projects and actions that were perceived by the co-workers as illustrating laziness or a reluctance to 'pull their weight'. The following description illustrates data relevant to this category:

I think he was busy organising his social life, he'd do a few bits and pieces ... It's not something that stands out that he would come to me work-wise with work related questions. It was more he was always telling stories and carrying on talking to his mates, lots of emails. When he left, he always had lots of emails, so he was pretty busy doing not a lot from what I gathered.

It was not only at work that fraudsters were perceived as showing laziness, it was noted that one fraudster became lazy even with his own devious dealings:

What we learnt earlier on was that he diverted all the mail from all statutory authorities and the bank to his own post office box. And another later occasion, and we were able to confirm that. We had him identified as the owner of that box ... Because he was slack and lazy. So kept getting caught out in his own subterfuge.

Some interview participants described their first impressions of the manager in question and noted as a point of comparison with their later knowledge about subsequent, fraudulent behaviour. These particular participants remarked on the apparent oddness of the fraudsters during their initial contact:

Researcher: What were your first impressions when you first met him?

Co-worker: He's a bit of an interesting character. He was a sort of funny sort of guy.

The fact of seeing the manager wearing a mask is more of a time-related phenomenon, making sense of it afterwards. However, there are a few references that show that the co-workers actually saw acting, which is an important point in the impression management process but was explained or tolerated. And another co-worker remarked when the fraudster manager started work:

But that first day, pretty much I can only probably remember him wanting to be looking the part and acting a little.

And later, after a few years of working with the fraudster:

At that stage I sort of thought, you know, a few times I have seen him stack on a few acts.

Another component to the acting is the capacity to draw upon a range of persona to suit different contexts:

He seemed to be able to compartmentalise all these different aspects of his life. All his multiple personas. And interchange between them.

Furthermore, there was a kind of mask to adopt the role of a poser:

You could easily group [one of the directors] and [the fraudster] as posers, big time, la-di-da and hair and everything that went along with that.

To summarise, the data describe the experience of seeing a disguise at the time of working with the Arrogant Fraudster, and retrospectively naming it. This is a critical point in the findings, which will be discussed later. At this point it is important to note that several co-workers believe that they saw through the illusion but didn't realise the importance that could be attached to it.

TRUSTED

One of the additional constructs, which emerged from Question Data and relevant to the Arrogant Fraudster concept, revolves around the notion that the fraudster managed to be so well disguised that the manager was totally trusted. This ranged from making an easy employment decision upon entry, there seemed nothing apparently wrong, that some of the co-workers felt that they were sucked in as they trusted him and left him unsupervised.

The employment decision was centred on trusting the incoming accounting manager to help make the company grow. One respondent was thankful he had no say in the responsibility for hiring. Even an innocuous behaviour such as buying a house, which was later seen to be associated with fraudulent activity, seemed perfectly normal in another case. Data relevant to trust also contain examples of outside colleagues being perceived as being gullible for accepting the fraudster's actions or stories:

> *In fact I think, that is exactly why the manager of the local bank here, who ultimately did this transaction for him, probably got sucked in.*

> *So I am sure he was probably er ... gullible thinking 'Here he is, coming from a [charitable] organisation, talking to me and I understand all about his personality and probably sharing a bit about his faith or whatever.' And er ... He would have had no sense of [him being a fraudster].*

Rather poignantly, one upline manager described the fraudster's use of reason and logic to persuade trust in him:

> *He could persuade me to trust him. And I do remember something stuck in my mind, he sort of assumed responsibility to do something and I asked a question, 'Why should I trust you to do that?' and his answer was something along the lines of 'Well if you can't trust me around here, then I may as well not be here' something along those lines. Which at the time that is true, if you can't trust your accountant. You have to, you can't not, because if you don't, what's the point? The whole idea of having someone to do your accounts is to allow you to get on with other aspects of managing the business. You've got to sit there and trust your accountant. He's right he shouldn't be there. When that comment was made it always stuck in my mind.*

Apparent similarities between the Arrogant Fraudster and the co-worker also encouraged trust:

> *I viewed him to a degree as a work friend. A colleague. We were both males in our 30s, with young families, building up our businesses ... um*

> *Yeah, I relied on him, I trusted him ... a certain amount of here we both are sort of ... building a successful [business] working together.*

As discussed in reference to the interview data, a lack of supervision was also associated with the level of complexity and activity within some organisations:

> *Each to their own, they all made their own decisions. They were all too busy building stuff to be able to worry about it really and that was the biggest problem, they were too busy.*

Trust therefore allows the Arrogant Fraudster to work unsupervised with free reign in their work. Data demonstrated that the size and complexity of some organisations resulted in upline managers assigning specific tasks because they lacked the time and capacity to supervise. Other situations included sudden business growth and that upline management were far too busy. Similarly unforeseen events can overtake a business, as in the case of a fraudster who as appointed as an acting manager, and thus put in a position of control with access to the organisation's finance: also business owners could be unable to supervise as they did not know how.

A lack of management expertise also contributed to particular managers, unfortunately Arrogant Fraudster managers, being largely unsupervised. Data in this category described a range of contexts such as the inexperience of the business owners in accounting.

Relatively unstructured workplaces, particularly where work relationships were more like a family, also contributed to a lack of experience with close supervision. Furthermore, the unstructured nature of the workplace allowed one Arrogant Fraudster who was working on a contract basis between two businesses to come and go as he pleased and to be treated like an employee:

> *we even gave him keys to the office. He was a member of staff. He had cards, our business cards with his name on them. For all intents and purposes to the outside world he was an employee of the organisation.*

Other factors include low expectations of the managerial fraudster in some instances, with low expectation of revenue from purely keeping a branch business, revenue neutral:

> *He'd submit monthly, income and expenditure things. There were never great profits there. But you get, you're developing a client base, and you know, you never think that it's going to be hugely profitable. I thought, expand your client base and you are not losing money, we would keep it up and maintain it. And to a degree he realised that as well.*

Dangerously the accounting function was seen as low priority work and particularly bookkeeping was seen as low priority 'and payroll and bookkeeping was a minor administrative matter'. This suggests that small business owners' training in basic accounting is imperative as a way to offset fraud, and this is referred to later in recommendations.

The 'fooling everyone' bubble is how the co-workers described the skill with which the Arrogant Fraudsters hoodwinked so many people, not just in the organisation concerned. They deceived outside institutions such as banks, customers' with their bank accounts, suppliers, the taxation departments, pension funds and even unions with their membership fees. Although this is an obvious characteristic now, it wasn't at the time of working with the manager. Or was it? The information is very interesting here as there were some little glimpses which were ignored for many reasons.

A wolf in sheep's clothing and being seen as harmless was another essential part of the disguise, and again had many nuances. Competence was a necessary part of their disguise, although this is not so in all cases. One Arrogant Fraudster used the device of being the joke in the office, being labelled as bit of an idiot. Another fraudster would use the joke device as a way of avoiding difficult issues:

> *he'd brush everything off as though it didn't matter, just laugh it off. He'd laugh everything off. Even when they put pressure on him with regard to work it's another thing that really stood out to me that really.*

All of the Arrogant Fraudsters, as reported by their co-workers, had worked out a system of being able to defraud their host organisation within weeks of arriving. They were adept at hiding their deception by creating false creditors, using suspense accounts, journaling monies out of the double ledger system and then managing the 'error' reports. Some used very sophisticated methods, whereas others used simple ways that an accounting clerk could easily identify. If there was an outside institutional creditor demanding money, for instance the taxation office, then some fraudsters would respond that the taxation office had made an error – the height of audacity in most peoples' eyes. Ordinary creditors simply had to wait until eventually the Fraudster paid some of the outstanding debt. The Arrogant Fraudster has the dangerous ability to deceive anyone.

> *Yeah, I thought I was [a good judge of people]. I know I've got a knack for, if I come across someone who's a bad egg when I first meet them, I can just tell. I know I've got good intuition like that and it's always been right but that's why I was so ... he hid it well.*

The co-workers realised in hindsight that the Fraudster had put on a front to deceive them: this was perceived as putting on a mask and not revealing who he really was. This is a testament to the power of the impression management perpetrated on the co-workers, not only wearing a mask but the successful image that went with it. Two cases reportedly dressed up to go to work beyond the accepted level of office wear. One woman fraudster wore expensive jewellery and outsiders reported later to the co-worker that she had her hair styled every week. Whereas a male fraudster would wear a suit to work when everyone else was in more casual office clothing.

Some co-workers used the word 'persona' for the manager, while others said it was a mask, or maintaining façade or putting on a front. The Arrogant Fraudsters strove to give an appearance of being the friendly, happy family type, dropping information about their families into the casual office conversation. One had photos of his children on his desk. They often embellished their past and wove convincing stories about whom they had worked for and the high status of previous work. Co-workers were made to feel as if the Fraudster was doing everyone a huge favour by being employed at the organisation.

Their capacity of pulling off such a huge deception is shown in this account.

> *We had a super [pension] fund chasing him for seven months. And he provided transaction reports. 'It must have been there' [the fraudster would say], and they would come back and say, 'We can't see it.' And he would say: 'It must have happened there. Go and have a look again'. And then, after about seven months, as the employees wouldn't let this go, the money materialized [as the fraudster would put in his own monies to cover up].*

The disguise was even down to looking like they were doing important work.

> *Yes because I didn't know what he did. He always came across as he was always doing stuff and important. But when I look back at it, I still couldn't tell you what he did.*

To cleverly pretending to be without resources:

> *One of them [old cars that the fraudster used to drive] broke down in our car park and it sat there for 4 or 5 weeks. So it made people talking, and we said 'Can you tow it away please?' It was an embarrassment.*

No. No. No. No ostentatious signs at all.

Quite often the Arrogant Fraudster kept their ill-gotten gains out of view, so that using an old car was typical. Several had high-status cars locked away in a garage, using them only on weekends.

In answering a question about addiction, one recipient mentioned unexpected sides to the fraudster. It was quite a shock to the co-workers because the manager pretended to be a family man without such foibles. Such is the disguise that is maintained.

He had some subscriptions to some pornography sites including some transsexual sites.

Sometimes the mask was too thickly applied to satisfy one particular co-worker:

he always tried to show off, say share these impressive stories, you know, to put up this good mask in front of everyone, saying you know. Make people all around feel sorry for him perhaps, 'Yes.' Or think about 'What a great guy'. So I always say this, 'Ok, that is you, but … yeah.' You know? [laugh]

One subordinate co-worker described the fact that he had 'no inkling' of the fraudster's activities and could only conclude that the manager in question was honest.

'Look if you do that with the wages you won't have to pay payroll tax.' There was nothing … No inkling at all.

He certainly didn't tip me off.

The disguise was so strong that there were some references made to an Arrogant Fraudster having strong morals:

but he definitely had his morals and views and beliefs … you know. He was very strong with regards to that.

The morality shown is a very interesting aspect of impression management and will be returned to later in the discussion, as will the religious aspect. Putting on the show and acting the role is an astute co-worker's observation:

he was always a good actor, that's his nature.

Data relevant to the cultivation of a successful image was pervasive within the interview data. Interview participants' comments ran across a range of specific indicators relevant to the perception that a successful image was important to the fraudster, including being an ideal citizen or an active member of a church.

Another part of presenting well was being meticulous, a recipient describes how meticulous the fraudster was in everything:

> *Always well dressed. Extremely well dressed. Meticulous would be more the word. Meticulous to the point of almost ridiculous in that he would come to work in the morning take his jacket off, brush it down and put it on the hook and his desk was always spotlessly clean and he was an extremely tidy organised person ... Everything had its place. Everything was where it belonged. He knew where everything was.*

And as one upline manager said of his Arrogant Fraudster manager, he was taken in completely.

> *My only summary of him before the event, that he was probably just a nice guy.*

Having a supportive family, especially parents, was surprisingly noted for several fraudsters, so the charade worked just as well at home. Certainly a few parents could not believe that their progeny could have done what they did.

There were also data the included a variety of statements suggesting a sense of unfairness, one of the Red Flags. One co-worker proffered:

> *Maybe he had this sense of unfairness, 'How do other people achieve these things, you know, so that's why I have just got to get myself established.' I think that was his sort of attitude. Maybe that's what he thought he was doing. Getting himself established like everybody else.*

The Arrogant Fraudster used several means to hide things, having a jumbled mess of paperwork on a desk was one way of deterring the most zealous business owner. This was also reinforced by the Fraudster's expertise, which was also jealously guarded. Using the opposite tactic of having a bare desk every day also stopped people from prying as it imposed a barrier of authentic diligence. One fraudster performed the classic Red Flag of hiding things: he would do all sorts of tricks to avoid detection, even little things like closing down the screen of his PC. Only one case was exposed when he was away on holiday – a Red Flag is not taking holidays. However, the others took holidays as well.

MALEVOLENT

The co-workers perceived an underlying menace emanating from the managers concerned. This could have been thinly covered by an ingratiating attitude or resorting to manipulation, but mostly intimidation was used. This included threats or the actual use of violence. Violence could be physical, mental or emotional, but co-workers sensed that it was present.

Malevolence was witnessed by all co-workers of the Arrogant Fraudster. This was originally revealed in stalking-like behaviour to the company to ensure entry into the organisation. This was seen through manipulating board members before employment, offering a low price for the proposed work to be done, posing as an expert in a particular area when in fact they were not. Overall, they became such a good bargain that it was ridiculous to refuse. This activity demonstrated by all Arrogant Fraudsters led me to label them at first as predatory.

Power plays were cited with other managers or the board. These could be subtle or more openly deployed. The subtle power play tended to be focused on those co-workers upline while overt violence was displayed towards subordinates. He would use physical intimidation and threatened that he could win any physical fight against those who criticised him.

Other ways of using their malevolent power included switching on the charm to auditors for instance, and using authority invested in them by the board to ensure that people would obey the fraudster manager's instructions. A more subtle form of malevolence was seen in chauvinism, and one co-worker noted that with the fraudster she had to work with, this became worse over time.

This malevolent streak is even displayed in the predatory behaviour that was noted before the Arrogant Fraudster entered the organisation. Some participants related stories about the fraudster manager's entrance into the organisation through means other than a competitive advertised vacancy.

The stories indicated that some fraudsters intentionally used tactics to avoid a quality selection process, for example:

> *He was reasonably insistent and got back to me a couple of times and I said 'I will think about it and all the rest of it.' Er ... And then eventually in a weak moment I said 'Ah look, all right yep, I will take [you] on and see how it works.'*

Another ploy was to being useful as well as cheap to the business:

> *Well it is not so much the saying no bit, he had what we wanted he wasn't demanding a high salary and we thought that someone like that who has just got out of university freshly trained should be able to grow with the business. There was all sorts of good reasoning behind it. We could not afford a A$100K accountant.*

None of these strategies were noted as a warning to the organisation. Being too good to be true is usually not seen by a hiring panel as a process to inveigle entry into the organisation and be used to stay protected once inside.

Manipulation is another strand to the perceived malevolence. This set of behaviours included using trust to defuse any anxiety, being charming to get what the manager wanted, to exercising authority to getting things done. Subtle power plays were also cited as being used by the Arrogant Fraudster manager by getting rid of threats from others who knew the job well:

> *I hadn't been there long when he started restructuring and got rid of the other two ladies that were there that were doing bookkeeping type work. So it just was in the end myself and X after three odd months.*

This story concluded with the manager's protégé finally reporting to upper management about the possibility of a fraud.

INCONSISTENCIES

Reflecting on the two aspects so far, that one type of fraudster showed arrogance and having a disguise is not such an immense theoretical leap. Well-known fraudster managers who have reached legendary status, such as Jeff Skilling at Enron, have shown arrogance over a long period. Skilling was renowned for saying that he and his team were the smartest guys in the room. Nick Leeson always said that his word was his bond, even when bringing down Barings

Bank into administration. Any fraud investigator will tell you even more such stories. However, the final characteristic of the Arrogant Fraudster's impression management was a breakthrough for understanding their display and rhetoric and why it held up for years.

Delays

Over time, the co-workers became of small inconsistencies. This is based on two categories of data – suspicions and how the fraudster reacted to demands of their job. This is largely based on interviewees' stories about their growing realisation that a fraudster's actions were not right – an important aspect of the diminishing effectiveness of the Executive Impression Management over long periods of time. So strong is the impression management that in one case it took two years before further steps were taken.

Oddities

Little things were noticed at the time. However, the problem was that the co-workers could make no sense of what was happening: aberrations in the impression management process were excused instead of being picked up as clues. The typical audience reaction within the actor/audience relationship is that they will suspend disbelief. Excusing, using tact, covering up their mistakes are all part of the interaction phenomenon of impression management. However, there were no warning signs of being *fraudulent*, and this was remarked upon by many of the co-workers in their interviews.

> *But in essence, no warning bells, no-one that I spoke to gave really any indication of 'You need to be careful', or anything of that nature.*

When interview participants' described a long-term 'wariness', there appeared to the formation of an idea that something was odd in the fraudster's behaviour. The following comment was made by a recipient who speaks English as a second language, and pointed out something unusual:

> *But just think that really … um … made me raise question, or I just was wondering why, he [kept on talking to another manager in another branch] at the same time … I don't know if he was consulting, or asking help or ideas.*

In another case, an increasing sense of wariness led to some office keys being taken from the fraudster:

> *There were lots of little incidences. And that was what probably prompted me to put a trainee on in the first place: as his business was getting too busy, and it also prompted to me to say 'Eventually we will have you in an oversight role "X"' over the trainee as it were. To the point that I took his keys off him. Probably about a year beforehand. Because he didn't need to have them.*

Nevertheless, it still took a year before the situation crashed. Trigger events is a label given to data that describe more short term events and consequences:

> *[The fraudster] was behaving difficult, he was proving to be difficult over a certain request we'd asked him to produce job costing reports because we were getting suspicious about, not suspicious, but we were starting to wonder why the business wasn't making the profits it should be.*

Some interview participants described trigger events that were particularly related to financial indicators, such as unexplained discrepancies between profit expectations and account balances:

> *We could never understand why we didn't make enough money out of it. We were showing a profit but it wasn't sitting in the bank because he was spending it.*

In this particular case the external company accountant got suspicious:

> *[External] Accountant said 'I just haven't been comfortable for a while about this guy. I am just not sure if there is something going on there.'*

Another company pulled in an external accountant just prior to discovery of the fraud. In this case, the co-worker described particular discrepancies discovered after the external accountant was brought in:

> *And, yeah, we did a bit of forensic accounting and we found discrepancies between what was being reported to the [Tax Office] and what was being paid.*

And in finding the error an external accountant who used to previously work for the Fraudster Manager described how torn she felt:

> *He had the full security for everything all the passwords and full access to it. So he just could do what he wanted with it. And [when the security system] all changed and then when he asked me about that I thought, 'Oh', and with all the system changing, I thought 'Oh' and then I looked into it more [in the week preceding discovery].*
>
> *I had to work [elsewhere] on a Saturday because I was working casually …*
>
> *My Mum's noticed something's eating me and she's gone 'What's wrong?'*
>
> *I didn't want to say anything because I didn't want to suggest he's stealing when I didn't know and my Mum's like 'You ring those guys!'*

How the fraudster reacted to demands of his superiors is of interest. For the fraudster who was about to have a downgrade in his role, he actually increased his stealing:

> *It was during that period of time that the amounts accelerated dramatically. Some months A$80,000 he would steal.*

And for the fraudster who had pressure put on him about refusing to do project costings it rebounded on him and led to an external accountant being brought in:

> *So we asked for specific job costing reports to enable us to look at each individual job and he didn't want to do that or he made excuses why he couldn't do it all sorts of excuses and it dragged on and on and on, it went on for a year or two years. It might have even been longer, so in the end I got jack of it and I said 'Well, if you can't do it, I will get A back to do it.'*

It was in the data from the Question part of the interview that more corroboration was found for inconsistencies. One recipient used her own phrase, 'character compositions' or personality to describe how the fraudster differed from other people:

It's like OK. We all not feel well or something, but that's not for him. He just planned to have something else. That kind of character compositions.

Discussions of the fraudsters' characters were prevalent in some recipients' answers. One co-worker sought explanations about whether the fraudster harboured insecurities which would have caused causing the fraud, but finally concludes:

You could look back and say he was insecure, but I don't think he was. I think he thought that he was pretty good. ... But I can't understand really why he would coming from a family was really supportive and him being the golden child why he would feel insecure.

Whereas another recipient said when asked if there was anything else that was remarkable about the fraudster, responded that he was 'A bit lazy'. Of course this is not a fraud indication at all. But still a bit odd they said.

Another co-worker talked about another unusual aspect of his manager:

He was a bit 'funny', the previous manager told me that when he first came along he was told to go out and buy himself a chair, a nice comfortable chair. And I think that you know the budget was A$50 or a A$100 at the time. And I think that the chair arrived and it was A$450. And he nearly fell over backwards. It was I think nothing terribly special. But that was one comment that came up. You get X to do something, make sure you are very careful in what he does. Give him a little bit of authority .... ends up you know, much further.

A character trait that was interpreted as exhibiting a need for control by the Arrogant Fraudster featured in a relatively large amount of data. This extended to control over material possessions, community activities and close friends:

His cars, the vehicles he did drive were always clean. He was a meticulous, clean, well-shaved, groomed person. Liked everything around to be in its place. It's a control thing isn't it? It gave us the perception that he cared about the place and his job. Like I said, he did do his job. At the end of the day he did do his job, the accounts were done and everything was in order, he was just altering a few things in there to steal money, everything else was done, everyone was paid on time.

One recipient extended the metaphor of performance to include emotion as a performance and what the co-worker had to say is very revealing:

> *You could see people at moments of weakness, I could tell you like [the Boss], I've seen him as human, I mean you see them really angry, or really sad or just devastated or excited and you saw all these different things, but [the fraudster] was a bit, he just seemed liked he was always performing. You just dismiss, probably didn't take him seriously, because it's just [the fraudster] – carrying on. Where when other guys like [The Boss] or [the other Director] got angry, or whatever, you knew and saw the whole place, he'd really have effect. Whereas if it was [the fraudster], none of us took him seriously because he was always just performing, there was no … I can't say I ever saw or remember seeing him any different other than just being him like that.*

Another facet of controlling is making excuses and blaming others:

> *he was more of an 'excuses and blame' person not an 'apologetic and accept responsibility' person. That was one of his major problems. That was very clear, very difficult to deal with.*

Arrogant Fraudsters used blaming others to their advantage to cover up their fraudulent activities. In the Question component of the data a rather telling account was probed when 'blaming others' was referred to:

> *Ahhh! ... It was always someone else's mistakes.*
>
> *Oh no, he was very good at that … Very good at blaming others. Always. And then:*
>
> *[Fraudster:] 'I'll fix it up.'*
>
> *[Co-worker:] 'How did you go?'*
>
> *[Fraudster:] 'Sorted it out and this is what happened',*
>
> *Or:*
>
> *[Fraudster:] 'They credited it to the wrong account at the ATO.'*

> *Or:*
>
> *[Fraudster:] 'The superannuation [pension fund] for some reason lost the disbursement sheet. They just had it sitting in their consolidated fund, but it's fixed up now.'*
>
> *Oh it was constant, not constant, no it wasn't constant, it was regular. Enough for me to put on a trainee. Enough for me to take the keys. He didn't have to come in after hours, he didn't need to.*
>
> *But yeah, he was good at ...*
>
> *I call them Teflon people and I've come across them, not in a fraud sense.*
>
> *They are very good at ...*
>
> *Researcher: blaming others?*
>
> *Yeah.*

Another adjunct to controlling was how they dealt with threats to them:

> *They had a formal sort of gathering of our key staff to sit down and they do all sorts of things to try and get a team atmosphere going and [the fraudster's] attitude towards that was very very negative not participating at all. He obviously felt threatened by it.*

Control also extended over their subordinates:

> *He was the lord and master of his work domain.*

Controlling their own emotions was a feature of the fraudsters. A recipient describes what it is like to work with one:

> *Most of what you saw in [the fraudster] was very much like this, [signing a flat line with his hand]*
>
> *Researcher: Not spikey?*
>
> *No, no. Not spikey. No peaks and troughs. Very flatline.*

Inconsistencies were also apparent in descriptions of different behaviour when the boss was not present. One managing director describes how different the behaviour was when he was not around:

> *She did say that he would close things down, or say 'That's the way we do it.', or 'I want it that way'. 'I am only doing what the boss said', sort of thing.*
>
> *Researcher: 'My way or the highway' sort of thing?*
>
> *Yeah. He didn't share, obviously, as people would say 'What's going on?'*
>
> *So his behaviour to others was different to the behaviour to myself.*

One fraudster apparently exhibited quite different behaviours depending on the status of the particular colleague in question:

> *But you don't have to realise that he never tried to boss me around for example, but if you imagine if I put a staff member down there, they'd know the pecking order. In terms of where he ranked in the food chain compared to them.*

Most of the upline managers stated that they never saw bad behaviour from the fraudster, yet this was extant in the workplace:

> *Researcher: Did he treat people unfairly?*
>
> *Not visibly, but certainly those who were answerable to him, he was very unreasonable. The girls used to complain about how unreasonable he was and his attitude towards them.*
>
> *Researcher: How did you deal with that?*
>
> *I never saw it. I never saw it to be able to ... It was always say so. Tricky. It was never there in your face. It was always ... apparently if I wasn't here or had gone home early, yeah, you could expect a different [fraudster's personality], so as to speak.*

And some fraudsters were also described as holding different views in private:

But yeah, but those times, yeah, I would say, yeah certainly gave that impression. But privately though, her views were completely different.

One interesting point, which is inconsistent with the contented family man impression management, it appeared that some fraudsters were very careful to never let their home life 'meet' their work life. Recipients appeared to believe that this was associated with the different behaviours required of the fraudster in different contexts: One recipient explained:

Researcher: Any other times you spotted this, because you had other social functions?

Well no, because [the fraudster's wife] never came to any of them. She never came to our Christmas party, she never ever came to that.

The whole time I was there she didn't come to one, oh no, she went to one barbecue but the other times no.

On the discovery of the fraud, with the meeting with the full board, one fraudster had his wife sitting in his car outside:

His wife was apparently was sitting in the car downstairs in the garage, she never came up. So I don't even know ... that she knew about it then. I don't think he told her. Being him, he probably said 'I've got to come in for a meeting at work, there's some business that I need to do.'

But most kept their private life at arm's length:

To be perfectly honest, his private life was kept at arm's length. You would occasionally learn a few bits and pieces like this supposed house.

Almost inexplicably some recipients reflect their feelings of being confused seeing acts of genuine caring by the fraudster when later they found out that he or she was capable of deception and fraudulent behaviour, for instance:

Here's something that always strikes me, because he had ... one of his other passions was gardening, cause he followed in his old man's footsteps. His old man always had this rose garden business and [the fraudster] helped with that where they would propagate roses and sell them to nurseries. And he used to come in here occasionally and do all this gardening around the office. He did all that.

Why [should he do that]? I never do remember seeing how it was paid for or anything, but he did all that you know and it's quite a nice garden. They were a good choice of plants, conifers, they don't grow quickly, they don't take much looking after, they're nice thick green, they've got colour. He did the whole lot from soil conditioning, mulch, the whole lot and looked after it. It was not unusual for [the fraudster] to walk outside take a breather and pull a few weeds out of the garden. So where does that come from? He did it with genuine care. It looked good and you'd think the guy cares about the place.

Little things like that are what can throw you completely.

Another fraudster was seen to be genuinely caring because 'he was looking after me', that is, the co-worker:

So, but he was friendly: 'How's the weekend?' 'How's the kids?' He came to my house, my 40th birthday, and give me a gift. He brought me things at Christmas and took me out to a function or two. So he was trying to be a bit gregarious there. Trying to look after me. I was friendly. I mean he was in his office, and wasn't chatty.

Another set of inconsistent behaviour displayed, was that the fraudster manager was found to be inept for the job. It was somewhat surprising that in some cases the skills did not match the job for which the fraudster was employed. This is described in 'didn't have a clue', which was a reverberating theme in the Their Stories data about one fraudster in particular:

[The fraudster] was actually brought in to provide the financial [expertise]. It was obvious that he didn't have a clue. I think he was out of his depth. I don't know, he didn't even understand the system here.

Other examples of being inept included comments about: being unable to do accounts, having everything in a mess, and not being thorough.

At a more general level, it was 'the little things' that contributed to patterns of inconsistency:

And he end up with better chair. Ahh, that's when I look at the other lady and thought 'No way! Not going to believe you with that. You are not going to get away it.' So little things, yeah.

Another co-worker said:

Little things. Only little things. Oh. Maybe things like, petty cash ... or going to buy the drinks or ... it was not anything that I didn't think [their boss] or the other bosses wouldn't know about. Pushing the limits I suppose a little bit.

Well as I said I heard he lied once. That came. I kind of had my little doubts. But OK, just not over a sick day. Little very little doubts.

Despite the existence of apparent inconsistencies, there appeared to be a tendency for upline managers to ignore the behaviour because it appeared to be unrelated to work. However, it was still an oddity which passed scrutiny.

Some particular inconsistencies did not manifest early in the employment period, but were noticed later. This was particularly the case with data that comprised the 'emotional abuse' category, which included recipients' comments about the fraudster being abusive, chauvinistic, sleazy and engaging in threatening behaviour. Most of this data aligned closely with similar categories which emerged from the unstructured interview data and only a selection of the data are presented below as examples of rich categories covering discussions of chauvinism and emotional abuse. The malevolence was ignored at first by upline managers but later regarded as inconsistent with a good manager.

Yeah, yeah, yeah, it was dominating ... actually I can recall um ... I can recall some of the staff saying that he was probably quite dominating. I think he was a bit threatening when he asked them to do things, it was like 'you will do this' or you know like ... do this or you're out, sort of thing. A bit threatening.

Researcher: So he wouldn't tolerate any mistakes from his staff?

No, especially if he had shown them once, twice, then it was 'then you're bloody stupid'. 'What are you incompetent? Don't you listen?' Yeah. I never saw it but that's what I was told.

Inconsistencies were also apparent in specific examples of lying and duping a line manager:

> *And then it just came out. 'He's not sick, he's lying.'*
>
> *And there was another transaction where he wrote a cheque for a deposit on a house that he was buying ... We all knew he was buying a house. And it was interesting how he did that actually. Just waited when I was on the phone one time at lunchtime, and just came up and said: 'I'm just rushing to get my solicitor, could you sign this cheque?' and that's what happened off he went. Course I knew he was buying the house I just assumed that he had money in the account, you wouldn't think to check, and that's what he did. Anyway, the cheque never got presented, it never went anywhere, but that was one that directly affected me, as I was actually a signatory on the [fraudulent] cheque.*

Another key component of the inconsistencies was comprised of risky behaviours. These behaviours are put together because they risk health and the safety of themselves as well as people around them. They include examples of amoral behaviours as well as alcohol and drug use, gambling and risky 'wheeler-dealer' activities. Drinking and drugs were discussed in several contexts, often as a suspected behaviour:

> *Some of the people thought that he had been on a drug, like speed or coke, as sometimes he would appear at functions with his eyes were a bit red, watering, and a bit distant and a bit out there ...*
>
> *Oh, she used to hit the sauce a bit apparently. Apparently, and subsequently when we searched the bottom of the drawer there was evidence of [drinking].*
>
> *Researcher: Oh, at work?*
>
> *Um ... um*
>
> *Researcher: But you didn't know at the time?*
>
> *No, no.*

Gambling seemed to be fairly common with the fraudsters. Interestingly one fraudster's gambling was never a health risk per se as it was money laundering not gambling. Money laundering of course would carry its own health risks:

> *I don't think he was a gambler I think he thought he was smart laundering the money at the casino. I don't think he was a gambler at all because I know what a gambler is .... and they lose. 'Cause they're victims for it, they love it. Real gamblers don't tend to have a lot of stuff. Like the detectives said, he didn't lose money at the casino, he made like A$70,000 by just putting it through the casino. He told the police he had a chronic problem and that he'd lost it all and when they audited it and went through all the [casino] footage and saw that he didn't lose at all. 'Cause he upset this detective and the detective decided he didn't like him and so he'd have a little bit more of a look into it.*

Being a wheeler-dealer is one of the Red Flags that Romney et al. had mentioned.[3] As one co-worker said about the manager's contact with other superiors.

> *I know that they spoke a lot. And it appears that [the fraudster], yeah, ... got the support of this guy. But this guy knew nothing about what [the fraudster] had done, but he knew [the fraudster] was talking about it. And they were talking about investments generally, and they were all ... they were both wheeler and dealers in how to get the best value out of things and the best opportunities. He had a real alliance.*

QUESTION DATA

The data from the questions regarding theories about narcissism, psychopathy or Red Flags and so on, supported the emergence of four constructs relevant to the concept of Arrogant Fraudster. In some cases the data are closely aligned with specific questions asked of co-workers. For example, it could be expected that themes such as arrogance would develop via the direct question:

> *Did you think that he or she was arrogant? Yes or No.*

3 Romney, M. B., W. S. Albrecht, and D. J. Cherrington. 1980b. Red-flagging the white collar criminal; potential fraud situations have common characteristics, according to a survey of published cases, which can be used as early warning signals to prevent actual acts. *Management Accounting* 61 (9): 51–56.

However, it was not anticipated that the constructs of disguise and inconsistencies would emerge from these data, and certainly not to the extent of the many descriptions that were related by the recipients in this section. Significant additional data from this part of the interview were added to the patterns of behaviour that develop over time – which were labeled as inconsistencies. These are little things that are noticed by the recipients, little things that do not necessarily add up to anything, but nevertheless are there. The malevolence construct was enriched with data describing observations about long-term and risky behaviours. Although it did not relate to one specific question, the issue of trust emerged as an important area of data.

In general terms, the question data provides additional support or nuances to categories and constructs, which emerged from Their Stories. The concept of Arrogant Fraudster is strengthened by the categories that emerged from the Question component of co-worker interviews.

At this point we will now look at the Likeable Fraudster. This type relied on fewer data, as there were a smaller number of co-workers. Despite this artefact the description is quite the opposite of the Arrogant Fraudster impression management that has been described in detail here.

The Likeable Fraudster

When I asked for a word to describe this type of fraudster manager, I was given Likeable. This is shown as one of the major constructs within the Likeable Fraudster concept, which contrasts sharply with the Arrogant Fraudster, is that of benign manager traits. This construct refers to being seen to be of good appearance, fair to others, being a good manager, honest and supervising, and it was mentioned that the Likeable Fraudster type was trusting of others and they trusted him.

Co-workers spoke of their good relationship with the Likeable Fraudster manager and there were a variety of ways in which this was explained. Good relationships were associated with activities from after-work drinks to generally being sociable with the staff, having several seemingly deep work relationships within the organisation.

The Likeable Fraudster is perceived as honest and being a fair manager to all as well as being able to keep his eye on the staff. There was a distinct nice side to the Likeable Fraudster. Laughing at mistakes that were made, is one of them:

> *Yeah he did. But he would laugh it off, 'Sorry about that!'*

Even after correcting mistakes of subordinates one Likeable Fraudster would say 'only joking' after everything:

> *He always used to have a giggle after everything, you know, like say 'I'm only joking', or ' I don't mean it so don't take it to heart' sort of thing.*

When quizzed a bit further, the co-worker replied that the executive was loved by staff:

> *Researcher: Did any of the other staff take it to heart, the joking?*
>
> *No, everybody loved him. He was really loved. Everyone just thought he was great.*

Not only loved by their staff, apparently they also loved their families:

> *Researcher: He had a son didn't he?*
>
> *Co-worker: Yes.*
>
> *Researcher: What was he like to them?*
>
> *Co-worker: Oh, adored them, he absolutely adored them.*

Finally, the last trait of the benign manager traits construct is a reference to how one of these managers was perceived as trusting as well as trustworthy – a giver and receiver of trust:

> *But he was very trusting, I fully trusted him. I believed everything he said. Maybe I'm just gullible. He was just very trusting, trustworthy.*

INCONSISTENCIES IN THE LIKEABLE FRAUDSTER

Like the Arrogant Fraudster, one construct which stands out on its own, but very distinct from all the other data relevant to the Likeable Fraudster, is the difference in behaviour when a spouse was present:

> *Researcher: So there really was a marked difference between his behaviour around her and his behaviour around [the staff]?*
>
> *Oh definitely. He was much more relaxed around us.*

This was so strong that he would curtail after-hours drinking with this manager's wife:

> *I don't think he wanted her to socialise with us whereas she was quite happy just to have a drink with us, but he didn't want her to. He said: 'No, no this is our last drink we're going to go home.' But we'd planned to have a couple, you know.*

There are no more references to this construct, but tentatively, this behaviour is seen in both types of fraudster.

PUTTING ON A FRONT

Another similarity to the Arrogant Fraudster is that the Likeable Fraudster would also put on a front. This construct emerged from four areas including hiding the problems well, lying and pretending and also quite unexpectedly, having a trophy wife.

Hiding activity seen by the co-worker and is clearly part of the Likeable Fraudster's impression management.

> *But with him I used to think he was hiding behind his glasses.*

These data refer to experiences and feelings after the fraud was uncovered and were not known at the time. This quote explains this:

> *Researcher: Did you ever feel as though: 'I should've picked it up, I should have realised?'*
>
> *Co-worker: No.*

> *Researcher: Why was that?*
>
> *Co-worker: Because he hid it very well you just wouldn't have known. it would have been impossible to pick up unless someone was close to him ... So I didn't feel that I should have. We were workmates, not best mates after work.*

The managerial fraudster's capacity to 'hide well' was also referred to in relation to one instance in which a gambling habit was extremely well concealed:

> *Researcher: You didn't know about the gambling?*
>
> *Co-worker: No. Well yeah, we didn't know that was why he stole that. We didn't know anything [the investigators] didn't tell us anything.*
>
> *Researcher: Did you put two and two together at all, in those chats before you got officially told?*
>
> *Co-worker: No. Well [a new manager] come and told us, she was sitting with us and she said 'OK, this is what happened.' So she sat there and told us all how he did it. He obviously had an addiction. She didn't know herself how he actually did it she said I think he was fiddling with [an] account. That's how he's done it. She wasn't sure.*

While some fraudsters were perceived to be adept at hiding their actions, it appears that there were cases where true feelings of the Likeable Fraudster were perhaps disclosed to a trusted few:

> *Researcher: Did he ever speak about his true feelings at all?*
>
> *Co-worker: I think he did with the branch manager, I think he did because they were quite good friends.*

Lying is a construct that emerged from data that was related to strategies about hiding the fraud. Lying could involve leading others to believe certain stories that might rationalise particular actions:

> *Researcher: Did others in the workplace say something similar to you?*
>
> *Yeah. Yeah. We all thought he had problems in his marriage and that's what I think he led us to believe as well.*

But I think he actually was.

Or being relatively straight forward lying about fraudulent activity:

He won like millions of dollars but he never ... and I remember saying to him: Did you have a win?' He said 'Oh yeah I had a win!' and I said: 'How much did you win?' I think he told me a couple of hundred but I think it was a couple of million that he won but he hid that of course.

Another data category within this construct comprised recipients' perceptions that the fraudster was pretending to feel normal:

He had an addiction. It would have been awful for him it would have been horrible for him to sit there and have to just feel normal. I don't know how he did it.

Interestingly the impression management was not complete, yet the audience of the co-worker did not suspect that anything was wrong.

Yes. I could see [he was putting on a front], I mean he was always happy, but I know I could just see it, I could see it in his eyes. There was something going on and I thought it was actually marriage problems …

Researcher: You say that you could see it in his eyes. Are you quite intuitive?

Yes. I just get a sense of something,

Finally, within there is some data relevant to co-workers' perceptions that the fraudster had a 'trophy wife' and that this was a part of the front that was put on:

Very materialistic I guess. Always well dressed and had to have the best of everything and very very attractive lady. Whereas he sort of ... they looked like the odd couple because he wasn't. He was totally different looking, I'm not saying he was ugly but he was not, she wasn't what I expected when she walked in the door.

Oh yeah, she had the best of everything. She didn't work but she'd go out and about and she'd have nice beautiful jewellery you know like, designer label perfume …

One recipient linked this with perceived marital difficulties:

> *I really do think he was having marital [difficulties] ... I mean obviously he had a lot on his mind but I think she was very, she just wanted more and more and more, she was very demanding, she came across as being very demanding and it was just draining him.*
>
> *You could just see that he loved her and he was trying to keep her ...*
>
> *You could tell the change in him as soon as she walked in he just turned into a bit grumpy I guess, not relaxed, a bit stressed.*

GAMBLER

Being a gambler was referred to in the Likeable Fraudster concept. I was somewhat surprised at the recipient knowing about the gambling of one manager before discovery:

> *He used to talk about how he'd go to the Melbourne Cup [a popular horse race in Australia] and he used to always have a bet.*

Being a gambler was described as having a bet every now and then. However, the betting behaviour was noticed online by some staff and minimalised by the manager, looking through the form guide and making wins.

As well as always be looking through the form guide:

> *Researcher: But normally when you spoke to him and you initiated the conversation, what would he do?*
>
> *Co-worker: Yeah when I spoke to him about that he would always be looking through the form guide.*
>
> *Researcher: Wouldn't look you in the eye.*
>
> *Co-worker: Yeah. Now that you say it, but I didn't think then. There were a lot of things that clicked with me afterwards.*

FEELING INFERIOR

There is a danger to co-workers by noticing that the Likeable Fraudster shares benign features with the Respectful manager type. Furthermore they do not seek a power over role with co-workers but manage their impression management through positioning themselves as lower than the co-worker.

This is demonstrated with the central construct to the Likeable Fraudster impression management, which is inferiority. This is based on how the recipients saw the executive fraudster to themselves. If they gave the impression of ranking higher than the audience they reflected this imbalanced power ratio and classified them as superior, if they classified themselves as lower then they would fall into the inferior type. Superiority has already been explained at some length in the Arrogant Fraudster concept. Inferiority emerged from four data categories, including being humble, lack of confidence and not like a boss, and the inferior positioning of the senior manager fraudster.

Being humble is seen when a recipient was asked a question if he thought the executive fraudster was arrogant:

> *No, no I don't think so. He was reasonably humble, I would have thought.*

There were many reasons that the audience felt was an appropriate excuse for the inferiority and a perceived lack of confidence was cited as a reason for this positioning:

> *I don't think he was very confident. He came across as being like he lacked a bit of confidence in some areas but in other areas yeah he was quite confident. Just a little bit not very confident He was confident with customers like because he put on I suppose a bit of ... cause like he was the bank manager and so he'd always go up and have a bit of a chat but, he just was very confident when it came to talking to the big wigs of the bank sort of you know. He'd get an email about a teleconference, [he'd say:] 'Here we go.' Every time you walked past the office he was never talking he was always listening, so I don't think he really contributed much to the conversation with his employers. So I think in that sense he wasn't very confident.*

Lack of confidence was also associated with shyness by co-workers, avoiding eye contact and being withdrawn, not laughing much.

Other data revealed that co-workers felt that the fraudster manager they were discussing did not really feel or act like a boss. This was discussed in terms of both a lack of authority and relatively relaxed work habits in not doing much at all at work.

> *He never ever made me feel, that he's the boss and I've got to do it. He'd always asked .... 'You don't have to do it, but if you want to, do it.' He wasn't like he was the boss at all. You don't have to do it but it would be good if you could. It wasn't: 'You're doing this. This is what you get paid to do.'*

In fact Likeable Fraudsters do not manage much at all. Several co-workers felt that their fraudster manager did not look or act like a manager.

One hint of the underlying negativity was noted as a degree of intolerance, which was surprising to the co-worker as the manager concerned appeared to get along with everyone so well. This would appear in chauvinistic remarks, displays of male arrogance towards females and even racial prejudice was demonstrated:

> *With the indigenous [people], he used to ... little remarks, 'Oh he's black you know'. So yeah, it was sort of like: 'Oh here we go. It's pension day they're all going to come in take all their money out and then come back in and abuse us because they've got no money left. Typical blacks', you know, little remarks like that.*

In emotional terms co-workers also noticed mood swings and unhappiness. In the reference below the real cause of the weekly cycle mood swings was due to the heavy betting the manager made on Thursday and Friday nights for weekend races with no or little return on Monday.

> *Researcher: Did you ever notice this pattern during the week on a weekly basis?*
>
> *Co-worker: Yes, that's why I thought it was marriage problems. At first I thought 'Oh it's Mondays.' I was the same on Mondays. But it got worse like towards the end and he didn't look happy in his job. I just thought maybe things were getting to him. I had no idea what actually was wrong with him.*

One co-worker mentioned that his boss didn't look busy and didn't stay for long in the office. and was cited as leaving the office:

> *Now I come to think of it he used to leave the [workplace] a fair bit during the day. He'd pop out for five or ten minutes. Oh I'm just going over to the shops, the newsagents or ... Because you know, he wouldn't have had the car, his wife always had the car, so he would always walk but everything was in walking distance so was the [betting shop]. Now I think of the times that he used to leave, there was times when I needed him to sign something and it's like where is he? 'Oh he's just popped out he'll be back soon' and then he'd come back in with the paper.*

To summarise, these data provide a picture of a manager not liking their work, being unhappy and perhaps showing behaviour that may be somewhat passive-aggressive by not working particularly hard or for any length of time.

Chapter 5
Eventual Destruction of the Illusion

What was noticed in hindsight was the building up of pressure in the Likeable Fraudster. The stress build-up prior to discovery of the fraud began a few months before the discovery of the fraud:

> *Researcher: Did you see a difference in that last six months?*
>
> *Co-worker: Oh definitely. Yeah. He was a lot quieter than normal and didn't really want to socialise all too much. A bit withdrawn.*

What has been found in the co-workers' data is that the maintenance of the illusion takes its toll on the fraudster executives using a disguise. The illusion weakens and cracks or strips finally appear.

Strips

Breaks appear in the disguise over time due to the build up of pressure for the fraudster. Generally they take the form of what one recipient described as 'little things' and these are referred to as 'strips' by Goffman in *Frame Analysis*.[1] Here he explains that communication is organised into primary frameworks, which give an understanding to both parties about what is being said, why and how. Primary frameworks relate not just to words but to everything that is implied, including motive and intent in the communication. Each interaction is made up of a collection of strips, which Goffman defines as

> *any arbitrary slice or cut from the stream of ongoing activity, including here sequences of happenings, real or fictive, as seen from the perspective*

1 Goffman, E. 1974. *Frame analysis, an essay on the organization of experience*. Boston, MA: University Press of New England. Original edition, 1974.

> *of those subjectively involved in sustaining an interest in them ... it will be used as a starting point of analysis.*[2]

Given that each strip is nuanced (because it forms the primary framework), when coming across a strip that fails to fit the framework, there is a shift in consciousness.

> *It is what a person feels who begins, rightly or not, to think that the strip of activity he is involved in has been constructed beyond his ken [understanding], and that he has not been allowed a sustainable view of what frames him.*[3]

Goffman goes on to say that suspicion and doubt can now occur, but it is in reference to the framework of meaning, not necessarily the person. One co-worker described this moment, regarding an incident of the fraudster manager purchasing an office chair, which cost four times more than expected. The explanation given by a fraudster manager did not fit with the image of a good manager that he was trying to produce:

> *Ahh, that's when I look at the other lady and thought 'No way! Not going to believe you with that. You are not going to get away it.' So little things, yeah.*

However, this did not lead her to denounce the manager as a liar. The connection that it was suboptimal, in fact it was dangerous to have a financial controller and acting general manager of an organisation be a liar, did not occur to her or anyone else around her. She was only talking about the specific lie of the chair. She was a not a gullible woman, in fact far from it, she demonstrated her gift of intuition in many of her answers. She, like the other co-workers, failed to connect the dots due to the strength of the impression management from the fraudster.

Little Things

Each co-worker of either fraudster type noticed an out of context strip. They described it as a 'little thing' that was odd or incongruent and was noted in their interviews. All of the oddities were seen exactly as Goffman predicted, as

2 Ibid., p. 10.
3 Ibid., p. 122.

being within the framework of a manager, and not related to the person as a problem of integrity:

> *Little things. Only little things. Oh. Maybe things like, petty cash ... or going to buy the drinks or … it was not anything that I didn't think [their boss] or the other bosses wouldn't know about. Pushing the limits I suppose a little bit.*

The problem, it turns out, is that the co-workers cannot understand the importance of these 'little things'. Some of these strips occur immediately on entry of the fraudster into the organisation. Most are noticed over time and maybe as early as two years before the actual discovery of the fraud.

A most interesting aspect of these strips is that the fraudsters themselves can become sloppy in their fraud activities (e.g., forget to pay certain creditors). This means that when they are out of the office on holidays, sick leave etc., their system is liable to fall apart. This point is tendered in the Red Flags indicators of fraud where an individual fails or refuses to take leave.[4]

The study captured a list of strips that occurred with the Arrogant Fraudster cases that were seen as odd but not accorded any weight by the recipients, including:

- Exaggerating their importance with customers and colleagues.
- Wearing expensive jewellery or clothes.
- Lying over little things, for instance taking a sick day off when well.
- Spending considerable time out of the office to chat with others.
- Never bringing their partner to the office functions.
- Being able to deflect critical questions by bluffing or joking.
- Tending the office garden (this is a reverse strip).

4 Romney, M. B., W. S. Albrecht, and D. J. Cherrington. 1980b. Red-flagging the white collar criminal; potential fraud situations have common characteristics, according to a survey of published cases, which can be used as early warning signals to prevent actual acts. *Management Accounting* 61 (9): 51–56.

- Using an old decrepit car (another reverse strip).
- Losing personal items and being extremely angry.

For the Likeable Fraudster the strips were more inclined to be emotion-based incongruities, such as racial intolerance and moodiness. I suspect the Likeable Fraudster fails to give respect to all and keep up a happy mood due to the underlying pressures, which reflect increasing unhappiness with themselves.

Pressure Increases Over Time

One of the issues is how the Arrogant Fraudster managers managed to keep up the façade for so long. Some of the fraudsters kept up their clandestine activity for many years. Certainly inconsistencies started to appear, and this leads the upline management to start having suspicions and or doubts about the executive in question. There seems to be a psychic toll on the fraudsters in the upholding of disguised impression management, with increasing anxiety showing in frequent hand washing, growing uneasiness by upline managers with extra supervision covertly put in place and in one case, important office keys removed. For the fraudsters themselves it was reported that there was an increase in risky behaviours including fights in public houses or taverns, increasing rates of absenteeism and taking higher amounts out of the business's funds.

An interesting area that has come up through analysing recipients' responses in developing the 'Becoming Aware' framework is the amount of signs that were given to the fraudster that the upline management were beginning to become suspicious. There are notably two cases where the fraudsters would have known that time was running out, but they still continued their frauds. Some recipients have rationalised this by thinking that perhaps they wanted to be caught.

A more plausible explanation that arose from the supplementary interviewing of fraud investigators for triangulation purposes was that in their experience the fraudster absolutely believes that they will get away with it through their superiority at beating the system. A sense of superiority is a previously identified theme for the Arrogant Fraudster group, and those who were signalled that time is running out were indeed seen as superior and arrogant by their recipients.

Moreover, the defrauding behaviour has parasitic overtones. Seemingly, there is no need to change hosts until the blood runs dry. One fraudster was noted for varying amounts he stole depending on revenue, being careful not to take too much in lean times.

When confronted with the discovery of the fraud, the Arrogant Fraudster managers rely on their previous use of trustworthiness in bargaining with their employers. They either fight the case vigorously, or if they own up, they do so because the amount detected is smaller than what they actually stole. They do not show remorse according to the recipients, unless that is used for mitigation purposes in the courtroom.

Long-standing Illusion

The fraudster group hoodwinked, bluffed, lied and cheated their organisations of millions of dollars. Yet apparently the co-workers saw nothing untoward, because the impression management given was (almost) efficient. The shortest period of fraud was six months and the longest was eight years. Clearly then, the impression management mechanism as used by these fraudsters was extremely effective. Goffman refers to fraudsters and con men in *The Presentation of Self in Everyday Life*, but only as 'one-off' actions. In this study however, the actions were long term. Criminals, Goffman says, would have their own dramaturgical demands and expectations, for instance Chicago gangsters are gangsters and are not disguised. Because his work was applicable to many scenarios and he suffered a relatively early death, there is no guide to what Goffman would have thought about these lone managerial fraudsters. But as we have seen, Goffman says there are strips to any frame, and the strips emerged over time according to the co-workers.

The Cracking of the Illusion: the Process of Discovery

At the first point of discovery the Arrogant Fraudster, as Goffman predicts, shows signs of their true self. Fear is quickly masked by old techniques of trying to re-establish trust. If those fail, then power plays and manipulation come to the fore. As it happens there are a number of instances caused by the process of discovery of the fraudsters' activities, over time. This leads to a three-stage illusion-shattering process for the Arrogant Fraudster.

INITIAL CONTACT

There is an initial contact with the fraudster, which alerts them to the fact that people have discovered their ruse. The response appears to be very minimal, usually one word 'Oh' and that is it. Another fraudster responded with a plain 'Oh,' to a telephone request to come in to the office. Another on the other hand, offered a very non-committal 'Oh. I wondered when you would see that' when the first fraudulent transaction was discovered.

This moment appears to be very short, and the fraudster retains the old illusion, while thinking rapidly. There is little external sign of what is going on with these fraudsters to their co-workers.

INTERIM STAGE

Then there appears to be an interim stage of dealing with the shattered illusion. One fraudster says: by telephone:

> *I thought you would call me about that.*

Another co-worker reported a highly unusual reaction of the manager being stone cold serious. This was from the fraudster who had normally used the impression management tactic as the joker in the office. His seriousness was so extraordinary that the recipient remembered it quite clearly several years later.

FINAL STAGE OF ILLUSION MAINTENANCE

The fraudsters continued the illusion, even though they knew that everyone had seen through it. This very much describes the final stage of illusion-keeping that the Arrogant Fraudsters tried to uphold. It came at the stage of formal confrontation between business owners and their Arrogant Fraudster employee, which was held days or weeks later. All fraudsters try to keep up the old illusion or try a new one.

For instance, one Arrogant Fraudster came in prepared with a 'confession' which was tantamount to an explanation – as there was no admission of guilt to a fraud, and his plea of not guilty was maintained right up to the last moments of his trial. Another exclaimed: 'Charge me! Charge me!' When this did not happen, she explained that she was dying of cancer. Finally, seeing that this had no effect on the co-worker, she fell to the floor in what appeared to be a catatonic state and had to be hospitalised.

Finally, another's reaction was to admit guilt to the smaller amount that he was accused of stealing. He immediately made an offer to repay and to leave the company. This was a restitution impression-management strategy as the amount that had been discovered at that point was merely 3 per cent of the overall fraud.

DISCOVERY PROCESS FOR THE LIKEABLE FRAUDSTER

It was explained by the fraud investigators (later interviewed in the study) that in their view it was the Arrogant Fraudsters' arrogance that made their discovery a threefold process. To suddenly be exposed is such a shock to them that they appear to give a response quite slowly, as immediately they are not superior anymore to those around them. They don't take this in for a while and try other devices.

However, for the Likeable Fraudster the discovery process was reported in two stages. One recipient described the manager as having a moment of complete exposure of his feelings of fear to her, which he then quickly tried to cover up. The illusion in the perpetrators' mind appears to be shattered immediately at that point, and it was only a matter of days afterwards that the second stage occurred when he turned himself in. For another Likeable Fraudster, his moment of illusion-shattering was also initial and complete, reporting that he felt it was 'game over' and finally some weeks later in this case, the second stage of turning himself in. There appears to be no attempt at a drawn-out illusion maintenance activity as with the Arrogant Fraudster. In fact, it almost seems that the Likeable Fraudsters were waiting for the moment when they would be found out. It is at this point, however, that the Likeable Fraudsters think seriously of killing themselves.

INCONSISTENT IMPRESSION MANAGEMENT IS USUALLY OPEN

The fraudsters, both Arrogant and Likeable types, are the only managers who create the disguise or illusion. Other (non-fraudster) managers, both Malevolent and Benign, are not worried about disguising or hiding, they are transparent with their impression management. The Respectful executive impression management does not have any illusory component in it. The audience trusts the actor and the actor performs as per expectations.

BALANCING IMPRESSION MANAGEMENT STRATEGIES

Jones and Pittman[5] point out that there is always a careful balance when an individual uses particular strategies. Ingratiation impression management has to contend with issues of authenticity and sincerity or the behaviour is seen as sycophantic. Self-promotion is based on selling competence and the self-promoter must achieve performance in that competency or risk being seen as incompetent. Jones and Pittman remark that the stronger the claim the more likely the case that the competence is actually weak. However, they are most likely to get away with it if they promote a successful appearance and background. This could explain why so much effort in the impression management process was spent on establishing a successful appearance to those on the receiving end of the fraudster Executive Impression Management.

Table 5.1 Impression management strategies of all of the Inconsistent executives

	Reported impression management upwards	*Strategy ⬆ upwards*	*Reported impression management downwards*	*Strategy ⬇ downwards*
The Arrogant Fraudster				
Superior	Efficient, effective	*Self promotion*	Exaggeration	*Self promotion*
Superior	Moral, religious person	*Exemplification*	Bullying and lying	*Intimidation*
Superior	Efficient then got sloppy, aggressive 'bluffing' response to cover up errors.	*Self promotion*	'My way or the highway', 'sweatshop'.	*Intimidation*
Superior	Competent, conscientious	*Self promotion*	Got rid of competent staff. Abused blue-collar males. Trained staff to low level.	*Intimidation and Self promotion*
The Likeable Fraudster				
Inferior	Reasonably competent, senior	*Ingratiation*	Nice boss but with 'problems'	*Ingratiation*
Inferior	Competent senior	Ingratiation	Nice boss.	*Ingratiation*

5 Jones, E. E., and T. S. Pittman. 1982. Toward a general theory of strategic self-presentation. In *Psychological perspectives on the self*, ed. J. Suls, 231–262. Hillsdale, NJ: Lawrence Erlbaum Associates.

The exemplification strategy is quite different, derived from 'seizing the high moral ground' and wanting respect by projecting integrity and moral worthiness. This is fuelled in part by the projection of feelings of guilt and shame if the impression management is unwarranted, and therefore its intent is to obtain power and control. Users of this impression management strategy can be criticised as being hypocritical or sanctimonious. Although this was not openly stated about one fraudster, it was certainly implied from the data.

UPWARD

Fraudster managers use a mixture of self-promotion and exemplification impression management strategies to their upline manager. Self-promotion is a preferred strategy of Arrogant Fraudsters, and even the most affable of them in the study was reported to have links with organised crime and subsequently used powerful threats to his upline manager when he was exposed.

The exception is the Arrogant Fraudster who used exemplification, which proved to be particularly effective in the religious setting of the organisation she was in. The upline recipient of that particular fraudster impression management did not mention this aspect, in fact he seemed to have been taken in completely by the exemplification strategy, as he thought that she was a highly moral person but excused her ineffectiveness in the role in which she found herself; she was simply a wrong hire.

The Likeable Fraudsters only used the ingratiation strategy upwards. They clearly used a strategy of being liked by their line managers or boards as a way of handling their communication with their superiors.

If the motive of each impression management strategy is taken into account, there is a need for respect from the audiences of self-promoters and the exemplifiers, whereas the ingratiators want to be liked. Again this helps explain the data, the ingratiators demonstrated clearly to their recipients that they wanted to be liked by showing benign characteristics upwards to their management. However, where the ingratiators came into their own was in downwards impression management to their subordinates as they stayed with the strategy that worked for them best, whereas the other non-ingratiators changed tactics accordingly.

The self-promotion and ingratiation upward strategies are highly dangerous for an upline manager. The truth will not be seen for several years. They ensure that the impression management is so complete that their supervisors, including boards of management are taken in. Personally I think this explains why whistle-blowers have such a difficult time in exposing the frauds. Going to a senior manager to complain about the fraudster is to go against the rock-like impression management. This is so strong an illusion that it will be some while before the senior manager can believe it. All upline managers reported that they could not believe the whistle-blower in the exposure of the fraud.

They grasped at straws, such as errors possibly being made by the whistle-blower. In order for an upline manager to believe and take action, irrefutable evidence has to be provided, otherwise they simply will not believe it. Once they believe it however, all hell breaks loose with the wrath of broken trust.

DOWNWARD

The self-promoting Arrogant Fraudsters mostly used intimidation as a strategy for subordinates but there was some reporting of self-promoting downwards. This is an interesting result, as they appear to not need to have respect from those employees who work with them. It would seem that the more powerful figure (upline management) produces the greatest need for respect. However, impression management strategies to subordinates produce a need to dominate and abuse by intimidation, thus appearing dangerous.

This seems to indicate that the Arrogant Fraudsters using Inconsistent Malevolent impression management who use self-promotion upwards, will mostly use intimidation downwards. Einarsen[6] has considered the vexing question of downward intimidation behaviours including: bullying, counterproductive behaviour and managerial aggression in the workplace and refers to this as destructive leadership. Insightfully in 1999, he wrote about the conclusions of an earlier study[7] that: 'The three main reasons [for bullying] were competition concerning status and job positions, envy, and the aggressor being uncertain about his/her self.'[8] This observation fits neatly in with the upward self-promoter/downward intimidator strategies that have been witnessed by co-workers of malevolent managers in this investigation. Furthermore, the interviews with fraud investigators uphold this proposition: many of fraudsters they had dealt with in the past used promotional tactics and simultaneously bullied their staff. One investigator thought that about half

6 Einarsen, S., M. S. Aasland, and A. Skogstad. 2007. Destructive leadership behaviour: a definition and conceptual model. *The Leadership Quarterly* 18 (3): 207–216.

7 Einarsen, S. 1999. The nature and causes of bullying at work. *International Journal of Manpower* 20 (1–2): 16– 28.

8 Ibid., p. 20.

of the fraudsters he had dealt with were of this dual impression management strategy type.

The ingratiators, that is the Likeable Fraudsters, on the other hand are more consistent in their impression management strategies. They use ingratiation upward as well as downward, as observed by the co-workers in the study. The strategy of downward ingratiation by a manager means that it is possible to keep followers in control and according to one study produced a moderate influence on employees.[9] Certainly the Likeable Fraudster manager who provided drinks after work every day for his staff was able to do this quite successfully.

Interestingly, those managers who imposed a superior relationship mostly used self-promotion upwards and intimidation downwards in this sample, whereas the executives projecting an inferior relationship through their impression management used ingratiation both upwards and downwards.

BLOWING UP THE MYTHS – APPLICATION OF THEORY PREDICTORS

Using the overall basic theory indicators of impression management, social psychology, psychopathology and the Red Flags, the data revealed a relationship of recipients' responses which was negative or positive.

The 'Red Flags' appeared to reveal little between the two groups of fraudster and non-fraudster managers. In contrast to the two precepts of impression management, morality and authenticity show some relationship with the two groups of recipients but in different ways. Morality is more detectable with non-fraudster executives, whereas authenticity is more noticeable in fraudster managers. The fraudsters trade more in the currency of trust, which is the foundation of authenticity, rather than demonstrating morality. The other groups of psychopathology and social psychology indicators are only slightly more noticeable with the fraudsters than non-fraudsters. When looking at individual items the fraudsters and non-fraudster executives demonstrate differently (see Table 5.2).

Overall, non-fraudster executives apologise, admit their weaknesses, are conscientious and work long hours. They also have 'less moderate' but still have some marital difficulties perceived by the recipients. Whereas the fraudsters are more likely to be hostile to people who touch their office things,

9 Yukl, G. 1992. Consequences of influence tactics used with subordinates, peers, and the boss. *Journal of Applied Psychology* 77 (4): 525–535.

Table 5.2 Top five differences on individual theoretical themes

Indicator	*Non-fraudster executives*
Apologised	Very high
Admit to weaknesses	High
Conscientiousness	Moderate
Work long hours	Moderate
Marital Difficulties	Less Moderate
	Fraudster executives
No one to touch their things	Very high
Surround themselves with 'yes men'	High
Take shortcuts	High
Always right	Moderate
Superiority	Moderate

e.g., computer, filing cabinets, are more likely to surround themselves with 'yes men', take shortcuts and consider themselves always right and superior to others. The next list of factors for the fraudsters would be: being a good actor; narcissistic; arrogant; variable performance and disregard of others. It would seem therefore that the recipients were able to see some of the psychopathic tendencies with this group of fraudsters. There were some items that bore no indication either way. All executives were considered to be sociable, even though there were at least two who showed signs of introversion. And both groups demonstrated moral behaviour and views, with neither group showing signs of greed to the recipients.

The two questions regarding being able to apologise and demonstrating a preference for people to stay away from their things are the better descriptors for this group of non-fraudsters and fraudster executives respectively. However, there is the caveat that this is from a purposeful sample and not random, so inferences to the general population cannot be made. One interesting observation is that self-monitoring was not seen by many recipients, and it is suspected that this behaviour is more connected to the impression management types associated with ingratiation upwards and downwards.

ATTRIBUTIONS OF AUTHENTICITY AND MORALITY

Executive Impression Management is based on Goffman's work and predicated on authenticity and morality of the self. The findings indicate attributions of these qualities and these attributions are strong and lasting.

Authenticity

The only type that is perceived as truly authentic is the Respectful executive, whose impression management type is seen as consistent and benign. The recipients' phrase 'What you see is what you get' about the Respectful executive in question, is a modern way of talking about authenticity. The theme of the Respectful executive certainly demonstrates support for what is implied by authentic leadership. Etzioni[10] explains that authenticity is where the outward appearance and the underlying structure are both responsive to human needs. This is supported in the Respectful type; whereas inauthenticity, Etzioni states, is unresponsive and only maintained as an institutional front see Table 5.3. Being authentic is also linked with high self-esteem[11] which was reflected in the recipients' descriptions of the Respectful executive impression management showing respect for and encouraging others.[12] Authentic leaders have also been found to be self confident, self-aware, reliable and trustworthy, with an attendant moral perspective.[13]

Table 5.3 Comparison of attributes of the pre-conditions to impression management

Executive impression management type	*Authenticity*	*Trust*	*Morality*
Respectful	Present	High	Yes
Likeable Fraudster	Co-workers only	Downward projection	Disguised downwards
Arrogant Fraudster	Upline manager(s) only	Upward projection	Disguised upwards

10 Etzioni, A. 1968. Basic human needs, alienation and inauthenticity. *American Sociological Review* 33 (4): 870–885.

11 Kernis, M. H. 2003. Optimal self-esteem and authenticity: separating fantasy from reality. *Psychological Inquiry* 14 (1): 83–89.

12 Avolio, B. J., W. L. Gardner, F. O. Walumbwa, F. Luthans, and D. R. May. 2004. Unlocking the mask: a look at the process by which authentic leaders impact follower attitudes and behaviors. *The Leadership Quarterly* 15 (6): 801–823.

13 Ilies, R., F. P. Morgeson, and J. D. Nahrgang. 2005. Authentic leadership and eudaemonic well-being: understanding leader–follower outcomes. *The Leadership Quarterly* 16 (3): 373–394.

Authenticity: the Respectful Executive

Nonetheless, Ilies, Morgeson and Nahrgang advise that: 'However, instances may exist where expressing one's true self results in severe social sanctions, or where projecting a powerful image of one's true self requires monitoring behaviors for the purpose of self-presentation.'[14] Interestingly, the participants in this study did not observe these two situational responses in the Respectful impression management, although several recipients observed that problem clients received short shrift from the manager. Losing some income may not be the serious social sanction that Ilies, Morgeson and Nahrgang implied. And one recipient reported that her Respectful executive who used the consistent benign impression management at one point lost a major customer through telling them the truth of their situation; he ensured that no staff lost out on their bonus income as well. So there is some doubt as to whether the situation of severe social sanctions would actually impinge on Respectful Executive Impression Management, and this is possibly due to the underlying strength of consistency.

As for self-monitoring of behaviours in order to modify impression management, this was observed by only two recipients of non-fraudster executives who did not give off the Respectful impression management in any case. It therefore appears likely that the Respectful executive's impression management does not change under stress or circumstance.

Trust: the Arrogant Fraudster

Trust is the key to what the fraudster is able to project very well upwards with boards and owner-managers, displaying an aura of trust created by their self-promotion strategy. Upper management even trusted the executive who was described as incompetent who was claimed to have 'not enough of a clue' about his work. Being outwardly very religious, which suggests adherence to a strict moral code, was one fraudster's modus operandi to engender trust. Once the outward impression management which has attributions of morality is delivered, a deep trust follows quickly. Obviously, this particular set of circumstances would only work in a setting that preferred a strict religious moral code. However, most businesses are run in a more secular fashion and assume a moral code in what could be described as an individualist self-interested fashion. This depends on all of society adhering to a commonly agreed set of principles. However, in a conflict view of society several moral

14 Ibid., p. 380.

codes can exist side by side, as typified in the maxim 'There's one law for the rich and one law for the poor.'

Morality

Normatively, morality would be internalised and become part of self-regulation and self-discipline so it is guided from within, not from external influences.[15] When the semi-structured interview questions were asked outright about executive morality, there was a mixed response. It was assumed and taken for granted to be in place by recipients of the Respectful executives, and in the Question Data part of the theme, there is a construct referring to them as having a moral character and being seen to operate ethically. Co-workers talked about a moral character in terms of honesty, being generous, doing work in the community, country values and having ethics and honour. It would appear also that transformational leaders share characteristics of these Respectful executives. Bass and Steidmeier[16] state that to be truly transformational a leader has to be grounded in virtue and moral character: this of course describes the Respectful executive but it is not characteristic of a manager giving off inconsistent impression management.

Morality: the Arrogant Fraudster

It is only the Arrogant Fraudster type who is sometimes assigned as immoral. The relationship between the Likeable Fraudsters and their co-workers seemed to be so beneficial and strong that morality was assumed, as one recipient reported:

> *He was honest except for one thing [the fraud].*

Morality is not the sole domain of executives using Respectful executive impression management. The mixed response to questions about the fraudster's impression management before discovery of the fraud was due to their adopting a disguise. One executive claimed morality on the grounds of being religious and was generally accepted as such.

> *That was the thing that was really obvious. [speaker's emphasis:]* Really strong Christian faith!

15 Ryan, L. V. 2000. Moral aspects of executive leadership. *International Journal of Value-Based Management* 13: 109–122.

16 Bass, B. M., and P. Steidmeier. 1999. Ethics, character, and authentic transformational leadership behaviour. *The Leadership Quarterly* 10 (2): 181–217.

Another co-worker mentioned:

> *but he definitely had his morals and views and beliefs … you know. He was very strong with regards to that.*

Borrowing the benign characteristic of morality is part of the Likeable Fraudsters' disguise. Although recipients were able to detect the non-fraudster executives slightly better on this construct, it is only classified as 'moderate', which demonstrates the strength of disguise. Looking for immorality in a person in order to detect possible fraudulent behaviour would therefore be quite ineffective, as one recipient pointed out:

> *There were never occasions where you thought, [from the fraudster] let's put a little bit extra on the invoice, or let's not deduct that from their wages, or let's not pay that person's super or …*

The disguise of morality in their impression management proved to be very successful.

Morality as a Precondition

In order for self-presentation to work however, the impression management has to be moral. The reader may remember that it is one of the preconditions for impression management. It is assumed that the audience will be able to detect immorality and consequently withdraw from the audience act of reciprocation. Like Goffman, recipients of the fraudster impression management assume that morality (as well as authenticity) is in place unless indicated otherwise. And unfortunately for the organisations that were defrauded, there was no indication. It was assumed that the fraudsters were moral.

AUTHENTICITY VERSUS MORALITY

Perhaps then the fraudster may instinctively know that they do not have to work as hard on morality as on authenticity (and therefore gain trust). There are no reports of fraudsters going out of their way to establish their morality, except for the religious fraudster. However, the fraudsters do go out of their way to firmly establish their authenticity, which appears to makes them more detectable on this factor than non-fraudster executives. And maybe the reason for the fraudsters to be more relaxed in instilling morality with their recipients is because morality exudes from the self.[17] This seemingly paradoxical state of affairs means it is important to review the self as a concept in impression management to understand this complex arrangement.

THE SELF

The self is deemed to be an empty space devoid of impression management and reaction to the outside world. It is seen as the moral private place of the essence of the individual, often referred to as the phenomenal self.[18] Impression management has been said to be an activity that serves the self in projecting the self as believable and beneficial to the recipient.[19] When it is not, it is said that impression management quickly changes to try and reach equilibrium about the self. This is almost a homeostatic activity, which is not sensed or even made conscious. Perhaps this happens when we believe the lie that we have told. However, there are others who view the self quite differently.

Tseelon[20] presents a postmodern view of the world, where impression management is not seen as used for the purposes of trickery: it is purely an interplay with others' impression management. This judgement is much closer to Goffman's perspective of impression management in that it exists only in the social interaction itself and reflects the inner self to others.

To extend this argument further, to say that a manager gives off benign or malevolent Executive Impression Management does not mean to say that the executive themself is benign or malevolent. When stress occurs individual beliefs about the world change.[21] The data are peppered with references about an 'us and them' fracturing of their world, whereas the Respectful executive impression management was cohesive. The recipients of Tyrant and Mediocre impression management reported this in many ways, e.g., favouritism, being exclusionary to others and high-pressure tactics. The world would seem to be a partitioned place to these executives and their only way of dealing with it is to divide and conquer. It is the way

17 Bandura, Albert. 2002. Selective moral disengagement in the exercise of moral agency. *Journal of Moral Education* 31 (2): 101–119.

18 Ibid.

19 Schlenker, B. R., and M. F. Weigold. 1992. Interpersonal processes involving impression regulation and management. *Annual Review of Psychology* 43: 133–168.

20 Tseelon, E. 1992. Is the presented self sincere? Goffman, impression management and the postmodern self. *Theory Culture & Society* 9 (2): 115–128.

21 Bandura, Albert, Gian Vittorio Caprara, Claudio Barbaranelli, Concetta Pastorelli, and Camillo Regalia. 2001. Sociocognitive self-regulatory mechanisms governing transgressive behavior. *Journal of Personality and Social Psychology* 80 (1): 125–135.

that this person has learnt to deal with the world. Goffman is most insistent that impression management is dealing on the outer of the self, with the world as the self knows it. But this is not a private self or a public self. It is *how* individuals make sense of their world. The interesting thing about this aspect is that it is non-blaming. These are only facets of how individuals respond to their world. To quote Goffman,

> *This suggests that while persons usually are what they appear to be, such appearances could still have been managed ... The implication here is that an honest, sincere, serious performance is less firmly connected to the solid world than one might first assume.*[22]

The Self: the Arrogant Fraudster

A staged confidence game requires all the tricks of the legitimate. Indeed, as this investigation has found out, in the co-workers' eyes the two types of fraudster impression management display strips or cracks in the veneer of the disguise over time. What is seen is not a powerful character who is trustworthy and authentic, but rather, albeit momentarily, fear which is described by Goffman as an indicator of weak character. These fraudsters are still operating within their impression management type, disguising their view of a highly fractured world with the mask of Respectful executive impression management. This is the contrivance that gives them away. If the Arrogant Fraudster used open impression management, they would have had less chance to stay in a Respectful impression management-dominated organisation, that is, at the executive management team or board of directors' level. The fractured attitude and behaviour would not be tolerated. A fraudster using Arrogant Fraudster type of impression management uses the disguise in the belief that this disguise will work better than their authentic self.

The Self: the Respectful Executive

As seen earlier, underneath the fraudsters' impression management one would *expect* to see a weak person, not a strong character. Similarly, the self of an executive showing Respectful impression management would be *expected* to be a strong character, however, this may not be the case. For example, an individual could use benign impression management yet be weak, despite the impression management offering goodness, trust and authenticity to co-workers. In fact, the Emperor in the fairy tale was described as being a good

22 Goffman 1959, op cit., p. 71.

and trusted ruler, but the tailors found his one weakness, his love of high fashion, and exploited it for their own ends. Displaying Benign Executive Impression Management does not mean that the individual is good. It only means that they are showing consistency, trustworthiness and morality in their impression management to certain people. For the Likeable Fraudster it was the bond made with certain staff.

REAL CHARACTER

The real character according to Goffman is only revealed at 'fateful moments'. This is explored in studies by Woods and Jeffrey[23] and O'Connor[24] in the revelation of character in different settings: in teaching and adolescence. They researched what is seen as identity at a fateful moment in time. Going one step further, it could be argued that these two conditions, of character strength and the Respectful non-fraudster Executive Impression Management reflect these forms. Goffman considered that the character was instilled in the person and was unlikely to change over time.[25] The investigation found evidence of weak characters in the fraudsters. However, as noted earlier there is some research[26] that indicates that there are four categories of impression management approaches if an individual is 'found out' in a public predicament. These include: using excuses, justifications, concessions and denial. It would be expected from this study that the fraudster manager using Inconsistent impression management (Arrogant and Likeable Fraudsters) would use such strategies. And indeed that was precisely what the co-workers of fraudster managers reported. A manager using Respectful impression management would be expected to only use apologies,[27] which implies genuine self-awareness and having the humility to learn.

This observation concludes the exploration of the executive impression management types and the recipients' attributions of authenticity, morality, trust and self-esteem, view of world to each type and strength of character. The next chapter will now explore Executive Impression Management to generate

23 Woods, P., and B. Jeffrey. 2002. The reconstruction of primary teachers' identities. British *Journal of Sociology of Education* 23 (1): 89–106.

24 O'Connor, P. 2006. Young people's constructions of the self: late modern elements and gender differences. *Sociology* 40 (1): 107–124.

25 Goffman, E. 1967. *Interaction ritual: essays on face-to-face behavior*. New York: Pantheon Books. Original edition, 1967.

26 Konovsky, M. A., and F. Jaster. 1989. 'Blaming the victim' and other ways business men and women account for questionable behaviour. *Journal of Business Ethics* 8 (5): 391–398.

27 Tucker, S., N. Turner, J. Barling, E. M. Reid, and C. Elving. 2006. Apologies and transformational leadership. *Journal of Business Ethics* 63 (2): 195–207.

a possible explanation of how and why the fraudsters have such a distinctive impression management type.

Chapter 6

The Basis of the Types

To reiterate, five themes of executive impression management emerged out of both sets of data: Their Stories and the Question Data. These themes appear to be differentiated types of executive impression management and are as follows:

For the fraudster executive recipients:

1. Disguised Inconsistent Malevolent Superior (The Arrogant Fraudster)

2. Disguised Inconsistent Malevolent Inferior (The Likeable Fraudster)

From the non-fraudster executive recipients:

1. Consistent Benign (The Respectful Executive)

2. Inconsistent Malevolent Superior (The Tyrant Executive)

3. Inconsistent Malevolent Inferior (The Mediocre Executive)

There are three issues concerning the data that must be explored before a framework can be developed, regarding the positioning of the recipient and the executive in their impression management relationship. However, before this discussion takes place, there are certain theoretical issues that have come out of the research that inform insight into executive impression management:

- Consistency/inconsistency of impression management

- Power in the workplace.

The unique focus of this investigation is through engineering the study from the position of the co-worker receiving the impression management given off by fraudster managers. The data are solely from the perspective of the audience.

This means that for the first time, there is an opportunity to identify and discuss what impression management is like from the recipients' point of view.

Two Types of Fraudster

Having only two types of fraudsters is not extraordinary. Romney, Albrecht and Cherrington found two types of fraudsters: those who had a criminal history and others who had no history of deviance. This led the authors to conclude that one type will steal at the first opportunity and the other will only steal when 'the level of desire overcomes his inhibitions'.[1]

This is the first mention of two distinct types of fraudsters that I had found in all my research. Another researcher, Michael Levi, also suspected there were two types,[2] but these two voices are lost in the hubbub of people wanting to make a living out of white-collar crime, the forensic accountants, auditors, fraud investigators and the occupational associations who support them. This early finding about white-collar criminals seems to have been lost due to the fact that in the recent surveys, the fraudster characteristics are gathered together to present a single profile. If the surveys had taken into account the two types as the originators of the Red Flags found this investigation would only be corroboration of that fact, and intrinsic enough to be deeply involved with the persona and executive impression management that the fraudster gives off.

UNIQUE 'LENS' OF THE RECIPIENT

Turning to the co-workers. Using the exceptional opportunity of the recipients' perspective, there are theoretical consequences about the view of the recipient for the themes of impression management that emerged from the data. This problem only relates to the four themes of Inconsistent executive impression management, and in particular the Arrogant and Likeable Fraudsters.

1 Romney, M. B., W. S. Albrecht, and D. J. Cherrington. 1980b. Red-flagging the white collar criminal; potential fraud situations have common characteristics, according to a survey of published cases, which can be used as early warning signals to prevent actual acts. *Management Accounting* 61 (9): 51–56, p. 54.

2 Levi, Michael. 1988. The prevention of fraud. In *Crime Prevention Unit: Paper 17*, edited by K. Heal. London: Home Office Crime Prevention Unit. Available online at: http://collection.europarchive.org/tna/20080205132101/homeoffice.gov.uk/rds/prgpdfs/fcpu17.pdf (Accessed 14 July 2009)

If, in a given situation, a co-worker is a subordinate and a favourite of a manager giving off impression management, is it possible that this recipient would have described that executive as Benign whereas others, those who were not favourites, would have described received impression management as Malevolent. Or to put it in the context of the study: is it possible that their 'lens' of the recipient is distorted by received favouritism? Or vice versa: could their lens be warped by non-favouritism and feelings of jealousy?

Reviewing the data and subsequent findings this did not in fact happen. There are reports of others being favourites, but not the recipients themselves:

> *You know, she had her favourites, she was allowed to have her favourites. ... Well it was a very exclusive group and I didn't become part of the exclusivity.*

This is in accordance with the literature on favouritism.[3] It is reported that negatively based favouritism (as opposed to positive discrimination measures, for example, to increase the number of women at managerial levels), is typically used by authoritarian managers. It is seen as unfair and the favoured are seen as management 'toadies', also that this practice conceals problems, ignores merit and produces irrelevant performance goals. Furthermore, favouritism works against the distribution of justice in an organisation and the resulting social comparison it elicits, and results in stress and feelings of injustice, particularly if the issue is handled insensitively.[4] Furthermore, Khatri and Tsang[5] argued that the crony can be fast career-tracked, but it produces an ineffective organisation as a result and they did not recommend this.[6]

Despite the negative impact for the organisation, ingroup membership is rewarded by transactional managers by establishing a sense of trust with followers through the application of conditional rewards under the guise of patronage.[7] Favouritism and patronage therefore seems to not alter the lens of

---

3 See Dasborough, M. T., N. M. Ashkanasy, E. Y. J. Tee, and H. H. M. Tse. 2009. What goes around comes around: how meso-level negative emotional contagion can ultimately determine organizational attitudes toward leaders. *The Leadership Quarterly* 20 (4): 571–585; also, Fisher, J. E. 1977. Playing favorites in large organizations. *Business Horizons* 20 (3): 68–74; and Greenberg, J., C. E. Ashton-James, and N. M. Ashkanasy. 2007. Social comparison processes in organizations. *Organizational Behavior and Human Decision Processes* 102 (1): 22–41.

4 Greenberg, Ashton-James and Ashkanasy 2007, op cit.

5 Khatri, N., and E. W. K. Tsang. 2003. Antecedents and consequences of cronyism in organizations. *Journal of Business Ethics* 43 (4): 289–303.

6 Ibid., p. 298.

7 Fisher 1977, op cit.

the recipients. Possibly, favouritism would have been disclosed as part of the impression management from their executive if they received such a status, it would have been expected to be conditional and temporary as well as noted in the relationship.

NATURE OF CONSISTENCY IN IMPRESSION MANAGEMENT

The issue that comes to the fore is that favouritism and patronage only happen with the inconsistent forms of impression management and the resulting managerial behaviour is seen as such.[8] For example the favourite, depending on the needs of the executive, may be quickly replaced with another. Turning to the findings, the managers who had favourites, as reported by the recipients, were said to be inconsistent in their impression management, confirming what Dasborough et al. had reported earlier. Co-workers talked about differential treatment in examples of inconsistency:

> *he doesn't actually treat her the way that he treated me ... but you know if you do things like that then you're not going to be favoured afterwards whether you keep your job or not, so either way it was going to be pretty unpleasant for me.*

The primary concept that stands out from the findings is that recipients noted the consistency or inconsistency of the impression management that they received. This is significant because it is reported that it creates cognitive and emotional difficulties for the co-workers. For example, one co-worker reported emotional shock in receiving inconsistent impression management. Consistency therefore seems to be a very important issue to co-workers.

This is in alignment with Goffman's self-presentation theory, because consistency is the foundation of impression management. The actor's performance will fail once the audience detects inconsistencies. Goffman tells us that the audience will use tact to cover up any embarrassment for the actor for these reasons: 'Audiences are motivated to act tactfully because of an immediate identification with the performers, or because of a desire to avoid a scene, or to ingratiate themselves with the performers for purposes of exploitation.'[9] But these are used when there are minor discrepancies. In fact, Goffman explains that we expect the opposite, no discrepancies in the act,

8 Dasborough et al. 2009, op cit.

9 Goffman, E. 1959. *The presentation of self in everyday life*. New York: Anchor Books, Doubleday, p. 232.

referring specifically to social status: 'we expect that the differences in statuses among the interactants will be expressed in some way by congruent differences in the indications that are made of an expected interaction role.'[10] If that expectation is not fulfilled and there is perceived incongruence, the audience will not believe the actor's performance. Therefore, consistency in impression management is paramount. However, for audiences of those executives who expressed inconsistent impression management, congruency was not received. These executives' impression management was reported as inconsistent.

This is an interesting finding as it is the first indication that impression management can vary by its consistency.

Does it put Goffman's theory of impression management at risk? The mainstay of the theory is the audience's responsibility to keep the actor honest, in that they will always see through any inauthenticity. In the cases of the executives giving off inconsistent impression management, the audience appears to be unable to be held accountable for their responsibility.

After the shock of receiving inconsistent impression management, the audience is unable to manage the inconsistencies of dealing with the actor in the usual way. They do not, or are unable to, take the final step of uncovering the sham. This may be for two reasons as expressed through the recipients' voices:

- The possibility of losing their job if they are subordinate to the executive.
- In the case of the business owners/board members, they want to keep the competence of the inconsistent impression management manager in place to maintain the status quo.

Regardless, all recipients of inconsistent impression management are stymied in taking the next step of seeing through the façade and calling off the act. Yet Goffman predicted that the audience should in fact have the upper hand in the social interaction no matter how many encounters there are. This is due to the initial exchange of information where the audience has its expectations already in place and the actor wishes to catch up.[11]

10 Goffman 1959, p. 24, op cit.
11 Goffman 1959, pp. 14–15, op cit.

The result in this study is that the co-workers ignore inconsistent impression management and furthermore quite dangerously do not accord it any value. This was classified as merely oddness, personality quirks or just being a bad boss. This exposed impedance to impression management requires further consideration.

Consistency is Benignly Consistent

It is only in the Respectful form that managers are seen as consistent in their impression management. This constancy does not change over time, as one recipient noted when working with her executive for 14 years. Respectful managers are described as confident, hard working, of moral character and respectful to staff, as well as being consistent. This finding parallels Block's study[12] where she found that transformational supervisors were associated with consistency in the organisation.

Not only is consistency consistent, it is also benign. The literature over the last ten years suggests support for the notion of managerial consistency as being a positive condition in the workplace. For performance-related criteria, McKay, Avery and Morris found that positive consistency from managers' and subordinates' perspectives had higher sales performance than those of a negative frame.[13] And there is some evidence that consistent executives who have consistently minded subordinates achieve expected sales results.[14] Yet consistency is ignored as a prerequisite in managerial employment recruitment, promotion, their key performance indicators (KPIs) and even in selection criteria into MBA programmes.

For associated characteristics of positive managerial consistency, Sanders, Dorenbosch and De Reuver found that there was a higher affective commitment by employees within consistent managerial environments.[15] Jernigan and Beggs

12 Block, L. 2003. The leadership–culture connection: an exploratory investigation. *Leadership and Organization Development Journal* 24 (5/6): 318–335.

13 McKay, P. F., D. R. Avery, and M. A. Morris. 2009. A tale of two climates: diversity climate from subordinates' and managers' perspectives and role performance in store unit sales performance. *Personnel Psychology* 62 (4): 767–791.

14 Soltani, E., P.-C. Lai, R. Van Der Meer, and T. M. Williams. 2008. Managerial approaches towards service quality: the case of three service organisations. *Service Industries Journal* 28 (10): 1399–1414.

15 Sanders, K., L. Dorenbosch, and R. De Reuver. 2008. The impact of individual and shared employee perceptions of HRM on affective commitment: considering climate strength. *Personnel Review* 37 (4):412–425.

found that managerial consistency related to higher moral commitment to the organisation from subordinates.[16] This was expressed in conjunction with showing concern for their subordinate's progress and supporting their staff with other managers as well as satisfaction with the manager's technical competence. Interestingly there is another reference to specific consistency behaviour in the workplace from Geller who found through focus group discussions that consistency was a component of trust.[17] In a commentary from a veteran of 40 years in management consultancy, Norris[18] found that consistency is the product of a good manager and with consistency there has to be courage. Given the sparse consistency literature, it can be summarised that employees increase moral and affective commitment as well as trust from the consistency of their managers. These findings correspond well with the co-workers' reports of their Consistent Benign impression management from their own manager.

The consistency of the Respectful executive impression management is stable even though Goffman proposed that there would be differences in how people use their impression management with various audiences.[19] For instance, a manager will use one impression management form to the board of directors, which may differ from the impression management that is received by subordinates.[20] However, the impression management used for either audience will still be consistent, despite being a complex social process with variation in content to different audiences. Gardner and Martinko emphasise that to be less than reliable will lead the audience to detect aberrations and therefore see through the impression management: consequently nothing else about this person will be trusted. Therefore consistency in all of its complexity of delivery is primary, paramount and necessary.

MALEVOLENCE AND INCONSISTENCY

The Arrogant Fraudster type of executive impression management in this study gives off malevolent impression management and these cases are classified as inconsistent in the eyes of the co-worker. The Arrogant Fraudsters

16 Jernigan III, I. E., and J. M. Beggs. 2005. An examination of satisfaction with my supervisor and organizational commitment. *Journal of Applied Social Psychology* 35 (10):2171–2192.

17 Geller, E. S. 1999. Interpersonal trust. *Professional Safety* 44 (4): 16–20.

18 Norris, D. B. 2001. The unreasonable and arbitrary manager. *Consulting to Management* 12 (3): 35–36.

19 Goffman, E. 1967. *Interaction ritual: essays on face-to-face behavior*. New York: Pantheon Books. Original edition, 1967.

20 Gardner, W. L., and M. J. Martinko. 1988. Impression management: an observational study linking audience characteristics with verbal self-presentations. *Academy of Management Journal* 31 (1): 42–65.

impression management changed over time and was so described in the co-workers' interviews. Inconsistency is a solid characteristic of the Malevolent forms of executive impression management. The literature has some support for the negativity that is associated with this type of inconsistent impression management. Tanure and Gonzalez-Duarte found evidence in a case study that executive inconsistency in 'discourse and practice' curtailed other support departments' roles in an organisation.[21] Also, Jernigan and Beggs[22] found that those managers who were not consistent, and 'alienative' to moral commitment, displayed negative behaviour such as being intolerant when an employee made a mistake. In addition, Snell and Wong[23] found that if a manager was wilfully inconsistent, then these managers were described as unconscientious; helpful to upline managers but not to others when the manager is not around; not interested in being harmonious in the organisation and untrustworthy in the stewardship context. Furthermore, respondents described this behaviour in their investigation as self-serving in some contexts.

LACK OF CONSENSUS IN INCONSISTENT IMPRESSION MANAGEMENT CONTENT

As it happened, a result of the sampling by convenience was that in some cases, the owner of the business was a co-worker and the fraudster manager reported to him, and another co-worker was a subordinate to the same manager. There was a marked difference in the impression management that was given off and received by these two sets of recipients. It was almost as if the recipients of the same executive's impression management were of two different people. The executive using Inconsistent Malevolent impression management upwards to owners or board members was self-serving in content. However, the subordinate receiving the downward impression management had negative occurrences. For the co-workers of the Likeable Fraudster there was a disparity between upwards and downwards impression management again, with ingratiation used in both instances. While this was not a focus of the study, it was expected as noted earlier that there would be slight differences in upward and downward impression management as mentioned by Goffee and Jones,[24] but the overall content would still be consistent. However, as previously demonstrated, the discrepancies that occurred between upward and downward

21 Tanure, B., and R. Gonzalez-Duarte. 2007. Managing people in radical changes (M&As). *International Journal of Manpower* 5: 369–383.

22 Jernigan and Beggs 2005, op cit.

23 Snell, R. S., and Y. L. Wong. 2007. Differentiating good soldiers from good actors. *Journal of Management Studies* 44 (6):883–909.

24 Goffee, R., and G. Jones. 2005. Managing authenticity. *Harvard Business Review* 83 (12): 86–94.

impression management only happened with the executives using Inconsistent impression management, not those using Consistent impression management of the Respectful executive.

In the latter case, superiors of the Respectful impression management type received positive content (but not self-serving) as well as the recipient who was subordinate. One of the interesting points raised is that when the manager gave off Consistent Benign impression management, all recipients were in accord about the executive. It could be that these Respectful executives are transparent and trusted, as well as being highly effective, which Norman, Avolio and Lufthans[25] demonstrated in a recent study.

Reflecting on the collective voice, it is as if the Respectful executives are glossed over. Yet when talking about the inconsistent executives, recipients are vociferous. Baumeister et al.[26] offer an explanation that somehow negative events have more impact on the psyche than positive events of the same type. They argue that bad events hold more value in our psyche than good events. It may be the result of pragmatism of survival.[27]

The Baumeister team reviewed a wide range of psychological phenomena, including impression formation, and came to the conclusion that perhaps this is due to evolutionary survival; that to not recognise danger, for example, could have had deleterious results. 'Survival requires attention to possible bad outcomes, but it is less urgent to good ones.'[28] They raise an interesting possibility that culture may find it useful to promote good events including love, a good marriage and a happy career, rather than negative ones, to generate conformity. Exceptions to this are not treated lightly, with social sanctions in place for instance, being unloved, experiencing divorce, having career failure or non-achievement. These exceptions are labelled as dangerous to the individual's sense of well-being, as these events in turn, it is argued, threaten the basis of society.

In this study, it appears that the good events are reported by the co-workers who are working with an executive who is consistent. The attention that the recipients expressed about the executives using Inconsistent (whether

25 Norman, S. M., B. J. Avolio, and F. Luthans. 2010. The impact of positivity and transparency on trust in leaders and their perceived effectiveness. *The Leadership Quarterly* 21 (3):350–364.

26 Baumeister, R. F., E. Bratslavsky, C. Finkenauer, and K. Vohs. 2001. Bad is stronger than good. *Review of General Psychology* 5 (4): 323–370.

27 Ibid., p. 323.

28 Ibid., p. 325.

Malevolent or Benign) impression management relates to the transgression of the social rule of being a good manager. Co-workers have reported that having a manager using Inconsistent Malevolent impression management in one's work life means being hypervigilant (to avoid wrath), general unhappiness, feelings of not being recognised and/or being emotionally and verbally abused. It would seem then that the primary characteristic in being a good manager is consistency, which may relate to the adherence to the allegory of consistency of behaviour in society.[29]

CONSISTENCY RELATING TO SOCIAL THEORY

Certainty and consistency is demanded in science, and to some extent in social science. Consensus theory is based on social rules, and conformity to those rules would be expected. However, some sociologists of consensus theory do expect conflict, but it is still seen to be harmonious and actually helpful for society in its emergence. For instance, Georg Simmel[30] saw conflict as an integrating factor, not one of disengagement. He argued that conflict contained in the 'struggle principle' was a necessary part with the 'unifying principle'. To put this very simply, without conflict, society would not unify itself. It is necessary for people to understand bad in order to achieve good, to use Baumeister's analogy. Essentially an individual is still connected to the other in spite of showing 'hatred and envy, want and desire'.[31]

However, conflict theorists would expect all social rules to be broken in the interests of power acquisition. Despite the consensus view of society being seen as the dominant theory of how society works, conflict theorists argue that society operates on conflict. There are power imbalances which create inequity, which in turn subjugates many and makes managers the puppets of business owners or large corporations. These managers would use negative authoritarian transactional behaviours to obtain conformance from workers,[32] and yet have positive impression management towards their own superiors, thereby using inconsistent impression management. Conflict theory therefore anticipates managers as agents of more powerful interests, using inconsistent impression management specifically positive upwards and negative downwards to their staff.

29 Boslego, J. 2005. Engineering social trust. *Harvard International Review* 27 (1): 28–32.
30 Simmel, G. 1904. The sociology of conflict. I. *The American Journal of Sociology* 9 (4): 490–525.
31 Ibid., p. 490.
32 Clegg, S. R., M. Kornberger, C. Carter, and C. Rhodes. 2006. For management? *Management Learning* 37 (1): 7–27.

However, it can be argued that in the daily running of consensus systems, certain things are lost. Argyris argues that is because some things become undiscussable and governing values allow unilateralism.[33] Organisations try to smooth over contradictions and strife, because they have an 'inability to discuss risky or threatening issues'.[34] Argyris thought that the problem lay with organisations themselves, but instead found that

> *It appears that most individuals in our society (and in many societies throughout the world) are taught, through acculturation and socialization, a set of values, action strategies, and skills that lead them to respond automatically to threatening issues by 'easing in', 'appropriately covering', or by 'being civilised'.*[35]

This is so inbuilt in their socialisation that people are unaware of their learned responses. Furthermore, 'they are unaware that they are unaware'.[36] A case of social blindness at the extreme.

Furthermore, Argyris and Schon[37] state that the consequences of their Model-1 theory-in-use (that is, the worldview and values implied by individual's behaviour, or the maps they use to take action) are that individuals can embark on a range of bad behaviours and inconsistency and be unaware of them. When applied to the fraudster manager this reflects the Inconsistent impression management and resulting behaviour that was described by co-workers. The Argyris and Schon Model-1 says that by minimising generating of expressing negative feelings, defensive norms such as mistrust and lack of risk-taking rule the workplace. Concomitant with Argyris and Schon's theoretical discussion, a recent empirical study[38] has demonstrated that the negative feelings of CEOs result in less risk-taking, which suggests that affect is also interlinked with this type of behaviour.

While Goffman is accepted as a consensus theorist, he has also been noted as a conflict theorist, as remarked earlier. His micro inspection of the minutiae

33 Argyris, C. 1980. Making the undiscussable and its' undiscussability discussable. *Public Administration Review* 40 (3): 205–213.
34 Ibid., p. 205.
35 Ibid., p. 205.
36 Ibid., p. 208.
37 Argyris, C., and D. A. Schon. 1974. *Theory in practice: increasing professional effectiveness*. San Francisco, CA: Jossey-Bass.
38 Delgado-García, J. B., J. M. d. l. Fuente-Sabaté, and E. d. Quevedo-Puente. 2010. Too negative to take risks? The effect of the CEO's emotional traits on firm risk. *British Journal of Management* 21 (2): 313–326.

of daily life allows the power imbalances to be illustrated, for example, with the actor trying to control the audience through his impression management. As Baumeister et al. argued,[39] the audience adjudication happens so subtly with the recipients of Consistent Benign impression management that the audience has made up its mind long ago, most likely at their first meeting, that 'all the boxes were ticked'. There is an equal balance of power, which is received, enjoyed and tucked away. Forgotten about, that is, until there is an unexpected violation.

The Role of Exceptions

Furthermore, it is the violations to consensus that make the Inconsistent Malevolent and Benign managers stand out. And this is exactly what Goffman saw, that to prove impression management exists in all of our social interaction, it was the violations that should be investigated.[40]

The finding of Inconsistent Malevolent impression management given off by managers supports that the accepted rule that society is marked with co-operation and reciprocation. Furthermore, it is the exceptions that cause outrage and discomfort to the recipients.

Far from saying that impression management has a failing, the theorist himself, Erving Goffman, had the foresight and intellect to understand that it is the exceptions that prove the rule. And these exceptions are the managers who are creating power imbalances for their own needs. This includes emotional abuse to others as well as defrauding the organisation. After some considerable debate, Chriss[41] arrives at the same conclusion that Goffman insisted upon, that if acting is insincere and inauthentic, it must be coercive. Coercion can be subtly manipulative, as with the Likeable Fraudster, or openly superior and malevolent, as with the Arrogant Fraudster. Either way it transgresses society's norms of social interaction. This state of affairs allows the inconsistent manager to act, secure in their power base of being the person who holds the co-workers' (both upline and subordinate) economic future in his hands.

39 Baumeister, Bratslavsky, Finkenauer, and K. Vohs 2001, op cit.

40 Goffman 1959, op cit., p. 15.

41 Chriss, J. J. 1995. Habermas, Goffman, and communicative action: implications for professional practice. *American Sociological Review* 60 (4): 545–566.

THE NATURE OF POWER USED IN FRAUDSTER IMPRESSION MANAGEMENT

Goffman anticipated control over people through impression management. The executives through their impression management also asserted their power positioning to the recipients. Despite the attempt, the final determination of how that positioning is received and evaluated remains with the recipients.

If we are talking about the abuse of power as a feature of managerial fraud, I must introduce the most widely used taxonomy of power in organisations – French and Raven's classification of power in the workplace.[42] The two authors described five types of power. Originally used for supervisor–subordinate relationships, the taxonomy has now been developed by Raven and other scholars to 14 types of power, covering all power relationships in daily social interaction.[43] However, the variations reported are subsets of the original five used in the workplace. Managers may have great power in that they can fire an individual, but they need not resort to such an extreme measure in order to make use of their power, possession of the threat of termination is the actual lever for power in the workplace. The original taxonomy is: reward power is founded on compensation, coercive power on compliance, legitimate power is having the justifiable right, expert power relies on superior knowledge and referent power is based on the subordinate identifying with the power holder. Informational power, which is power in organisations based on information, was added by Raven later,[44] and is used to explain why an individual should comply. This is possibly accounting for 'the need to know' basis. According to Elias,[45] Raven later developed a power-interaction model, which identified motivation to influence, albeit positive or negative; assessment and choice of available power bases; implementation and after effects.

Coercive Power

Using French and Raven's typology, some fraudsters appeared to use coercive power to maintain compliance by subordinates. Typically, coercive power can

42 French, J. R. P., and B. H. Raven. 1960. The bases of social power. In *Group dynamics: research and theory*, ed. D. Cartwright and A. Zander, 607–623. Evanston, IL: Harper and Row.

43 Elias, S. 2008. Fifty years of influence in the workplace: the evolution of the French and Raven power taxonomy. *Journal of Management History* 14 (3): 267–283.

44 Raven, B. H. 1993. The bases of power: origins and recent developments. *Journal of Social Issues* 49 (4): 227–251.

45 Elias 2008, op cit.

result in bullying and sometimes verbal threats, to ensure that compliance is gained from the subordinate. If a person fails to comply they will suffer stress from coercion and could ultimately lose their job.

Expert-based Power

Expert-based power is where individuals use their superior knowledge or skill to gain compliance. Originally this was seen as purely in a positive sense, but later others pointed out that there could be a negative form of expert power. As Elias states: 'knowledge may be used in such a fashion (i.e. negative expert power) that strictly benefits him or herself, resulting in resistance to the influence attempt'.[46]

This is illustrated through the following incidents from the data. There were three owner-managers in the study, and they did not suspect that anything was wrong. It was not until one fraudster refused to give reports and another kept on making gross mistakes that after a long period of time, at least one year, and two years in another case, that suspicions started to be aroused. Those suspicions were not of fraud, but only about their competency. And this indicates what the true power was – negative expert power.[47]

The fraudsters displayed competency at the beginning, indeed were brought into the unsuspecting organisations solely due to their expertise. As long as their expertise was not exposed, the fraudster executives' power base remained intact. The employer wanted to keep the Arrogant Fraudster in place: in their minds losing such expertise was deleterious to the company. This probably explains why the upper management of the fraudsters kept them *in situ*: their expertise was still valued. One fraudster used this very well to his advantage by protesting that the statutory bodies (for example the Australian Taxation Office) must have had their facts wrong, and this was believed.

If the owner-managers had supervision and accountability protocols in place,[48] the problem of using the impression management of competence to

46 Ibid., p. 272.

47 Chang, J. J. S. 2008. An analysis of advance fee fraud on the Internet. *Journal of Financial Crime* 15 (1): 71–81.

48 See Higson, A. 2002. *Indications of Fraud in SMEs*. London: Fraud Advisory Panel. http://www.fraudadvisorypanel.org/newsite/Publications/Publications_research.htm (accessed 31 August 2009) and Coram, P., C. Ferguson, and R. Moroney. 2008. Internal audit, alternative internal audit structures and the level of misappropriation of assets fraud. *Accounting & Finance* 48 (4): 543–559.

hide the fraudulent behaviour would have been discovered far sooner. As it was, the frauds went on for a very long time. Spot audits would have also found mistakes in the books of at least three fraudsters. However, it must be stressed that an outside detailed auditing process went on for many years for some of the fraudsters, and it failed to penetrate the negative expert power held by them. One of these 'experts' defrauded in excess of A$15 millions.

As seen with credit card fraudsters,[49] the managerial fraudsters relied on this negative expert power to pull the wool over peoples' eyes. They also relied on:

- Ineffective review systems
- Getting rid of the threats of other perceived experts in the organisation
- Training subordinates to be unquestioning
- Recruiting compliant subordinates
- Providing gibberish to confuse the owner managers. This was used in different ways by four fraudsters
- Messy, incomprehensible reports
- Keeping any questions at bay through joking and diverting behaviour
- Giving reports that only showed half the picture
- Asserting that other organisations, notably statutory authorities, were wrong.

Power for the fraudsters was the tool to organising their fraud. Without negative expert power their disguised Inconsistent impression management activities would have been quickly exposed.

49 Chang 2008, op cit.

Referent Power

Referent power, as described by French and Raven,[50] is a positive form of co-worker identification, that followers will comply as they identify with the supervisor. There is an example of the use of latent referent power used in a grooming context in the data. An accountant who used to work with an Arrogant Fraudster was brought back in to do project reports that the fraudster was refusing to provide. She was not beholden to the fraudster to keep her assignment. It was the owner-managers who would decide whether she remained employed or not. It is still interesting to note the angst that the accountant suffered, and the supposition on the fraudster's part that she would keep quiet about a fraudulent transaction she had found. In that social interaction he was using referent power and hoping that due to their years of working together, she would show some loyalty to him. After an internal struggle of some hours, which demonstrates the strength of the affective power that he had over her,[51] she went ahead and exposed the fraud on the advice of her mother, who was outside the fraudster's power base in the workplace.

The Likeable Fraudster impression management typically uses referent power to establish control over their subordinates. The case of the executive offering free drinks after work is establishing such a power base. Notably too, when the fraud was exposed, the affective power remnants were so strong that all the staff left over a period of six months.

50 French and Raven 1960, op cit.
51 Raven 1993, op cit.

Chapter 7
The Two Fraudster Typology

Unlike the earlier approaches using a single profile, such as KPMG Forensic's 2007 *Profile of a Fraudster Survey*, this investigation of what the co-workers saw has resulted in a dual typology for the managerial fraudsters.

Executive Impression Management as a Core Process

As we have seen there are two relevant aspects that are common to the five types of Executive Impression Management: being consistent or inconsistent and the exertion of power in their impression management. This will be discussed with reference to the Arrogant and Likeable Fraudsters.

CONTINUUM OF CONSISTENCY

With this in mind, a continuum of consistency of impression management can be formed from the data (see Figure 7.1). With the inconsistent managerial forms that do not steal and are openly inconsistent, for example having favourites, to the benign form of management who are openly inconsistent, the fraudster managers lay in the middle of the continuum with their disguised consistency.

The Disguised fraudsters try the wolf in sheep's clothing act of donning the disguise of a manager exuding Respectful Executive Impression Management. As noted by the co-workers of the fraudster managers, there were definite inconsistencies over time. Consistency of executive impression management must therefore form the principal element of the conceptual framework. A true Respectful manager would never be inconsistent, as discussed earlier. From this basis the secondary issue of the use of power in impression management was considered.

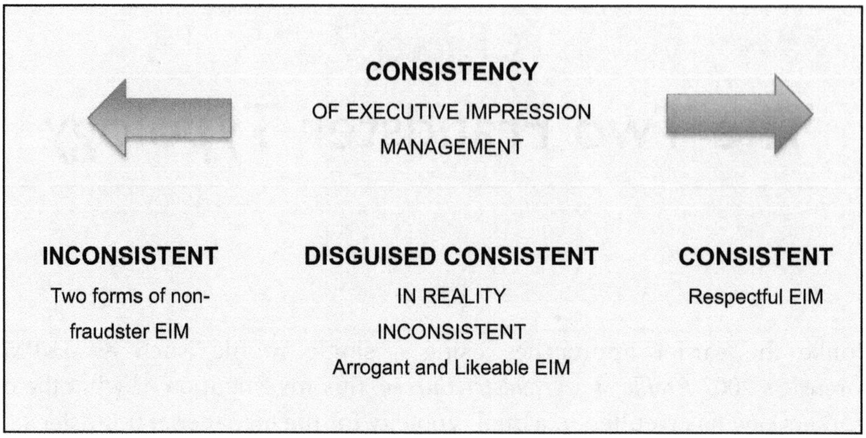

Figure 7.1 Continuum of consistency of Executive Impression Management

EXERTION OF POWER IN EXECUTIVE IMPRESSION MANAGEMENT

Although the perceptions of the managers are outcomes of the consistency of impression management, there is still another dynamic at work in the core process. It relates to the power relationship that the recipients receive through their own lens. As Goffman noted despite the motives of the actor, the impression management process is essentially one of control of the audience. The actor does this mostly by conforming to the 'definition of the situation' and 'by expressing himself in such a way as to give the kind of impression that will lead them [the audience] to act voluntarily in accordance with his own plan'.[1]

Control, and therefore power, are seen by Goffman as neutral and can be applied for moral or immoral purposes. At this point it is worthwhile to consider the three types of executives: those using the Respectful Executive Impression Management and the fraudsters using Disguised Inconsistent impression management.

1 Goffman, E. 1959. *The presentation of self in everyday life*. New York: Anchor Books, Doubleday, pp. 3–4.

Power: Respectful

With the Respectful executive impression management the situation is defined through a power relationship of legitimacy and equality.[2] The use of power with others was reported as:

> *he bases them on their own merits and treats everyone equally.*

This treatment is respectful and invites reciprocation from the recipient's own free will:

> *He treats the receptionist the same way he treats his [business] partner. So everyone is easy. Which is nice.*

Equality marks the benign relationship, which in turn induces the control mechanism of consensual voluntary reciprocation:

> *He can be, [persuasive] if he wants something done. I won't say overly, he does it in a nice way.*

Consensual, participative reciprocation therefore distinguishes the power of the Respectful impression management.

Power: Inconsistent Impression Management

However, with Inconsistent impression management, the opposite occurs. Reciprocation involves exercising control over co-workers. The managers using Inconsistent impression management do not use equality or consensus; they use coercive power (therefore inequitable), either subtly (the Benign form – The Likeable) or overtly The Malevolent form (the Arrogant Fraudster), to make co-workers do what they want them to do. For instance those who worked with the Arrogant Fraudster reported that they used their superiority to push them into doing their tasks.

> *He took great pride in thinking he was like my mentor and he was teaching me and all this.*

2 French, J. R. P., and B. H. Raven. 1960. The bases of social power. In *Group dynamics: research and theory*, ed. D. Cartwright and A. Zander, 607–623. Evanston IL: Harper and Row.

Note that Likeable Fraudsters were described as using a cleverly restrained form of coercive power by making themselves appear inferior to the recipient to create reciprocation. This is extremely important for co-workers to understand, they were just as manipulated and abused as those who used power over them.

Not to over emphasise the point, it is essential, Goffman argued, that there are checks and balance to the power arrangement of impression management. This would be in a form where the audience would detect the relationship being imposed and respond appropriately. No matter how the actor may wish to have his power acknowledged through the use of impression management, the final decision rests with the recipient who has the right to agree or disagree with their power relationship.

In an equal and just world the recipient can choose to end the relationship. However, this is not the case in inequitable relationships, no matter how much the recipients counter. Goffman describes this well in *'Asylums: essays on the social situation of mental patients and other inmates'*.[3] Recipients are locked (literally) into reciprocation, which generates all sorts of passive–aggressive behaviours, for example ignoring what has taken place, or in the case of mental patients, outrageous actions to seize control of the power of the interaction.

Power: the Fraudsters

Fraudsters, however, use the Consistent Benign impression management of the Respectful manager as a disguise. However, it is the power relationship that they assert over co-workers that demonstrates their Inconsistent impression management. For example at discovery; to certain subordinates who were groomed to receive favours; or to others who are seen as of no use in their game plan, and therefore treated inequitably, even though they attempt to maintain the Consistent Benign impression management to those who are considered important to deceive, the business owners, boards and so on.

A small example of the disguised coercive power is seen with the co-worker who knew that the fraudster had taken advantage of his position by buying a more expensive office chair and lied to cover his actions (an inconsistency):

3 Goffman, E. 1962. *Asylums: essays on the social situation of mental patients and other inmates.* Chicago, IL: Aldine.

> *Yeah, but again I didn't at that time, you know, argue with him, or disagree because [of] what he was doing, I didn't interfere with his work.*

This quotation reveals the inherent control being exerted over the co-worker: it appears to leave the individual with little choice but to go along with the outcomes of the manager's impression management. The fraudster's power is in terms of coercion. Looking at the different mechanisms of power produces an understanding of executive impression management (see Figure 7.2).

Respectful (Consistent Benign impression management) managers employ equality as their control mechanism and rely on consensual and voluntary reciprocation. The fraudsters' Executive Impression Management will mostly use consensus but in certain circumstances will necessarily fall back on coercion as their modus operandi, marking themselves different from a truly benign manager.

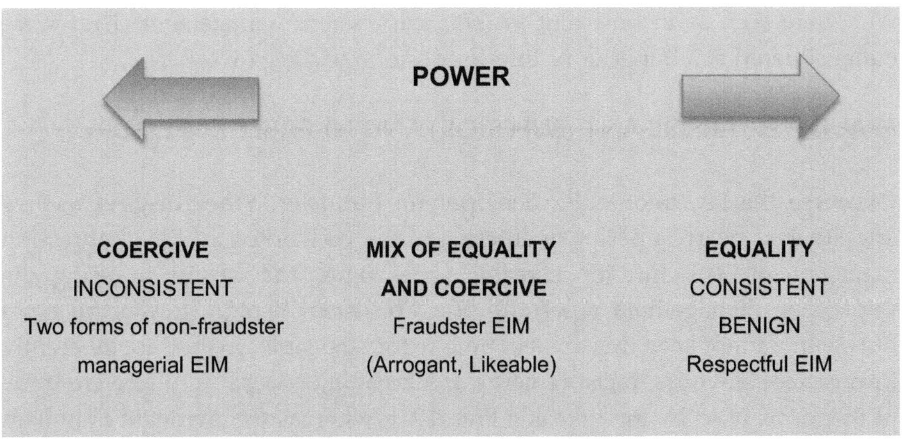

Figure 7.2 Power mechanisms employed by executives using differing Executive Impression Management

Power: Inconsistent Subtypes

Two variations of Inconsistent impression management emerged. There is a Superior quality to it as well as an Inferior (see Figure 7.3).

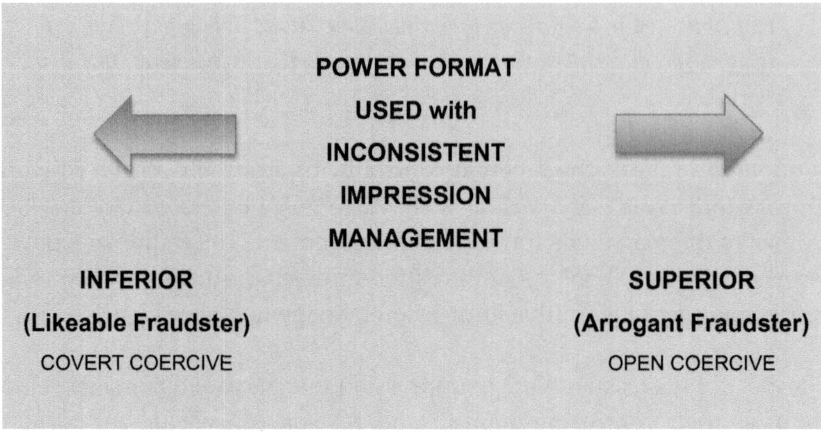

Figure 7.3 Dimension of power relationship (exerted on the co-worker) of inferior and superior fraudsters

For the co-workers in the study, there was no middle ground for managers who were seen as inconsistent in their impression management. They were either situated in a Superior or Inferior position to the co-worker.

FRAUDSTER: ARROGANT (SUPERIOR) AND LIKEABLE (INFERIOR)

Of course, this lays another burden upon the fraudster in their disguise as they are either at heart Superior or Inferior to the co-worker in their impression management. The Inferior Likeable type comes the closest to using the impression management repertoire of a Consistent Benign (Respectful type) but again, cannot keep this up over time or for all people, so they are inherently inconsistent. Favours, racist remarks and breaking company rules were some of the forms used by the Likeable Fraudster, whereas the Arrogant Fraudster used arrogance and malevolence to maintain and support superiority over the recipients.

The key analytical insights for the Inferior theme are that the impression management is markedly benign to recipients, also the disguising aspects of the Inferior are restricted to covering the fraud only. There was no indiscriminate lying reported, however there were many appeasement behaviours. The Likeable Fraudsters' stress centres on not measuring up to role expectations and being found out, rather than creating the successful image which Superiors tended to do as well. In addition, expressing unhappiness was not mentioned in relation to the Superior fraudsters either. Finally, there is a complete absence of any display of superiority, and more a display of being humble.

THE INTERRELATIONSHIP OF CONSISTENCY AND POWER

There is an interplay of consistency and the usage of power in the concept now called Executive Impression Management. The construction for the overall core process of the Executive Impression Management process as it emerged from this study is outlined below in Figure 7.4. It is imperative to understand this when detecting disguised fraudster managers.

The relationship that the manager exerts in impression management gives the tone or style to what is received by the co-worker. If the impression management is truly consistent (upwards and downwards) the co-workers perceive the manager as benign. They are viewed as good managers with good work practices; they show respect to the recipients and trust them accordingly. The recipients reciprocate willingly to the invitation of equitable power. The problem is that the fraudsters mimic the Respectful executive, and it is only small inconsistencies over time that reveal the proposition that the manager may not be benign, whereas the Respectful executive is unwaveringly consistent to everyone.

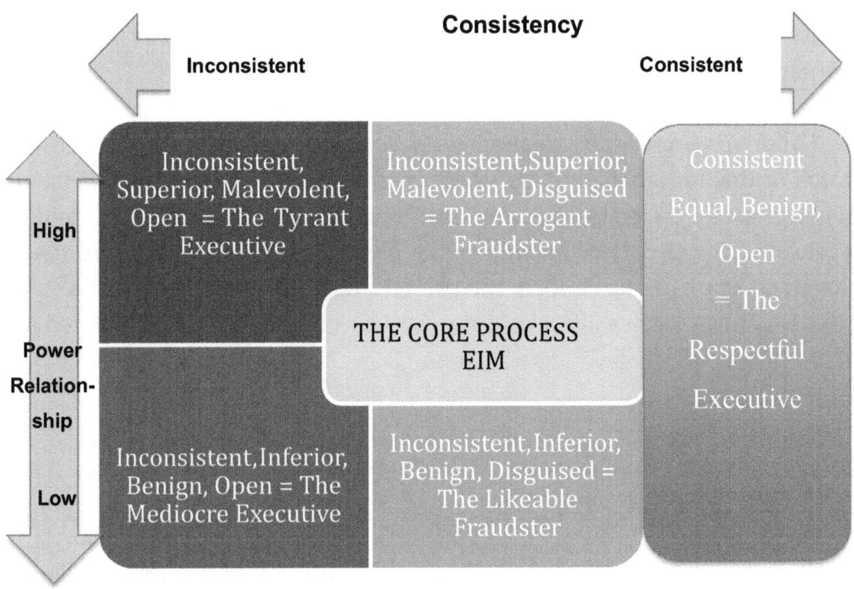

Figure 7.4 The overall core process of Executive Impression Management

The fraudster managers are placed in the central area of the model, because they were seen to be consistent at first, but over time inconsistencies appeared. In some ways, the fraudster executives' impression management is extremely malevolent: they cause great harm to the organisation. Small businesses find it difficult to recover from the money being stolen. However, in big business, say a bank, what is a few millions lost compared to the billions that they report in profit? The harm will be to the co-workers and their inability to cope with the emotional abuse that has been wrought by their trust being destroyed. However, what is being measured in this core process of impression management is the degree of inconsistency, not the harm itself.

UTILITY OF THE CORE PROCESS

This study is the first to report differentiation through identifying types and attributes of Executive Impression Management from the co-workers' point of view. From the data, it has been possible to identify consistency and power relationships as central to the executive impression management process. However, there are no other studies available to embed this in the literature, apart from what has been raised in the issues section of this chapter on consistency and power. This may be because no studies have come from the point of view of the recipients of impression management. Ginzel, Kramer and Sutton[4] developed a model of how an organisation's (outside) audience will interact with the organisation, but this audience is able to 'call the fraudster manager's bluff', does not have to stop due to the power of fraudster manager and can terminate the relationship at will.

Other research when dealing with audience is primarily focused on the status of the audience, which influences the type of impression management that is given by the actor.[5] For instance, it was found that high-status audiences receive more strategic or Machiavellian impression management from actors.[6] However, this does not inform the present discussion of the co-workers' point of view. An extensive literature review has taken place on these items, and

4 Ginzel, L. E., R. M. Kramer, and R. I. Sutton. 1992. Organizational impression management as a reciprocal influence process: the neglected role of the organizational audience. *Research in Organizational Behaviour* 15: 227–266.

5 Gardner, W. L., and M. J. Martinko. 1988. Impression management: an observational study linking audience characteristics with verbal self-presentations. *Academy of Management Journal* 31 (1): 42–65. In addition, Gardner, W. L., and B. J. Avolio. 1998. The charismatic relationship: a dramaturgical perspective. *Academy of Management Review* 23 (1): 32—58.

6 Weinstein, E. A., and L. S. Beckhouse. 1969. Audience and personality factors in presentation of self. *Sociological Quarterly* 10 (4): 527–537.

apart from what is cited there are no other indications of literature applicable to the model on the core process of Executive Impression Management.

The discovery of the audience (co-workers) not being able to reciprocate in the usual manner is due to the power hierarchy of the workplace and therefore distortions occur in the impression management process. This means that the whistle-blowing effect of the immediate co-workers is stopped dead. This is of primary importance in any investigation and must not be ignored. They are unable to blow the whistle, either because they are mesmerised by the fraudster or, if they are a subordinate, fear of losing their job.

WORKPLACES AS IMPERFECT ENVIRONMENTS

What is different here from daily or normal self-presentation is that executive impression management is tied to the power structure of a workplace. The workplace is the theatre where the actors are on stage, with various types of audiences observing their performances.[7] In ordinary, day-to-day impression management, the audience is able to play the role of check and balance to the actor's performance, by not only evaluating what is being acted in front of them, the controllable part of the actor's performance, but also what the actor is 'expressing' or 'giving off' inadvertently (the uncontrollable part of the performance). Once the two parts of the impression management are evaluated as analogous, the audience will accept the performance.

In the workplace, the theatre is different. Because of the power distortion in the workplace, it is quite possible that abnormal impression management could occur. For example, gender differences in impression management in the workplace have been identified in a review of the literature by Guadagno and Cialdini.[8]

Developing five concepts of executive impression management that are workplace linked is therefore in tune with the special power dynamic that can occur.

7 Collinson, D. 2006. Rethinking followership: a post-structuralist analysis of follower identities. *The Leadership Quarterly* 17 (2): 179–189.

8 Guadagno, R., and R. Cialdini. 2007. Gender differences in impression management in organizations: a qualitative review. *Sex Roles* 56 (7–8): 483–494.

The imperfect workplace allows the actor to have power over that person by virtue of the ability of being able to dismiss individuals from their position.[9] Because workplaces are hierarchical, there is always someone above a recipient until the top role is reached, and even there a board of directors is answerable to shareholders.[10] This means that almost everyone in the organisation has some extra power that a normal audience does not possess. Furthermore, the higher up that person's role is, the more power that person has over the lives of the co-workers. Therefore, if a higher executive does not behave well to a recipient in an impression management sense, the recipient's reactions are limited.[11] Thus the normal role is altered and the recipients are unable to articulate disbelief during the performance, which is a noted cause of stress for the recipient.[12]

USAGE OF IMPRESSION MANAGEMENT THEORY BY CONFLICT AND CONSENSUS-BASED THEORISTS

In the literature review two schools of usage of impression management developed. This is important for the fraud investigator to understand. If the investigator comes from a particular school of thought, for instance, a consensual society with individualism as the primary concern, it could mean that the investigator will overlook discrepancies in impression management due to his adherence to the notion that 'Everyone is allowed to be different, it is ok.'

One aspect that emerged from the data is that the fraudster managers used power for their own advantage. Social exchange theory predicts reciprocity.[13] None is received according to the data but the audience maybe satisfied that there is an implied reciprocity in the Arrogant Fraudster's impression management. This is reflected in the Emperor's New Clothes fairy tale, whereby the tailors who are the fraudsters used power over the Emperor and his courtiers by knowingly fabricating a story that anyone who could not see the new cloth was unfit for high office and stupid. This co-opts their own power into the new cloth, which enables the tailors to succeed in their fraud.

If the Arrogant Fraudster cases are considered, each employed power in their own ways for malevolent purposes. One gained it through community

9 French and Raven 1960, op cit. and Gioia, D. 1983. Perceptions of managerial power as a consequence of managerial behavior and reputation. *Journal of Management* 9 (1): 7–27.
10 Vredenburgh, D., and Y. Brender. 1998. The hierarchical abuse of power in work organizations. *Journal of Business Ethics* 17 (12): 1337-1347.
11 Collinson 2006, op cit.
12 Elangovan, A. R., and J. L. Xie. 2000. Effects of perceived power of supervisor on subordinate work attitudes. *Leadership & Organization Development Journal* 21 (6): 319–328.
13 Emerson, R. M. 1976. Social exchange theory. *Annual Review of Sociology* 2: 335–363.

positions and support. Another gained it from younger employees and Ph.D. students who were sponsored from India. One used religion for power, and another deliberately used his position where the owners and employees had little managerial knowledge and he could use jokes and deflective tactics to never be questioned in his work. The authentic reciprocity was not there in each case, as they used the power that they sought to be installed and remain above their normal rank. In a mutually consensus society, fraudsters would be deferent to their bosses; heads of units would be compliant to their headquarters, and religious people would surrender to their God. To do otherwise is labelled as deviance.[14] Unfortunately this is not the case, or so it would seem to me: the consensus view of society is normative in intent rather than realistic of our way of life. Dictators still run countries, powerful multinationals control huge assets and markets and so on.

Using critical conflict theory in impression management, there is an allowance, indeed expectation, that some people will wish to dominate others for economic gain.[15] This fits the data much better. It means that the Arrogant Fraudsters acted entirely as would be predicted by critical theorists, in that they sought personal wealth and attained it by the subjugation of others. The theorists view conflict as a fact of life. However, it is not quite a perfect fit with the fraudster's behaviour encountered in this investigation. Critical theory permits the means to an end for those who are treated inequitably in society. Nevertheless, in this study the fraudsters did not come from poverty, in fact quite the opposite. One fraudster came from a wealthy background, another was given many extra benefits by his parents as compared to his siblings, a third came from a land owning family, and another fraudster had an established status in local society. If the investigator takes the conflict view of society he could easily overlook the 'Robin Hood' effect of taking assets from a business if the manager concerned was poor or had outstanding circumstances (namely righteous causes) to leave well alone. If the reader considers this proposition outrageous, then look at how cases are selected to be investigated by the police. Naturally all cases are investigated, but some more so than others and it is beyond pure expediency. There will be a value base or worldview underlying the decision to investigate.

Fortunately, impression management as an activity fits within both consensus and conflict theories. Consistent benign executives are those who

14 Horowitz, I. L. 1962. Consensus, conflict and cooperation: a sociological inventory. *Social Forces* 41 (2): 177–188. http://www.jstor.org/stable/2573609 (accessed 25 April 2010).

15 Gardner, W. L. 1992. Lessons in organizational dramaturgy: the art of impression management. *Organizational Dynamics* 21 (1): 33–46.

consensually reciprocate in society and by social exchange theory would expect and earn reciprocation in terms of referred power, given by those around them in the organisation. Those managers who give inconsistent impression management will ultimately be found out by their audiences, provided of course that there is an equal distribution of power between actor and audience. As there is no equality of power in the workplace between managers and their staff, the impression management process is distorted and shut down.

POSSIBLE REASONS WHY THE PREVIOUS FRAUD MYTHS DO NOT FIT

When comparing manager fraudsters with non-fraudster managers, the co-workers did not observe the psychological, Red Flag predictors outlined earlier. As expected, non-fraudsters were more detectable in regards to morality, but fraudster managers were better at displaying authenticity to their co-workers, which is used to enhance their disguising activity. It was in their interest to push and promote authenticity to the recipients with overtones of attributed trust. The surprise in looking at Table 7.1 is that the non-impression management theories were not upheld by the co-workers, namely: psychopathology predictors, social psychology factors and the Red Flags.

There are some slight differences of the rate of detection between the theories, with the Red Flags the least noticeable by co-workers of fraudster managers. Red Flags do not appear to indicate fraudsters, they apply to both groups of non-fraudster and fraudster managers. There were a small number of predictors showing in the Consistent Benign managers group of co-workers, for example, marital difficulties and works long hours, but very few other indicators.

When the subgroup of fraudsters is inspected separately there are even fewer signs to their co-workers, but then, these fraudsters are the masters of disguise in their Executive Impression Management and this would be expected to some degree.

However, when the data were reviewed for the comparison between the Respectful type and all Inconsistent executives' impression management both fraudsters and non-fraudsters together these predictors were more prominent for the managers using the Inconsistent Malevolent form of executive impression management. Indeed, recipients of the non-fraudster executives using Inconsistent Malevolent or Benign impression management assigned the list of predictive behaviours in the semi-structured interview guide more to managers using Inconsistent impression management than the fraudster group of recipients.

Table 7.1 Likelihood of fraudsters and non-fraudsters exhibiting signs of different literature based explanations, according to the co-workers

Type of theory	*Overall responses*	*Comment*
Impression Management:		
Morality	Medium	Non-fraudsters are moderately more likely to be more detectable of their morality in co-workers' eyes.
Authenticity	Medium	Fraudsters are moderately more likely to be detected as authentic.
Psychopathology	Low	Fraudsters are slightly more likely to be detected as psychopathic.
Social Psychology	Low	Fraudsters are slightly more likely to be detected using Social Psychological indicators.
Personal Red Flags	Lowest	Fraudsters are only very slightly more likely to be detected through the Red Flag approach.

PERSONAL RED FLAGS NOT WORKING

What was unanticipated in this result is that so many of the managers using the Inconsistent Malevolent type of Tyrant impression management of the non-fraudster managers group were assigned Red Flag predictors by the co-workers. If the reader remembers the Swiss experience of how the room shuffled out of embarrassment, this finding is now not so extraordinary.

This leads to a possible explanation of why the different theory indicators do not work. The scholarly work on Red Flags has produced varying results for any of the predictors when applied to fraudsters,[16] bearing in mind of course that personal characteristics are only a small part of the many items on the Red Flag list. And one of the originators of the Red Flag approach has questioned their efficacy, as there are very few studies that have validated them.[17] Yet many scholars and practitioners still urge the use of Red Flags[18] (see

16 See Pincus, K. 1989. The efficacy of a Red Flags questionnaire for assessing the possibility of fraud. *Accounting, Organizations and Society* 14 (1/2): 153–163; as well as Zahra, S. A., R. L. Priem, and A. A. Rasheed. 2007. Understanding the effects of top management fraud. *Organizational Dynamics* 36 (2): 122–139.

17 Albrecht, C. C., W. S. Albrecht, and J. G. Dunn. 2001. Can auditors detect fraud: a review of the research evidence. *Journal of Forensic Accounting* 2 (1): 1–12.

18 For instance Grabosky, P., and G. Duffield. 2001. *Red flags of fraud*. Canberra: Australian Government, Australian Institute of Criminology; and Weisenborn, D., and D. M. Norris. 1997. Red flags of management fraud. *The National Public Accountant* 42 (2): 29–35.

Grabosky and Duffield 2001; Weisenborn and Norris 1997), as well as the top four accountancy firms and professional associations like the Association of Certified Fraud Examiners and they are enshrined within the recent Securities and Exchange Commission rules in the United States.

The fraud predictors that most reflect the Inconsistent Malevolent Executive Impression Management are the Social Psychological factors of sociability,[19] persuasibility and manipulation. Depression was the least noticed factor by co-workers. This is closely followed by authenticity factors, which reinforces the earlier view in this study that some managers use Inconsistent Benign impression management to engender trust, which they use for their own malevolent purposes. Signs of psychopathology, the Red Flags and morality of their impression management predictors were the least seen by the co-workers of fraudster managers. Again it ties in with how strong the impression management is with the co-workers.

PSYCHOPATHS AND THE FRAUD TRIANGLE

Reviewing the fraudster recipients on items, Arrogant Fraudsters show a sense of superiority and arrogance, but Likeable Fraudsters do not, which puts a strain on narcissism's explanatory power of fraud in previous research. Psychopathology appears to be a better fit with the Arrogant Fraudsters. The Likeable Fraudsters are closer to those described by Cressey with the unshareable problem, opportunity and rationalisation of the Fraud Triangle.[20] Some work in an organisation for many years without committing fraud, some as long as 20 years, they just need the trio of circumstances – unshareable problem, opportunity and rationalisation – to fall into place.

Impact of the Fraudster's Disguised Impression Management on Co-workers

The data that formed regarding the impact of the Disguised Impression Management on co-workers is revealing in understanding the strong emotional reaction that was felt by them. Betrayal of trust was foremost in the retelling of their stories, as well as disbelief as to what had happened. Every single person interviewed had no idea of the fraud, and all talked about their emotional

19 Sociability can describe ingratiation and self-promoting activities of the fraudsters' impression management strategies.

20 Cressey, D. 1973. *Other people's money: a study in the social psychology of embezzlement*. Montclair, NJ: Patterson-Smith.

reaction to the discovery. The emotions included being shocked, angry and disappointed. Business owners wanted revenge but this was also seen in other staff in small businesses. Continuing pain was mentioned, and some recipients were still feeling emotions like anger some years after the event.

A few co-workers talked about trying to be positive and reaching some sort of acceptance of the calamity that had happened to them. This gave them a sense of control and it included forgiveness of themselves in the adage, repeated several times, 'We all make mistakes'. How the recipients reacted emotionally depended on whether they had liked the fraudster or not. Disliking the fraudster meant that only shock and disappointment were felt but after that life carried on as usual. However, liking the fraudster whether Arrogant or Likeable, had ramifications and would make the co-worker revisit childhood trauma and other times when their trust was first violated.

The CAT Model of Emotions

It is important for the investigator to understand the consequences of the emotional harm. Over the years I have developed a model that helps with understanding people's emotions. This helps to understand the reactions such as violation of trust. This process has nothing to do with Emotional Quotient theory developed by Goleman.[21] His theory is based on training managers to understand that emotions are traits that we all share. Not only should we be aware of our own emotions, we should also be sensitive to others' emotions in the workplace. It is proposed that the more the individual is aware, the likelier there will be a better management practice built on sound relationships. Criticism of Goleman's theory says that it is not a true or statistically valid measure of emotions.[22] The critics state that it has little predictive value. Independently I have developed concepts that emerged out of my own recovery process from the devastating effects of maternal deprivation.

This theory is not to measure emotions per se (although it can be done) but to identify the underlying life force or energy that drives us to certain behaviours. I have used this theory on hundreds of managers within my consultancy practice and found it to be particularly useful to explain how trauma affects our current and future behaviours. It has not been tested by

21 Goleman, Daniel. 1995. *Emotional intelligence: why it can matter more than IQ*. New York: Bantam Books.

22 Locke, Edwin A. 2005. Why emotional intelligence is an invalid concept. *Journal of Organizational Behavior* 26 (4): 425–431.

psychology academics because it has not attracted their interest, but those who need to identify future behaviour which is harmful to others need to understand behaviour have to look at new and different theories. My ideas are reliant on the Connection Appreciation Trust model of emotional energy that I developed. It attracted attention from the anti-terrorism forces, in particular aviation security. The full expose of the theory has already been given in a chapter in an aviation security textbook.[23]

It is my belief that we have a life force within us. Some call this Chi or Qi. Perhaps it is our soul, I do not know. The life force or emotional energy as I refer to it, is either negative or positive. We are born with positive energy but as we grow up we become stressed by a variety of events, some of which will be traumatic. It is also my belief that the earlier the trauma the more it determines our lives. As I am an adoptee I learnt from the adoptee counselling movement that separation from the mother is the worst impact a human can experience. This is because the infant believes that the mother is part of themselves. The withdrawal of the mother creates a 'Primal Wound'[24] and this creates lifelong behaviour patterns for the child. My own life history contains events that would be seen as traumatic, the emotional and physical abuse from an adoptive father, earthquakes, being caught up in a civil war and being a few centimetres away from armour piercing bullets that lodged into the wall next to me and so on. I have seen horrible things that most people would not experience, but none impacted me more than my original trauma of being separated from my mother. Having a loving adoptive mother ameliorated some of the wound, but not all. The Primal Wound is all-embracing and underlies every behaviour.

During 1998 I experienced a recovery process that took a couple of years to absorb and I had to start from scratch about basic things that the reader would not even think about. For instance, what did I really like? As opposed to what I had grown up with thinking I should like – and as other people around me liked doing. Creating my identity is part of the healing process and as I put this together I had to think very hard about my feelings.

Of course I laughed and cried like any other person, but those responses were not really mine, they were adaptive to avoid the eternal torment of rejection. This is the primal wound that Nancy Verrier refers to the splitting

23 Sheridan, T.A. 2008. Emotive profiling. Vol 1 pp. 74–88 In *Aviation security management*, 3 vols, edited by Andrew R. Thomas. Westport, CT: Praeger Security International.

24 My heartfelt thanks to Nancy Verrier whose book has helped countless adoptees to understand what happened to them. Verrier, Nancy Newton. 1993. *The primal wound: understanding the adopted child*. Louisville, KY: Gateway Press.

of the infant–mother body and the infant taking responsibility for the harm, which ends in thoughts that the mother abandoned the infant because they did not like them. If scepticism arises for the reader, I suggest that you read the literature on maternal deprivation and the effect of parental rejection upon a child's psyche: the evidence is there.

The child's brain begins growing *in utero*. Noises, vibrations, even a distinction between light and dark are absorbed and put into frameworks of sensations. Once the baby is born there is an overwhelming sensorial input. To use a true but anecdotal example, I was in a seminar where Dan Popov recounted the following. It is regarding a child at the age of 8 who made serious attempts at killing herself and is a sobering story to reflect upon. Popov, a psychiatrist who was involved with the child, began a round of interrogative interviews with the mother and father and their highly intelligent daughter. Trying as hard as he could he could not figure out what was the underlying cause and therefore could not help them. One day alone with the child with the parents outside, he asked her about her earliest memories. She eventually reluctantly told the therapist that she remembered her father looking at her and the look on his face was dreadful, not smiling but almost fearful, it was not like the face of her mother which was warm and smiling. The parents were called back into the room and told of their daughter's earliest memory.

The parents were aghast when they realised that this memory was when the child was merely two days old. Her father was out of town for the birth and came home as soon as possible on the delivery of their first and only child. As it had been a traumatic delivery, mother was kept in her hospital bed and the father was taken to the neonatal unit where the new babies were kept. He looked down on his new daughter whose head and face was disfigured from the use of forceps and suction cups from the difficult birth. He remembered vividly looking at his child and feeing horrified. The nurse put the baby into his arms and he struggled with trying to deal with all of his negative emotions of anger, fear and sadness. The image of the father rejecting his child stayed in his daughter who grew up trying to please her father. As she had abilities and intelligence she became the 'A' student in everything she tried. But as she grew up she felt that it was never enough, that he was always revolted by her looks. She then started to self-harm and eventually tried to kill herself.

This recounting of the impact of a father's face when first seeing a newborn is very interesting because it goes against the old idea that a baby is born with a 'blank' brain. There is much more evidence than this one anecdote, but suffice to say the impact of one event so early on can have deleterious effects on the life of an infant. This certainly is revealing how early trauma creates likelihood of negative emotions about oneself later in life.

As stress progresses eventually the individual becomes more impacted with its effects, and so the baby who was born with positive energy resorts to using negative energy and its resulting behaviours to survive. Once an adult, the traumatised individual uses primitive coping mechanisms to tolerate daily life. In effect, the individual is suffering from Post-traumatic Stress Disorder (PTSD). This will be mostly unrecognised by all around the adoptee, including the individual themself. They are destined to live a life that is difficult, does not achieve its potential, repeats the cycle with their own children and dies sad and probably lonely.

Such is the power of stress in our lives. The more stress the longer and harder the impact on our behaviour and this is shown by the emotions of that individual. The markers will be present, but the understanding is not: that is why I have put together a model for us to understand.

The emotions are based on three dimensions, that of Connection, Appreciation and finally Trust, hence the shortened acronym of CAT (see Figure 7.5).

On the left-hand side are negative emotions and on the right-hand side positive emotions. Depending on where we are in life and how we feel we can pin down our emotions in a reasonable and logical manner, even if we are blind to what we are doing.

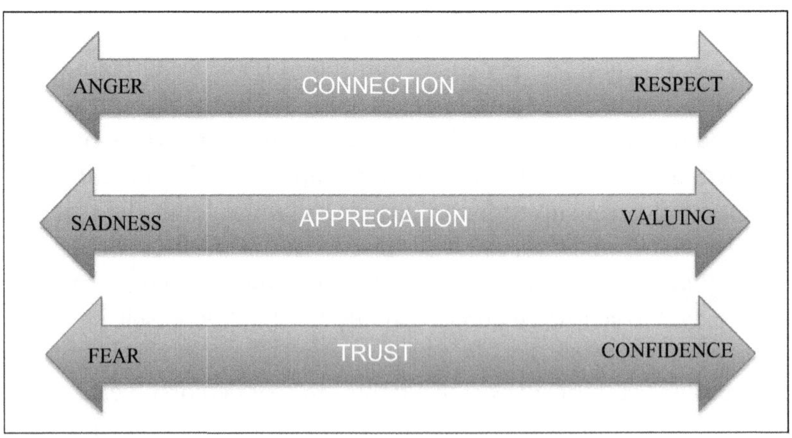

Figure 7.5 The CAT model in the workplace

The first dimension, Connection, is the primary emotion that is used when we meet someone for the first time. Appreciation forms from what the person is able to bring to the relationship, and finally trust forms. With these three elements the relationship is felt to be good and positive. This can be applied to work relationships as well as family and friends.

I am quite convinced that the positive emotional energy versus the negative is similar to and linked with the emergence of the Jungian Shadow when an individual is stressed. The behaviours seen by others are not pleasant. These can include using anger with people. Appreciation when negative is exhibited in greed, envy, minimising what others are worth and so on. Finally the Trust dimension is seen in the negative or Shadow, as being fearful. In an extraverted person this will make the individual appear aggressive and disagreeable, not a person who can be trusted to do anything properly. However, if the Shadow is introverted, the individual will be angry at themself, the negative emotions show through as guilt, shame, low self-esteem and interestingly equally likely not to be trusted, but this is not seen by those around the individual.

For the reader to understand better, this was how it happened with me. As I am normally an extravert, the Shadow for me would be the inverse, so introversion rules in my dark side. I was filled with self-hatred, guilt and shame. I had long-term depression (sadness) which nobody picked up, and I certainly could never trust anyone. Caring people could have said really nice things to me, but to no avail. I would interpret the kind words in those three dimensions of anger, sadness and fear. It is not a very nice life, but it was perfectly normal for me and the only one available.

I also felt there was nothing wrong, which is a brilliant example of self-deception. As I lived through it for over 40 years of my life in this manner, someone telling me that 'Oh-oh Terry, this is what you are really like' would never been believed by me. Goffman says that it takes a life crisis to see the real person. In my own way I had a 'good' crisis, which is a very long story but the fact that I was depressed was revealed to me after a car accident injury by an ordinary GP. However, this fact of depression opened up all sorts of possibilities as I tried to connect pieces of my life history. Very soon I realised that I had been depressed all my life. I then put together my own recovery process, which I knew was in some way connected to the fact of my adoption. It turned out it was not the adoption which was the primary trauma, it was the separation from my mother when I was four days old that was behind it all.

When I started my recovery I had to deal with constructing my identity, even down to what was my personality? Fortunately the gold standard of personality types is still the Myers Briggs Type Inventory[25] and it turns out that I am an Extraversion, Intuition, Feeling, Perception (ENFP) type. My natural drive is to help others, take up a cause and be creative. This has lent itself to my being an innovative researcher, as clearly demonstrated in my methodological approaches as well as seeking answers to humanitarian questions. It is from this motivation that I have written this book. Interestingly, my writing did not flourish until after my recovery, and I really enjoy doing this as a small attempt to help others. It fits perfectly with who I am. My adoptive mother even at the age of 96 years old still says: 'We never guessed that you would have been a writer!' This is the bittersweet crux of not knowing your heritage, I am quite convinced that in my ancestors, one at least must have been a happy writer/ investigator.

To unravel the odd things I would feel, I would take long walks to think about my feelings at length. I could understand and locate the differences between good feelings and bad feelings but the rest was a jumble. I had to learn from scratch what I felt. The muddle of hurt had to be deconstructed and was then built up into a coherent model of understanding. Practically all readers would have taken this knowledge as part of identity, the being of you. Not for me, I had to analyse it piece by piece. This understanding of the three dimensions and how they work together has been an amazing discovery to me and I began to apply it in my work.

At first I used it with unemployed managers and found to my utter amazement that my CAT model was successful for others. It explained so much in such a simple way, that even the most angry, disappointed and fearful managers understood it. And because it is non-blaming it takes away years of confusion, blame and anger projected onto the self and others. To say it was life-changing is to understate what happened. Furthermore the changes were sustainable and happiness creating. Almost all of the out-of-work managers (91 per cent) found a better life for themselves, they reported they felt a release to be the real them, leaving their stressful persona behind. We tend to define ourselves in our work, now being successful in knowing who they truly were, they were eager to set out on their individual road to being less stressed and more happy.

25 Myers, Isabel Briggs with Peter B. Myers. 1980, 1995. *Gifts differing: understanding personality type.* Mountain View, CA: Davies-Black Publishing.

If it could help western individuals in Australia, Switzerland and the UK, I found that it also worked with Asian people as well, after being required to deliver my training in Singapore for their Ministry of Defence. From understanding the cross-cultural implications that all humans have the same emotional base, I knew it could also explain the terrorists as we knew them in the first decade of 2000, from the 9/11 disaster and the Al-Qaida training camps and their intent to destroy the western industrialised democracies. As my model can accurately predict the emotional base of an individual, it could be applied to work with identifying them, because they were outwardly the same as some of the managers I was assisting. I knew that I could identify that they were too fearful to be identified for who they really were, deep down inside. I can base this assertion is by looking at their behaviour to see what they are hiding, looking for the aberrant facts.

Most people using my model when pressed to put themselves on the CAT scale are amazed to find out that they were deluding themselves. What I found was that the lowest common denominator of the emotion measured was actually the true overall indicator of where that person was. I found that the lowest indicator was the truth. This was done by applying it to myself first and later by many people admitting to me in confidence that yes it was true that is where they truly felt they were, but didn't want to admit it to themselves or others.

All sorts of trauma came to light in these sessions, child abuse, sexual molestation, physical abuse, neglect and abandonment, drug use, self-harm and so on. I found that I could use this model as a non-hurtful way of letting someone understand that this was not their 'fault', that it was only life's circumstances that have made them react this way. Being collected into a refugee camp and living an existence which is denied of freedom, witnessing your loved ones being killed or abused is one of the best ways to make a terrorist, in my view. Here I am not talking about the terrorist leadership, only their agents. The leadership to me is akin to the Arrogant Fraudster in behaviour and attitude.

BLIND TO OUR BEHAVIOUR

I had also theorised in this model that people would be blind to their darker behaviour. This is precisely what Jung had said about the Shadow, that people are unaware that they are using that part of their personality. Most managers who operate in the negative energy side that I have counselled using this model were actually blind to their behaviour. Therefore fraudsters will be operating in this mode. We have found that at the point of discovery the Arrogant Fraudster will deny what they have done and maintain the illusion as long as possible, sometimes over years. The Likeable Fraudster, however, knows the game is up and now everyone knows how despicable they truly are, they believe. Their self-destructive behaviour at this point is indicative of this. So if they are blind to what they do, can they be rehabilitated? Could a co-worker sit next to the thieving manager and feel comfortable?

With the CAT model there is the force of stress, which pushes us into negative behaviour. However, what is little known is that the counteracting force of motivation allows the individual to change from negative to positive behaviour. This is done by the 'bridges over troubled water'. On the Connection dimension we can move from Anger to Respect through using Compassion. On the Appreciation we can cross the bridge using Comparison and finally we can use the bridge of Competence for the Trust dimension.[26] How it works is that by using Compassion people are able to disarm the antagonist by finding some small point that they can genuinely respect. Guru I Gede Prama,[27] a well-known and well-respected Buddhist monk living in Bali with a degree in organizational psychology, uses the power of Compassion in meditation work. By doing this pain will be lessened, heart rates are slower, adrenaline reduced and endorphins will be released. From repeating this exercise you will achieve compassion for the fraudster. Compassion is so powerful that it stops wars, feeds millions of hungry people and provides happiness where there was only hatred. In the western world we have forgotten how to use it.

26 My thanks go to Gordon Hobday for the naming of the bridges in 2004.

27 Prama, Gede. 2013. *Songs of compassion*. http://gedepramascompassion.com/author/gedepramacompassion/ (accessed 30 July 2013).

Chapter 8
Rehabilitation Possibilities

If we are compassionate enough, can a fraudulent manager be turned around? We know that ideally we should use compassion with these damaged individuals. One type (Arrogant) appears to have a biological imbalance of the brain, creating a lack of empathy on their part, so every action is purely for self-gratification. This type would be unlikely to secure our compassion. Therefore we must put boundaries into their workplace. The Likeable Fraudster can access our compassion more easily as he is likely to have been traumatised in his early childhood. But letting a fraudster return to an organisation requires considerable thought.

Arrogant Fraudster

While compassion for the fraudsters was not the focus of the study, I do have some evidence that intuitively fits with the managers involved and also the experience of participating in the running of an outreach treatment facility for mentally disturbed adolescents (my apologies on the nomenclature of the 1970s) in Canada. I was part of an experimental team who had various treatment options for these jailed anti-social teenagers and among them were psychopathic adolescents. For the latter group we found that individualised treatment planning was the best option. It had far better outcomes than jail, where they were ordinarily placed because they were classified as a danger to society. What the programme ensured was 24/7 supervision with educational and recreational components as well as therapy with skilled psychiatrists. The programme put in place boundaries that did not exist before in the teenager's life and they stayed in place, sometimes for years. The cost of doing this was very high, but the programme's outcomes were good within the treatment phase. The problem would have been upon their graduation into the community with the same unstructured life patterns as before, and the old behaviours would return. Unless society acknowledges that non-serial killer psychopathy is less harmful, I doubt if the resources would ever be committed again to turn around such behaviour.

What has to be fundamentally acknowledged is that a psychopath is not likely to change. There is no need to, their world is all about 'myself and my wants'. There may be reduced fraudulent activity as they get older but I think this is more to do with less opportunity rather than any reformation of character. We have seen certain individuals being incarcerated and they set up fraud schools in prison. Their egocentrism is met by adulation by other inmates due to their notoriety and the ability to be a type of Robin Hood – stealing from the rich (anyone else) to help the poor (the fraudster). This certainly does not induce change, in fact quite the opposite occurs, as the behaviour is rewarded by the fawning of inmates and unfortunately often by prison officers too.

Bernie Madoff is a good example of this effect. He is the person that conducted the world's largest Ponzi scheme, a fraudulent investment operation where the operator, an individual or organisation, pays returns to its investors from new capital paid to the operators by new investors, rather than from profit earned by the operator. He retained the rest, which amounted to $US18 billion. He is reported to be the top dog in jail and likes it to be that way, receiving certain privileges that are denied to others. In Australia we saw socialites having picnics with incarcerated financiers in low-security prisons. One could not imagine this happening to bank robbers, or drug barons, yet minimum security prisons continue to contain white-collar criminals.

One idea may be to have these psychopathic criminals, including Arrogant Fraudsters, separated from other inmates as part of their punishment. Depriving them of their audience would be a way to contain them. There are secure units for certain categories of offenders, largely for their own protection, such as paedophiles, police informants and corrupt police officers. They do not mix with the larger jail population and have separate exercise and eating facilities. But even those units have other inmates to act as their audience.

One particular problem with prisons is that they can become not only universities of crime but prime networking opportunities. Their activities can be funded by organised crime members with this mixing, so that fraudster managers get to know individuals who would become useful contacts upon leaving prison for perpetrating further frauds.

We have seen in this study a pattern of repeat offending, with Arrogant Fraudsters who offend while out on bail before trial. This brings in the importance of considering bail or remand for these managers. Remand is the best option to protect other corporate and employee victims of their crimes. However, as white-collar crime is seen as not as serious as other crimes and with remand centres full, the accused tend to receive bail until their trial. Of course remand for an innocent manager falsely accused would be traumatic, but again separation from the general prison population is a key to minimise the effect on the individual concerned. Having been to boarding school, where the nuns used to lock us into rooms, I can attest to the salutary effect that being locked up is not a fun way of living with personal freedoms denied. However, it was not seen as traumatic by us, or our families, it was in fact quite normal, and there was just as much locking us out of areas as there was of locking us in.

While there are similarities to old style boarding schools, prison of course is far more serious. Rehabilitation of psychopathic fraudsters is practically impossible. First of all this is due to their persistence of innocence, despite long and detailed trials taking place. If they believe that they are innocent they of course cannot rehabilitate their behaviour. In this study the Arrogant Fraudsters did not perceive that their behaviour is any different from anyone else. They would claim however that their intelligence and cunning is far superior to others, and again this perception would be a barrier to any rehabilitation that they could receive. This superiority is strong enough to be seen by all co-workers and is unlikely to bend in prison, in fact it would be quite the reverse. Having been a social worker one would expect that I would hold different and 'softer' opinions, but these options are not applicable to the Arrogant Fraudsters because their psychopathy prevents change. Once we have learnt more about the neural implications regarding the lack of empathy that these psychopaths show, we can consider as a society how we manage them in within the justice system.

My bet is on a biochemical imbalance in the brain that produces this abnormal behaviour, however the drug companies are unlikely to follow up on a counter-acting drug due to the perceived lack of customers. However, it has been estimated that 3 per cent of managers are psychopathic, which in any terms means a fairly large proportion of organisations and people will be damaged by them, and it would be enough of a case for the justice system who would benefit the most to promote at least some pharmaceutical research into this phenomenon.

Psychopaths do not change but the literature says that it is possible to harness their energy by diverting them into harmless projects with as few people as possible assigned to them. However, it does beg the question of who is going to supervise the psychopathic manager and how, as even the experts get fooled by them[1] and skills would be required beyond the average senior manager or chairman. My thinking is that most organisations would try to get rid of them because they do not have the time or resources to organise a safer haven for the rest of staff. In spite of the lack of resources some organisations are obliged by Duty of Care legislation to retain this type of manager, particularly if the fraud cannot be proved. A sideways move away from any financial controls with shadowing supervision may be judicious.

I am aware that psychopathic managers may be among the readership of this book. I am also aware that they are intelligent and creative people and they may resent this curtailment of their activities, but self-aggrandisement is to the detriment of the organisation and I would lean to a harm minimisation policy so that other staff are protected. The greater good in this case should not be used as a reason to contest a sideways organisational move. The chair has to have the good of all at heart and without the option of firing, which could easily be contested on the grounds of discrimination with psychopathy noted as a form of disability, sidelining may be the only compassionate option available.

The Likeable Fraudster

The Likeable Fraudster has a very different form of behaviour and one that I believe is treatable with the right therapeutic options. This because they have a particular event(s) that indicates emotional damage earlier on in their lives. We know from Albanese's work[2] that women operate fraud for different reasons than men, when it comes to gambling. It is the Likeable Fraudster that will want to have an extravagant lifestyle, be generous to all and sundry, and most likely to gamble the proceeds fairly quickly.

Arrogant Fraudsters secrete the money away and do not show it off to their employer. One fraudster used to drive an old battered car to work, yet in his garage (not at home) he had a BMW hidden away. His friends used to see him driving that car, but never anyone related to the workplace. Seeing the BMW would have been a strip or oddity for a co-worker, therefore it was carefully hidden.

1 Babiak, Paul, and Robert D. Hare. 2007. *Snakes in suits*. New York: Harper Collins.

2 Albanese, J. S. 2008. White collar crimes and casino gambling: looking for empirical links to forgery, embezzlement, and fraud. *Crime Law and Social Change* 49 (5): 333–347.

What is imperative for both forms of fraudsters is that they are never allowed access to funds again, in any capacity. Human beings are unpredictable and we always have to be careful in trust and stewardship situations. Do not put temptation in front of them. You would not expect a wheelchair-bound person to manage stairs, so don't expect an ex-fraudster to manage money.

Retaining the Likeable Fraudster in the workforce is actually a good option, even if convicted and imprisoned. It shows the rest of the staff that they work in a compassionate organisation. Do not forget that the Likeable Fraudsters are *genuinely* liked, even loved by all who work with them. I did not find a single situation where a Likeable Fraudster was allowed back to their workplace, but being forced out of their job and the commensurate shame of the theft and subsequent imprisonment leaves an indelible mark on their psyche.

Restorative Justice

It was Wozniak[3] who talked about restorative justice, and here it is appropriate to discuss the topic further. The Arrogant Fraudster will think up more devious schemes while in prison and will move on to their next victim. They will never want to return to the original workplace because they have lost their power over people. Neither do the staff want them there. So there is little fear of trying to work with an Arrogant Fraudster in terms of restorative justice. What little they will allow access to will be begrudgingly given up and they are not interested in restitution. Their sole motivation is to put themselves in power again.

Likeable Fraudster and Restorative Justice

However, it is entirely different for a Likeable Fraudster. The non-profit organisations lead the way in returning fraudsters back into their fold, but I have not seen evidence of an imprisoned fraudster returning to a non-profit organisation as yet.

I propose a different way of dealing with them using the CAT model, as the fraud was perpetrated out of their perceived lack of power and that they feel immensely inferior to others. An Arrogant Fraudster's self-esteem may take a temporary battering, for the Likeable Fraudster it is permanent and shapes

3 Wozniak, John F. 2009. C. Wright Mills and higher immorality: implications for corporate crime, ethics and peacemaking criminology. *Crime Law and Social Change* 51 (1): 189–203.

the rest of their lives. My solution is to return the Likeable Fraudster to their workplace but placed under strict supervision, with no access to money.

From this innovative experience with Project Options in Ontario Canada, I have the confidence to recommend this seemingly counter-intuitive way of managing Likeable Fraudster behaviour. For those interested in the Ontario Juvenile Justice experiment, I don't believe that this programme – Project Options is still in place. The problem with the one-on-one programmes is that they are very expensive and cost much more per day than a corrective or psychiatric institution. However, if the subject of the fraudulent behaviour is of high benefit to the organisation – often they have been in place for many years before this activity commenced and contain a wealth of organisational information and expertise – it may be a very good choice. My thinking is that the individual concerned will be highly (and genuinely) remorseful and will want to make good the harm that they have done. Often, if they cannot return to their organisation, they will seek ways of assisting the community through a variety of other means.

Normative Restoration

There are several types of restoration for a Likeable Fraudster that could take place in a compassionate organisation.

1. COUNSELLING

Frequent therapeutic counselling should be arranged, which can be easily operationalised under an employee assistance programme, with access to experienced counsellors. Be aware that the cause may very well be treatment by the Fraudster's own parents, decades earlier and therefore these individuals are suffering from long term Post-traumatic Stress Disorder (PTSD). Symptoms of PTSD include: intrusive memories, avoidance and numbing, and increased anxiety or emotional hyperarousal.[4] As the Likeable Fraudster returns to work there will be an increased anxiety about their co-workers response to them. This is the time that an exemplary organisation can use its values to reassure staff that the values of respect are functioning and not merely words.

4 Mayo Clinic. 2013. *Post traumatic stress disorder*. Mayo Clinic. http://www.mayoclinic.com/health/post-traumatic-stress-disorder/DS00246 (accessed 13 October 2013).

2. MEETINGS

Remember the poet and jurist Rumi's words: 'Out beyond ideas of wrongdoing, and rightdoing, there is a field. I will meet you there.' Put in place facilitated meetings where staff can meet with the Likeable Fraudster before commencement of work. This is in order to diffuse the strong angry feelings that will be present. There must be a restorative justice facilitator who is able to control the encounter. Consideration must be given beforehand to what the organisation and individuals' need to feel in obtaining restoration. It will be extremely unlikely that any stolen money can be returned as frequently it is gambled or given away. If any funds are available these will have already been returned upon discovery of the fraud as this is part of the Likeable Fraudster's pattern.

It gives the opportunity to co-workers and senior management to outline what the fraudster can do to rectify the situation. There are several ways that this can be done in a respectful and compassionate way. But first a list is required.

3. NEEDS LIST

An independent non-judgemental facilitator must draw up a list of needs from those most affected. These needs may range from explanation as to why the behaviour happened, the betrayal of trust that co-workers will feel, the anger towards the organisation in allowing the fraud to happen, reassurance that this will not happen again that systems will be in place to prevent this from happening. Co-workers of fraudsters need to be able to repair their trust with managers who will want to prove that they are indeed trustworthy, particularly the more popular managers.

4. RE-ENTRY

Remember also that the Fraudster will have experienced institutionalisation, which can result in reliance on others to tell him what to do and so on, and needs time to adjust to the new work situation. He also will have a lack of up to date information technology, even mobile phones, and will need skill upgrading, plus being informed of the new changes in the workplace, production and customers.

The cost of this return, for instance in increased supervision, will be nothing compared to the costs of losing valuable staff and the selection and training of new employees. At the point of discovery the co-workers will be in shock and will be judging the organisational response to the Likeable Fraudster. As angry as others may feel, it is best to control the situation by handling it respectfully and fairly. Not only is the Fraudster likely to commit suicide, others will be severely affected and could be equally liable to self-harm.

Meta analysis of the available evidence of restorative justice has found positive benefits to all.[5] Those benefits that are relevant to managerial fraud includes:

1. substantially reduced repeat offending for some offenders,

2. reduced crime victims' post-traumatic stress symptoms and related costs;

3. reduced crime victims' desire for violent revenge against their offenders;

The context of this process is seen here to be after imprisonment basically as a means for the other co-workers to reach some peace with the perpetrator. There are programmes in various countries that would use restorative justice instead of the criminal justice system however, for a psychopathic individual I would not recommend it, as it will be manipulated to serve the needs of the Arrogant Fraudster. This solution can only be applied to a Likeable Fraudster. Therefore it is imperative that a correct typing takes place with a trained consultant. The reader must be aware that psychopaths can mimic anyone they please, and seeing that a Likeable Fraudster 'gets off lightly' and is given a second chance, they will soon pick up what behaviours to use to convince you of something other than their true selves.

Caring for Co-workers

Post-imprisonment and before the re-entry into the workplace is seen as an ideal time for restorative justice, but if this can be done within the prison environment – rarely are these fraudsters are contained within maximum security prisons, on a voluntary basis with the proviso of a trained facilitator, the organisation is very likely able to reduce the turnover rate of key staff who

5 Sherman, Lawrence W., and Heather Strang 2007. *Restorative justice: the evidence*. London: The Smith Institute. http://www.restorativejustice.org/10fulltext/restorative-justice-the-evidence (accessed 3 April 2009)

suffered abuse of emotional manipulation by the Likeable Fraudster. In fact there can be PTSD symptomatology displayed by key members of staff and high rates of anxiety around their ability to trust. It will be exhibited in such questions as: Who can we trust? Rumination over the case, almost bordering on paranoia in some staff, will be prevalent. Most staff in my study left within six months because they could not tolerate working in an organisation that overlooked their needs.

The co-workers that we are referring to will be key staff, as in the study there were upline management, for instance board personnel, senior management colleagues as well as subordinates. A sudden high turnover rate of these personnel will be deleterious to the organisation, let alone when operating in a highly competitive environment.

Blaming others will be high, particularly if the fraudster was brought in on another's recommendation. Immediate supervisors will feel that they are gullible. Feeling duped is anger, where the manipulator takes power away from the individual. It can be internalised (self-blame) or externalised to others. Blame takes away responsibility for that involvement with the scenario and absolves them from guilt. These emotions are primitive responses to managing a crisis within. Guilt, shame (blaming themselves) and overt anger will be rife.

Expecting high performance after a fraud has been discovered will most likely lead to many people resigning, even those not directly affected. There is very little literature about the effect of a fraud on remaining staff, this study has accidentally uncovered the deep and long-lasting effect that remains with co-workers.

Loss of confidence is another area that co-workers expressed. Direct counselling to deal with lowered self-esteem, reduction of trust in others and the onset of depression are all indicators of the harm that the perpetrator has inflicted. Resolving issues is in the company's interest as well as the co-workers and lastly of course the Likeable Fraudster.

Unlike the Arrogant Fraudsters, who bully people into thinking that they are good at their work, the Likeable Fraudster will usually be good at their job. This is why they are so trusted. They have probably been in their role for years. Then something is detonated in their mind, and they begin to steal.

A Likeable Fraudster has the possibility of therapeutic change and reforming their lives once the initial, usually childhood-incurred trauma is managed so that the person can recover. The issue that comes to mind when considering a fraudster returning to work is working out when the company would know that there has been serious change within that manager and that they are now no longer a threat to the organisation.

This area is quite problematic as it would endanger others, let alone the stewardship of the organisation, to allow a 'pretending to reform' fraudster back into the organisation. What has to be set up is a normative framework for measuring the change of the individual. I think that one of the best ways to do this is by asking the simple question of: 'How will I know if change has really occurred?' and the resulting consideration of ideal behaviours that would preferred to be seen. This concept is somewhat beyond restorative justice, as here it is the consideration of what our own needs and the needs of the organisation require to recommence a trusting relationship.

If a set of behaviours are developed it is far easier to match the current behaviour to the expected. For instance, an apology is given by the fraudster. Would the apology be public or private? The more public the apology the better, but we have to be cautious of humiliation, as no behavioural change can occur if the feedback loop that our senses tells us that we are terrible people. A traumatised individual, particularly if this trauma happens early in life, will already know how awful they are as a person, as they take on the blame of the event upon themselves. Adding to that burden will not assist recovery and recommencement. To see a written apology to all within the organisation would be less humiliating and probably healing to all.

However, it is easy to say sorry, as we all know. Therefore expectations of certain behaviours must be listed. Behaviours that indicate change last over time, there is no back tracking in behaviour from the manager. Here it is important to understand that if there is the slightest incursion of the boundaries that the organisation puts in place the manager is subject to immediate dismissal, or if this is cannot be implemented for external reasons, then demotion is imperative.

I know from my research that co-workers wish to see the Respectful Manager behaviours. There are two components. The first is consistency of their impression management. The second is that the manager must feel equal to others and not demonstrate behaviour that exudes an inferior orientation. So if this manager was known for handing out freebies, such as a day off to favoured staff, or conference tickets, then this behaviour will naturally stop because there is no need for the manager to do this. It is good practice in a company to make it a clear policy that ingratiation will not be tolerated. If there are any ingratiating behaviours these must be freely reported at once. We know that co-workers can differentiate these behaviours and any reports must be investigated sensitively by management.

It is only fair to the manager to state what is seen as Respectful behaviour, then they have a goal to achieve. Unclear and insincere statements are unsuccessful as there is no ability to measure. Just like goals, the behaviours must be measurable and achievable. This allows the manager to know what is required, indicates that a boundary has been put firmly in place and that the previous behaviour will not be tolerated.

The key is the boundary to requiring any change in behaviour of others, assuming that the boundary is respectful of others and appropriate. Boundaries in management practice have a habit of being like waves on the seashore, they come and go and there is no homeostasis. A respectful manager will put boundaries in place with others and these are often seen as expectations, but they can also be transmitted through apocryphal stories to demonstrate the boundary to others.

If an apology is expected to be made in person, ensure others are there to witness the sincerity and appropriateness of what is said. Sometimes individuals commence their apology with blaming others or 'the system'. This is not an apology, it is excuse making. A sincere apology states that the action that was perpetrated was completely of their own making. The action was theirs and theirs alone. The fraudster has to take full responsibility. Of course there are explanations, as we have seen earlier in the case of childhood trauma. These are mere clarifications, not an apology. We know that Likeable Fraudsters show genuine remorse at the time of discovery of the fraud, and we can therefore expect true remorse if mistakes are made in the future.

In the workplace it is not for you to judge a person if they have received enough therapy. You are not qualified to do it. However, all co-workers are qualified to receive the impression management that is exuded by the remorseful manager. At an intuitive level they will know if the behaviour is genuine or not. One method of putting this in place is quarterly 360° evaluations for the newly returned fraudster. It will offer a space and time for the co-worker to reflect and give their assessment of the manager concerned.

There is immense pressure at times to take back a manager who has harmed the organisation. It can build up in those who are fair managers and others who feel for the managers concerned. This is problematical if you are the individual who has to make the decision for the manager to return. An email may sit in the inbox, or a discussion with co-workers may create anxiety. Most people will err on the side of caution and will not consider it. But for the manager who feels for that person it is a conundrum.

The manipulative fraudster manager may use his friends, powerful intermediaries or even family members to coerce the decision to be let back in, but remember that if you are being subjected to this pressure from them it is a sure sign that things have not changed. Once this type of manipulation does not work the manager may resort to other tricks. What you must understand that the bottom line is that the manager has not fundamentally changed so that you cannot allow this to happen as you have still the duty of care to his co-workers. It is better to ignore the pressure attempts than to negotiate your fairness down the drain.

Anyone threatening suicide is at risk, so it is important to realise that this may not be just a threat. Suggest immediate counselling and then you can talk to the person afterwards. Stalking by constant calling is a low grade but still effective, bullying measure that an individual feels may make the subject submit to his demands. This would be the time to report to the police if stalking behaviour happens. They may threaten to copy the business to set up in competition. Many commercial operations have confidentiality clauses to prevent a senior manager to set up like this. In most counties there would be legislation to assist in the prevention of such activity, but usually this is an expensive task and gives off negative publicity, sometimes it is better to ignore and remind oneself that mimicry is a compliment. It is far better to use your time and resources on producing better goods or services.

Sometimes this takes nerves of steel, but it is necessary. If you engage in conversation with the manager then that person will not let up until reinstatement. There is no point in talking to someone who is not interested in changing his behaviour, that is what expert counsellors are for and even they cannot achieve change unless the individual concerned really wants it and is present on their own volition.

Be aware of quick fixes. Rapid behavioural change does not happen to most of us. There are stories of this happening, for instance Saul on the road to Damascus, but in therapy we know that it takes weeks if not months and maybe years to unlearn destructive patterns of behaviour. It is literally re-programming a brain. The plasticity of neural pathways in the brain are now known,[6] but it still takes concerted repetition for any changes to be observed. It is also known that individuals who have had brain trauma such as strokes take quite a few weeks or months to restore a minimum level of functionality with healing neural reconnections. Just remember that a Likeable Fraudster may be the equivalent of someone having a stroke, and while we all prefer to have that person back to full health, the reality may be far different. Also consider that the age of fraudsters is averaged out to be in their 40s and 50s, the patterns that have been learnt in childhood will take a long time to be changed.

As someone who has undertaken this recovery process I can speak from a sample of one. It took me at least six months with constant daily repetitive cognitive tasks to undo the self-destructive patterns I had learned. Thereafter I had to maintain a keen eye on my behaviours and used daily reflection in journals to check if there were any signs of slipping back into old ways. I also talked with family and friends who I could trust to give me feedback if they detected anything untowards. What I can tell you is that the old patterns do reoccur when the individual is stressed. Depending on the severity of that stress it could be total relapse, but the interesting thing to note is that if the person is still wanting to change their behaviour, the recovery time becomes quicker as healing progresses. However, in the workplace and an observer of the errant manager, if re-entry is your decision then the goal posts have to be set evenly and firmly in place. Do not waiver or allow pressure to build up for you to change your mind. Also remain observant to any different forms of pressure from unexpected sources such as social media and so on.

Sense-making Explanations

This need is for the individual co-workers to make sense of the situation for themselves. The psychological harm that is created by the illusion of the Likeable Fraudster is extensive, and each co-worker has to explore their own feelings about the illusion. Gullibility is an anger response against themselves. Typical questions are replicated below, and the sense-making explanation is added.

6 Doidge, Norman. 2007. *The brain that changes itself*. New York: Viking/Penguin Group.

Q: How could I be so stupid?

A: You were not stupid; you were duped into an illusion that is so powerful that no-one could *not* believe it.

Q: Maybe I should have copied another employee who is low on trust with managers?

A: No, low-trust individuals are not successful in life, as they have to spend time and energy into checking and double-checking what is the 'truth'. This leaves little time for customers and organisational growth.

Q: My judgement must be completely wrong.

A: There is nothing wrong about your judgement, even if you were on the selection panel of this manager on entry into the organisation or even recommending promotion. This type of fraudster is not aware of what they can do, in fact if this information is given to the individual beforehand it would be strongly and vehemently denied. Such managers are blind to their actions.

Q: I liked the manager so much; we got on so well, how could he do this to me?

A: Try to understand that the fraud is a product of the manager's PTSD. It is not personally driven to make you mad or angry. It is like being caught out walking home on a country road in a thunderstorm. You didn't take an umbrella because the sun was shining when you left home. It was sheer chance that the weather turned like this and you got soaked to the skin. Shaking a fist at the rain clouds or weather forecasters does not make the rain disappear, walking home gets you out of the rain and you can recover safely.

Q: Who can I trust?

A: Everyone. However, what you must learn is that one breach of your expectations of a person, no matter what the accompanying story is, you must withdraw your trust. There is an exception to this rule if this person is highly valuable to you (spouse, blood relative or best friend) then give them a second chance outlining clearly what your expectations are. If that person crosses your expectations a second time, then withdraw your trust completely. Third and fourth chances do not change the wrongdoer's behaviour. I liken the process of the second chance to the possibility that the person receiving the behaviour expectation may be 'expectationally deaf' and may not have heard correctly. Third and fourth chances emphasise to the transgressor that you are a doormat, expect further incursions of all other expectations of yours and my suggestion is to seek therapy from an experienced counsellor. Quite probably someone in your childhood made you feel unworthy of receiving trust and you are replicating it later in life.

Q: *How can anyone trust me as I allowed in, or recommended this person to the organisation?*

A: See Judgement answer. You are a victim of an illusion. End of story. Move on.

Q: *My wife/family are angry at me and even seeking divorce because I have destroyed their future by letting the fraudster in.*

A: No point arguing this on your own. Seek an experienced couple or family counsellor. Usually the spouse's own childhood trauma comes to the surface in such a crisis. A person who truly loves you will be by your side no matter what. That person may not understand – let them read this book, but they will stay with you as they believe in you.

Q: *I don't know what to do, I cannot stay in the organisation or profession any more. I want to run away and be an artist/hippy/find myself.*

A: Remember that this is a short-term response to the damage that has been incurred on you. Take a sabbatical to refresh. If this is a confirming incident that you no longer wish to stay in your work role, then seek experienced career counselling to find your life's work. Airlines recognise these days that their pilots need time out after a crash, same with you and your fraudster manager. Time out is a good response. This may be a short-term reaction, let time heal the wounds, even write about your experience to help others and let your mind and body heal.

Q: I have an uncontrollable urge to kill or hurt this person.

A: This is a normal reaction to being hurt. We are trained by the media and socially to use violence to rectify a situation. Try to resist this urge. Remember that killing or physically hurting the perpetrator does not remove or solve the problem. However, it is likely to put you in jail for a very long time. Forgiving yourself is the first step to ridding these thoughts from your mind.

Q: I feel so terrible that I want to kill myself.

Note: If you have suicidal thoughts, you must see a counsellor immediately. Suicide merely puts an end to your own pain, but suicide hurts those left behind and will hurt far more and far longer than what you are going through now. Remember the analogy to the thunderstorm; it was not your fault that you got caught in the rain. Call a phone service dedicated to suicide to help you right now.

The best explanation that has been given to me when I wanted to sort out the irrationality of the 'thunderstorm' was that it would help me to help others. Writing this book is a consequence of that advice; also providing a counselling service to managers on their career development and choices. Not many understand the total breakdown of trust within a person and the isolation it gives, so your experience will help you, your family and friends if it ever happens to them. I guess that is what we mean by wisdom.

MY OWN EXPERIENCE OF AN ARROGANT FRAUDSTER

If you are tormented by feelings of gullibility then you will be interested in what happened to me while I was writing this book, after the research had been completed. I actually became a target of an Arrogant Fraudster myself. Considering that they are a low percentage I am surprised that this happened, especially as I was armed with the research and knowledge about this type of fraudster. We assume that once we have knowledge we are protected. However, this is not true. Even in my consultancy practice I can only indicate the screening out of a fairly high percentage. I know that I would be better than other people on detecting possible fraudsters, but I can never state with 100 per cent complete confidence that I can screen out all of them. I knew that from my social science background that it is impossible to assert 100 per cent on human behaviour.

So how did this happen to me, as a person who knows so much about Arrogant Fraudsters? I am writing this in my office in Bali and as I am doing so, a large lizard about 1.5 metres long crossed the garden and quietly slipped into the fish pond. My ornamental fish are beautiful and add much to ambience of the small garden. I was horrified that the reptile was obviously intending on a quick lunch. I have exactly 37 fish of various sizes and while I can't say that I know them individually I do receive much joy from watching and feeding them. I did not want to lose any of my finned friends to a hungry water monitor. So I watched and waited. The lizard hid under a bridge, completely submerged. As reptiles are air breathing, I knew that he had to come up for air at some point. Indeed, his head came up as he waited for an unsuspecting fish to swim by. I watched if he was going to take one and luckily he didn't. While I was watching him with his cleverly camouflaged skin and behaviour it made me realise that this was the same behaviour as an Arrogant Fraudster. They too lurk and wait for their next victim, camouflaged with an expertise that they know the right victim wants. Presumably the big water monitor would have stayed in the pond until his stomach was full. But he was interrupted by a Balinese friend who poked it with a stick to get the large reptile to move. He was successful and the lizard ran away with my friend in hot pursuit. Several months later the water lizard has not returned, and obviously learnt that the free lunch was not available at my office.

The similarity of the water monitor is quite striking. The Arrogant Fraudster watches and waits for his next victim. No one can see he is there because he is so well camouflaged by the mask he is wearing together with its appropriate behaviours. Most of the time the lizard was underwater, only revealing itself to breathe. Similarly the Arrogant Fraudster would have to drop his mask only when necessary – say opening an account and depositing money in a bank, and then quickly put on the mask again and return to his victim for more.

My encounter with an Arrogant Fraudster began with an unsuspecting request of a driver to take us to see the sights in Bali when my husband and I arrived for the first time. There are countless drivers in Bali willing to assist tourists. Our driver was conscientious at meeting our tourist needs and naturally whenever we returned we would call him. I noticed that he spent much time while driving developing a relationship with me, talking about things that he knew I was interested in. I was pleased at his response as I am an open person and naturally talk to everyone without any hesitancy. Slowly over the ensuing return trips he became my friend. I would give generous tips and met his wife and family. Over a period of two years I trusted him so much that when we wanted to put in an office, he was the one we naturally turned to make it happen. I had appointed him as our manager as he was already so demonstrably trustworthy.

Looking back I can now identify odd things that would have heralded his lack of trustworthiness. His wife was always very quiet, the children dutiful but again extremely quiet. Most Balinese are very friendly and extroverted and here I rationalised was an exception to the rule, but I had no alarm bells ringing. My thesis was done and dusted and I was very happy to begin the dissemination process about what I had discovered. Unbeknownst to me the driver had by now defrauded us of many millions of rupiah. And there I was, telling everyone that we can now detect fraudsters! It turned out that he expected and received commission from every facet of the renovation. At first he used to involve me to sit in long discussions with building suppliers so that I could see him achieve the best rate. Not knowing the language, I could only judge by the behaviours that I saw. All seemed fine, there was no indication of fraud, in fact quite the opposite, I thought we were getting the lowest price possible. He must have gained tremendous satisfaction from this irony. Humiliating me through my lack of language. One of the outcomes of this humiliation is that I am now learning Indonesian to prevent this from happening to me again.

After the building had finished we had to have a purification ceremony, and of course he was the one to lead it. Even the local priest looked askance at the continual singing by him, stretching out a ceremony that would last about 40 minutes to nearly 2 hours with our 'friend' in the star role. He had taken and passed a degree in religious studies specialising in Balinese Hinduism and could sing and recite many passages from his academic knowledge. It was this expertise that formed the basis of our relationship.

One day my husband and I with another local driver met him as were driving into the large city of Denpasar for me to attend a dentist. As an ex-taxi driver he said he knew all the back streets and short cuts to take. While I was in the dentist's chair, our trusted friend could not help himself and took over the driving, as he knew the city better. His arrogance then took over. Apparently he drove like a lunatic and took my husband to shops that he had commission arrangements with, rather than sourcing goods that were cheaper and better. On our way home driving across the mountains with me and an aching jaw, our local driver told me what had happened. My husband did not say anything he was so angry that he knew that he would say things against my friend that

I wouldn't like to hear. Finally, when we got home, I heard the whole story from my husband who by now was somewhat more even-tempered with what he had witnessed. Not only had the Arrogant Fraudster damaged the local driver's car without compensating him, but he treated our local man with great disrespect. In Indonesia manners are of utmost importance: the Balinese underpin their social relations with respect and even have different languages to indicate respect.

Immediately I was alarmed. This was not a purely jealous reaction towards our local driver. This was contrary to all that I knew with my friend. An inconsistency! I insisted on meeting with him to try to understand what happened. From that point on he feared the game was up and avoided the confrontation. However, when he did come up to meet me it was with tears and not understanding how I could switch off our relationship. I spent a couple of hours counselling him, which I do so successfully with many other managers. I used the tried and tested approach of the CAT model and pointed out how stress makes us behave badly which leads on to controlling others.

He refused point blank that I could help him. He conceded that whereas I maybe right about his past he has since changed his behaviour and now he is perfectly fine. After confronting him with irrefutable evidence he still would not accept that anything could be wrong. In a way, I was quite shocked that he was contesting my work and my theoretical model. I am more than willing to listen to helpful criticism about my work, but here in front of me, maybe for the first time ever, I was faced with someone who felt that he had done all the necessary work and that I must be mistaken. This may be due to fact that managers who I counsel seek me out for advice and my reputation is built on a very high success rate that I have achieved over the years. Arrogant fraudsters do not need help from helpful individuals like myself, they only seek power and control.

Since then he has tried to convince me that I had got it all wrong (first stage) then it was I had misunderstood him as I am from a different country (second stage). Neither excuse held with me, I knew what he was doing. He has since turned up a couple of times without first contacting me thereby ambushing me with tears in his eyes saying he cannot live without me in his life. His wife and children were distraught apparently as I no longer visited them (stage three). He then said he would kill himself as there was no point in living like this – as I meant so much to him (stage four). The emotional blackmail failed to work and he turned up once again unannounced and told me that he would move to the district that I was working in and do good works to prove to me that he was not a bad man (stage five). The last time he appeared I informed him that my husband will deal with him from now on and that as an ex-detective he would most likely call in the police. Frauds carry a long jail sentence in Indonesia and the prisons are not to the same standard as in industrialised countries, with the intake cells usually crammed with about 30–40 people.

The five stages that I encountered were ruses to escalate a re-forming of the relationship. Similarly the Arrogant Fraudsters did the same to their targets. They do everything in their power to regain trust and to make you doubt yourself if you are making the right decision. Likeable Fraudsters do not do this type of behaviour. They own up immediately and try to make restitution, and if that is impossible they are very likely to kill themselves. One Likeable Fraudster that I know tried to suffocate himself in a hotel room by tying his head in a plastic bag. He wrote his suicide letter and without hesitation he put the bag over his head. Tiny folds in the bag where the adhesive tape did not stick foiled this normally successful attempt. He was found unconscious by a cleaner the next morning and rushed to hospital. No one knew that he was at risk, it was the one and only communication to the rest of the world of his intention to kill himself.

I expect my Arrogant Fraudster to reappear as he thinks, like all other Arrogant Fraudsters, that they are so clever to outwit anyone, but there will be no interaction from me, his target. Over the relatively short time that we knew him, we think every contractor would have had to have pay commission to him. In the meantime, when we come across a wronged contractor we pay the right amount for the work completed out of respect to their help in the renovation. The Balinese in North Bali live on the poverty line and to deny them their full reward for their work is utterly inhumane.

How did he build up the trust in me, his target? Because as with all Arrogant Fraudsters, he used expert power. In most cases of fraud by such a career criminal they come in with a particular expertise that the organisation requires as no one else in the business shares it. From this promontory they hold power over all in the organisation. Usually the expertise is financial, most Arrogant Fraudsters use accountancy or have particular expertise in procurement.

With me, because he knew that I was very interested in the unusual workplace culture of Bali, he became my expert. I was researching for another book and needed to find out as much information as possible about the way Balinese conducted their workplaces. Most con artists who centre on females use the emotional route to their hearts and we hear dreadful stories in the media of women who have given away their life savings to these men. In my case I was not flirted with as I made it clear that my marital relationship was sacrosanct. I was not flattered or called lovey dovey things. Once when he called me darling, I told him never to do that as my husband would probably punch him on the nose. So the normal route to my female heart was closed and therefore he had to use other means to feed off me, and that was his knowledge of Bali.

Yet when I reviewed the evidence I had filed in my office, I started to think that with all these now obviously false account books and invoices, perhaps he was a Likeable Fraudster. His childhood was one of impoverishment and there are psychiatric problems in his family. Yes, I thought, he is too nice to be an Arrogant Fraudster. This demonstrates the power that they hold over you. To use another way of saying it, they bewitch you. I felt that he must have had some terrible event triggering his frauds. But no, there was no recent disaster. His mother had recently passed away, but that was after we were defrauded. He had even used that event to squeeze more money out of me, but I am thankful that I had nothing to give.

Slowly I began to realise that my friend could only be an Arrogant Fraudster with the unveiling of the most telling characteristic: he felt superior to our local Balinese friends. They did not share this vital information with me as they are too polite to speak ill of another. It was only when I had concrete evidence and after I started asking, that slowly the facts were revealed: inconsistency and power over people.

I feel quite confident that he will do exactly the same to the next foreign woman he can get his talons into. Just as the fish-eating lizard was chased away, this man has now been chased away. Both water monitor and my Arrogant Fraudster may observe at a distance my comings and goings but now both life-forms know that if I catch them it will lead only to punishment.

Previous Theories Don't Help

However, what is quite remarkable I still had doubts. Perhaps he is purely mentally ill? That all of this is down to psychiatric problems in the family? Perhaps his reaction to this dysfunctional behaviour was by targeting women for payback. His mother was unable to be emotionally present for him when he was physically abused by his father. But the problem with this way of thinking is that the intellect is diverted away from the reality.

If I consider him to be damaged by say, childhood neglect, then all we can do is provide therapy and hope that one day the wound heals and the behaviour stops. The proviso to this is that the fraudster has to come to terms with the damage and take steps to undertake therapy. The people who are sitting in the counsellor's waiting room have realised that they are in pain and that they need help. Similarly, those who come to me after a period of bullying or other emotional abuse in the workplace seek my help. But to date in my practice, I have never had a bully request assistance.

This is a very telling point. The literature tells us that bullies have received emotional harm in their childhood, which in turn causes them to bully. However, this knowledge does not stop bullying. They continue to perpetrate the cycle of abuse on others, and this includes the workplace. But how does this answer our problem of stopping bullying in the workplace? Cute corporate value statements hung on a wall in reception do not stop bullying. The early emotional harm literature tells us how and why it happens but fails to tell us how to stop it. The present theories are not able to predict bullying and certainly not the targets. The only way to prevent bullying is to intervene in childhood trauma. As this social intervention is against our values of our homes being sacrosanct, the perpetrators of the abuse will not allow the therapeutic interveners inside their home. This is why schools find it very difficult to stop bullying, it is almost impossible to stop the harm to a child which later leads to abusing others. The other problem is that we cannot predict accurately that such harm will result in the child being a bully. Not all children with emotional damage turn into bullies. Furthermore, it is possible that the intervention does more harm than good, for instance the practice of taking children away from their parents is known to have long-term deleterious effects on children.

So for a social theory to be of use to us it must have the following features.

It must give us an understanding to human behaviour. The theory must explain behaviour and finally it must be able to predict, with some degree of accuracy, the outcomes of the behaviour. However, such theories are confined to human behaviour and therefore cannot be precise as scientific theory. If you like, it can be seen as a fuzzy glass to look through rather than the clean glass of science. The debate about scientific theory is too large to be dealt with here, but suffice to say, most scientists believe that theory gives empirical results, which can be tested repeatedly to give the same result. Social theory does not have this inbuilt rigour, it obtains rigour in a different way, such as with the qualitative methodology used in this study.

We can now say with some degree of certainty that managerial fraud now has an explanation to the behaviour and we can understand the 'whys' and 'hows', with also, and this is the missing piece of the jigsaw for me, a degree of predictability. However, it is not a scientific phenomenon but one of human nature – a social phenomenon and cannot be said to be 100 per cent perfect in explaining and understand all of managerial fraud, just the most likely tendencies. Hard theorists stay away from social science for this reason, others stay and impose their 'scientific' methodology upon impossible data but as pointed out earlier, they cannot obtain the condition of randomness required for inference, therefore all of these results are questionable beyond pure description.

Executive Impression Management

My small contribution to theory with the Executive Impression Management core process has some predictive power. The variable of consistency is dichotomous. With consistency, the individual is either consistent or not, there is no middle ground of 'Sometimes he is consistent, sometimes he is not.' This type of fence-sitting statement is actually stating inconsistency. As with the variable of power, from the core process if the individual concerned is using power either over or under then he is using power. No power held over or under means there is equality. Again a statement saying that sometimes the individual uses ingratiation – not generally seen as a power tactic as here the individual is using power under (manipulation) he is still using power to control others. The co-workers refer to an air of superiority given off by those using power to control in this manner, they obliquely refer to an air of inferiority when the power is used to control others through passive-aggressive means such as manipulation, divide and conquer strategies, setting up exclusive groups of 'in' people and cutting the individual out of the tacit knowledge (and therefore power) base, are all designed to create control via means of inferiority.

If I was hiring an individual for say, an accounting position, I look for far more and quite different information than is the usual content of the interview and selection process. This is due to the two types: Arrogant and the Likeable Fraudster. By the way, a Respectful Manager, once given the explanation that any information retrieved in an interview makes for a better selection process, will have no problems with supplying it. If items that are sought through background check are of news to the applicant I share the information with him. The Respectful Manager is self-aware and will always want to have feedback of his performance and his history.

Arrogant Fraudster's Superiority

This Balinese 'friend' always felt superior to me. It was only until I put my foot down that he would then be forced to take my advice for a more mutually desirable outcome. At that point he would resort to passive-aggressive techniques to undermine me. I allowed him to remain superior to me as he kept using his expertise as the key: 'Terry you don't know how Bali works, I do.' This is a typical statement of how I felt I had to allow him to have power and control over me. Many respondents reported that the Arrogant Fraudster manager would do the same. One fraudster ran circles around his tradesman boss in giving 'up-to-date' financial reports.

The ultimate power game is played out by saying if you don't listen to what I say I will leave. This is pretty hard to take in the middle of renovation work. A walk out complete with workforce in a foreign country is difficult, is an understatement of what faced us, so compliance is enforced. This card is a dangerous one to play with a client or accountant, as angry company accountants or renovators can sabotage the operation in retaliation. But it is also dangerous for the Arrogant Fraudster to play this card as the subject of the take it or leave it attitude may actually do that. The danger is seen as minimal to the fraudster, as after all they are the ones who believe in their superiority.

Their belief is based on earlier reinforced behaviour that indeed they are superior to all. I have had people mention that this must be a cover up for their own insecurity. I disagree. This study has shown me that this type of fraudster is secure. He knows that if he bleeds you dry there are other targets that can be successfully approached. The research has shown that they are reluctant to move on, but they will if necessary and they repeat the same behaviour all over again.

Others who do not understand the pathology of this behaviour will say that as the fraudster gets older the behaviour subsides. There is no evidence for this in this study. The longest fraud perpetrated in the cases was 12 years. As he grew older he didn't relax his vice-like grip on the company, in fact he squeezed out larger and larger amounts of money.

Their sense of superiority beggars belief. Any competition is immediately disarmed and disposed of. This is necessary to retain their superiority to others. Having a smart person on the payroll criticising their behaviour will not be tolerated. All sorts of excuses are made to be rid of anyone that belittles them. They are so secure that they even brag about it to others. There is no 3 a.m. insomnia as they rake over their faults such as with the Likeable Fraudster. They are able to sleep well because they know that they are right and the rest of the world needs to be conquered. Nothing will shake them out of their thinking, their world is composed of themself and subservient others. If a new client does not bow to their superiority then it is their loss, not the fraudsters'. This flagrant superiority is however very subtle. The impression management techniques that are used are clever with the 100 per cent full beam on the target. If you are caught in the spotlight you will not know it or recognise it. We are as helpless as deer caught in the headlights. That was the brutal truth that I had to accept. I could only get to a point of realisation after he was exposed himself through an oddity – the occurrence of his driving like a maniac. It was only then that I saw the fraudster as he truly was.

I am happy about having this lesson as it made me understand how all-embracing and strong is the impression management of the Arrogant Fraudster. That is why the co-workers replied that they appear to be more authentic and therefore trustworthy than others. Face-to-face interviews are useless at detecting the Fraudster. Bob Hare[7] was himself taken in by a couple of psychopaths in trying to determine prisoners' pathology in his research. Because of this he has been criticised heavily by others who do not understand the power of the impression management used. To admit to this must have been extremely difficult for a professional who has made his mark in his field, but shows that his honesty is the clue to what these offenders can do.

People in other cultures who retain animistic beliefs explain this as black magic: that the Arrogant Fraudster has cast a spell and you can only comply and do what is determined by the Fraudster. To break the spell requires immense counterbalancing of white magic, because the hold is so strong over the individual.

Upon reflection, there were oddities about his behaviour which now seem so obvious, and I think that I should have picked up the clues. But I didn't and if I cannot do it, how can someone without my training and expertise pick up on the small clues? Remember that the Arrogant Fraudster appears more authentic than others, therefore it is impossible to weave away from the constant barraging of camouflaged emotional abuse in the relationship.

However, if this was an account by a person in an organisation with concerns about the odd behaviour of a manager, I would instantly recognise it due to the

7 Babiak and Hare 2007, op cit.

research that I have done. The magic spell of the manager's authenticity does not fall on me as I am an outside observer, I am not the target and exposed to the damaging behaviour.

From this experience I have even more understanding of people who have had the misfortune of having an Arrogant Fraudster manager. I understand the doubts, the humiliation, the emotional blackmail that is used by them and the assault on your own rationality. Remember my own questioning of my 'friend'? That is abuse so pervasive that I was unable to see it.

It is exactly because I am not targeted by the fraudulent manager that I am able to retain the informed observer status. I knew intuitively that I could not approach convicted fraudsters in my study due to their ability to recount stories of how hard they were done by and it was not their fault. This is the reason why I focused on their targets as the respondents. Now with this illuminating example that was given to me in the form of my 'friend', I can share the feelings that a target exudes. However, without my theoretical approach of using Goffman's impression management all that I learnt from the research would have been lost. The result is that we tend to rely on interesting diverse theories (for instance, narcissism, impoverished backgrounds and so on) that lead us astray from what is really at work – putting on a false appearance in order to dupe others to obtain power and control. And this is why we have not seen this before: it is only with Goffman's theory that we can now see what is truly happening and gain an understanding of what is going on.

To bring in an experienced consultant to assess the manager of concern is the only way to measure what is happening. Psychologists will give psychological explanations, criminologists will give theirs and no doubt the police will give theirs, but all fail to identify the fraudster *before* the act is committed and none contribute insight if a fraudster is found defrauding the organisation. The psychologists will say therapy, the personal Red Flags indicators will not be reliable, the police may say jail, but none can manage the fraudster and predict with accuracy that Executive Impression Management does.

Calling Targets Gullible

For clarification of the above incident I want to draw attention to the problem of gullibility. A person can only operate within his realm of knowledge. If there is no evidence, only odd little things that are easily rationalised away, there is no knowledge that the manager is a fraudster. The impression management process is so strong that we all operate in its zone of comfort. It works for us from the day we were born. The infant relies on mother coming when it cries. The young child relies on telling stories to prevent punishment, then later finds out this is not such a good impression management strategy after all. An employee in his workplace has to be seen to give off the right impression management or his work would be doubted.

It is the Arrogant Fraudster who camouflages himself, waits for the right victim and then walks across our personal boundaries of authenticity and trust. They really do not care what they do to others. For anyone thinking that I must be gullible, please think again. Due to my highly unusual upbringing I had developed a sixth sense of intuition if a person intended to harm me. This means I can walk into a meeting and immediately sense what is going on. This fact has led me to operate successfully in my practice and consultancy where others fail. Combine this with the statement that I do know much more than many people on managerial fraud, then for me to be taken in like this is truly exceptional. But such is the power of the Arrogant Fraudster. Never think that your organisation will not be touched by such a person; there are many out there waiting for such complacency.

My episode demonstrates their dominance. It is subtle, adept and betrays the trust of the receiver. Arrogant Fraudsters have learnt not to give the game away. After collecting the evidence for the study I felt a certain empathy with the co-workers of a managerial fraudster, however I did not appreciate the full depth and breadth of their destroyed trust until my own revelation with my 'friend'. Many of the study's co-workers spent sleepless nights agonising if they could have done anything better. My answer is a flat no. It is impossible if you are the target of an Arrogant Fraudster. I understand how it feels, as it is a pernicious invasion of their power over you and is a deceit of the worse kind.

Chapter 9
Case Applications

Re-telling my encounter of an Arrogant Fraudster enables the settling in of the impression management process and it does well to consider other examples. Over the years I have collected fraudster case studies. I have extended Executive Impression Management to include other types of managers, including a business owner. This demonstrates the portability and robustness of the core process to others in the workplace.

The Likeable Fraudster

An interesting example of a Likeable Fraudster is Russell Wasendorf of the Peregrine Financial Group who has been jailed for 50 years, essentially receiving a life sentence for fraud. Even with a sentence cut for good behaviour he would be at least 106 before he would be set free. He is convicted of defrauding over 13,000 customers of at least US$200 million through his Peregrine Financial Group, a finance brokerage based in Iowa, USA. The story of Peregrine is the oft quoted basement start and finally reaching the peaks of financial stardom with riches untold through hard work. The bare facts mark the rise of Wasendorf's climb to the top.

FACTUAL HISTORY

Russell Wasendorf was born in 1948 in Iowa. In 1969 he married his first wife and had a son, Russell Wasendorf Jr, but the marriage ended in divorce fairly quickly. At school he loved acting and while at university he developed film-making skills and later produced a winning documentary film on soybeans.

He married his second wife in 1976 but this too ended in divorce. He then worked in a local futures commodities magazine firm producing promotional videos. In 1980 he established his own competing futures local commodities magazine at the rear of a barber shop in his home town of Cedar Falls, Iowa. A year later his business was growing and by 1985 he bought a small brokerage in futures trading for local farmers. He forecast the stock market crash of 1987 and saved clients who listened to him from ruin in doing so. By the early 1990s he had moved office into the Chicago heartland of stock trading, a short stroll from the Chicago Board of Trade. Client funds under his control were about US$2 million at the time, but shortly after he opened Peregrine Financial Group (PFGBest) in 1992, the defrauding began. He created a ponzi scheme (like Bernie Madoff) with incoming client funds paying off other clients dividends and so on. By 1993 an investigator from the Commodity Futures Trading Commission had found irregularities: he ordered six more audits and it put Peregrine at risk.

Wasendorf's inevitable financial ruin was delayed by some remarkably unwise decisions of the National Futures Association (NFA) by offloading clients of one troubled brokerage to another. In doing so they turned a blind eye to the irregularities and added fresh funds into his cash flow, which were used to keep the wolves at bay. Only a year later the NFA fined Peregrine for false advertising and also for not keeping proper accounts of clients' money. This was settled by paying a US$75,000 fine to the NFA and the wolves were kept quiet. So quiet that Peregrine was able to do this twice more, receiving life-saving finance from accounts from other troubled brokerages.

In 1998 Wasendorf invited his son to join him in the Peregrine Group to implement an online trading system. His son eventually became President of PFGBest while his father tried all sorts of schemes to stay afloat. One of the schemes did pay off and brought in much needed funds. Peregrine rose to become one of the top ten of brokerages in terms of funds administered – cited at over US$200 million by 2006. After he had committed to building a large headquarters in his home town – Cedar Falls, Iowa – the crash happened with the impact of the global financial crisis.

On the 9 July 2012, Wasendorf Sr, tried to commit suicide outside of his headquarters in Cedar Falls. He failed but his suicide note alerted authorities and the ensuing evidence led to his trial and a sentence of 50 years imprisonment.

AN ARROGANT FRAUDSTER?

My curiosity was raised by the conflicting reports about Russell Wasendorf Sr, he seemed to be painted by the press as a Bernie Madoff – having the luxurious lifestyle, the jet, the flash headquarters and the fact that he joined one of the advisory boards of his regulators. Madoff had become the chair of his regulator as well. In addition, both had a son who was in the business and both sons were genuinely shocked on receiving the news about their fraudster father.

Millions of dollars were spent on a lavish lifestyle, corporate contributions to charities and so on. The similarities are striking. But my intuition and research tells me otherwise.

I began to research in depth, for it is my belief that Wasendorf (Sr, unless noted otherwise) is far from being an Arrogant Fraudster but a Likeable Fraudster. Madoff fits the profile of an Arrogant Fraudster, whereas Wasendorf does not.

A VERY LIKEABLE FRAUDSTER

The Likeable Fraudster is someone who uses organisational funds for his own use to build up his image for the most important people in his life. These people would likely include a spouse or a parent. Behind the eyes of this convincing executive is a severely wounded child. Possibly we will never know of the wounds, how they were incurred, or when. But there are identifying events that indicate a wounded psyche: several marriages and subsequent divorces, family breakdown, an overwhelming drive to be seen to be good in his home town. A Reuters article captures the behind the mask Wasendorf. Apparently he and his brother were estranged, as well as his own son, he remarried in a sudden wedding in Las Vegas and he had a 'seething resentment against establishment rivals in Chicago'.[1]

Using attachment theory I am always drawn to the childhood of fraudsters to see if there are any clues to what trauma, if any, the fraudster faced. Certainly his family were impoverished to the point of being homeless: Wasendorf's christian names are taken from a local pastor and his son who took the family in and gave them an attic to live in about the time when he was born. When Wasendorf was five, his father, a foreman at a meatpacking company, was dead. His widowed mother Ida had to look after the four children on her own. A church-going woman, his mother re-married in 1975, when Wasendorf was 27. However, there was no apparent stepfather when he grew up. But a more telling fact is her occupation: after 15 years as a test radio repair operator retiring in 1969, when Wasendorf was 21 she became a stockbroker, this fact was taken from her obituary in 1990 in the Cedar Rapids newspaper.

1 P.J. Huffstutter, Ann Saphir, Tom Polansek, and David Sheppard, Sep 24, 2012, Special Report: Iowa broker built empire on a lie concealed in a postal box Reuters. Available at http://uk.reuters.com/article/2012/09/24/us-wasendorf-life-one-idUSBRE88N0EJ20120924 (Accessed 1 February 2013)

Her youngest child obviously admired and emulated her, following her footsteps by using his natural gifts of persuasion and media skills, into the local securities industry. There is no hint of fraud or dysfunction until much later in life. Why would a young man pursue the same occupation as his mother? It would be very likely that he would have been close to her, and having no father she would have been a role model for him. His older brother Lewis was estranged from Wasendorf, so there has to be a prior dysfunctional relationship of some sort. However, there are no reports of Wasendorf making himself superior to others, his greatest need was to be good at his profession and be the 'home town boy' who made good, sharing his wealth with local charities and his university. Undoubtedly the grinding poverty in the early 1950s would have been highly stressful, as well as the loss of his father. There are pointers that the Wasendorfs were not a straightforward family.

- His father was a foreman of a meatpacking factory, which means he was relatively well-paid, and yet homeless.

- His brother's blatant disaffection and expressed dissatisfaction of life choices to his wealthy younger brother.

Likeable Fraudsters have an overwhelming need to look successful with all the trappings, even including a trophy wife. There is an underlying drive to endure that this is the case. The motivation for fraud comes out of severe stress. His mother died in 1990 after a short illness. He loved his mother very much, he mentions her (but not his father) to his new wife in his suicide note. The grief of losing his 76-year-old mother suddenly that summer would have been overwhelming. There is no mention of any prior illness in the death notice. It is my intuition that it is this grief that rocked him to the core, and an unsatisfactory business audit tipped the balance and he began to defraud in 1992–93.

Wasendorf himself admits that a 1992 investigation with a resulting six audits by the Commodity Futures Trading Commission was his crisis point:

> *I had no access to additional capital and I was forced into a difficult decision: Should I go out of business or cheat? [his suicide letter states]. I guess my ego was too big to admit failure. So I cheated, I falsified the very core of the financial documents of PFG, the Bank Statements.*[2]

2 Ibid.

It is that point that he was pushed into using other people's money for his own, to keep up the image that he was building himself. The façade began when he created the Peregrine Financial Group. If he had stayed a small town broker it would have been unlikely that the fraud would not have happened. But there again, he could *not* be a small town broker. He had to be an uptown flash broker, which he wasn't, and he had a seething hatred for the Chicago brokers who in his view belittled him.

Not being a psychiatrist, but used to seeing these types of profiles, it is my guess that the real hatred was against his father and other older males, including his older brother. This is more than feeling angry on missing out on a father in his childhood. He was made to feel small and useless by a living person, not a dead one. Very likely there was physical abuse and certainly emotional abuse in his childhood, his reaction later in life is typical of those who are made to feel powerless as a child. Wasendorf shows a primitive response by blaming others for his action. His outrage at the treatment he received from the investigator and the Chicago establishment caused him, in his own mind, to defraud. He states categorically in his suicide notes that he had no option.

Yet he did have an option, and that is to face the fact that he was a good salesman, but not a funds manager. His traumatic childhood had set him on a path to prove to himself that he was worthy of a lifestyle of the rich and famous. Whoever or whatever instilled in him as a child that he was unworthy, poor and trash, is the real perpetrator of the fraud. Someone, somewhere, in the 1950s, set the time bomb that was later detonated in 1992–93 by the death of his mother and the investigator's determination to find administrative errors.

What is remarkable is that while his suicide attempt was in 2012, he kept up the pretence for over 20 years. He must have been strong as an ox to do that, convincing his wives and son as well as the community that he was not doing any harm to anyone.

The suicide attempt was real and he had prepared for his death over a number of weeks. He married his third wife and made a will that she would inherit everything. He wrote notes to his son and new wife explaining what he did and why. He wrote that he had done it deliberately and why, taking responsibility for falsifying bank statements and so on. He apologised for his actions, and was remorseful about what he had done. This is exactly the pattern of the Likeable Fraudster when close to being found out, or when the tension becomes unbearable, they will give themselves up or commit suicide. Far from being like Bernie Madoff, Wasendorf deserves our compassion and with the 50-year sentence for his folly, he has lost absolutely everything.

AN ARROGANT FRAUDSTER? ENRON'S ANDY FASTOW

Using the Arrogant Fraudster methodology it has given me insight to possible behaviour. I had written the following in November 2011:[3] 'Originally faced with a maximum of 140 years in jail, he received lenient sentencing thanks to some good plea-bargaining based on informing on his colleagues (notably Kenneth Lay and Jeff Skilling) at Enron.'

Interestingly, Fastow was the only executive fired by the Enron board just days prior to the collapse, due to the board finding out that he made US$45 million for himself in his off-balance sheet deals. Apparently the board thought this piece of financial wizardry was excessive. So not only has he been able to receive a lighter sentence, he gets to keep almost half of his fraudulently obtained money, after giving US$25 million back to creditors.

From what I had researched in the media it seems that Andy Fastow would fit the type of Arrogant Fraudster. It was said about him long ago that his critics: 'labeled him "Fast Andy" and the "Betty Crocker of cooked books"'. People who grew up with him judged him as extremely ambitious and recall how he quarrelled with high school teachers over his grades.'[4]

Barboza goes on to say that 'Former Enron colleagues have called him prickly and a bully. They say that during angry bouts, he was known to leave profanity-laced messages on the voicemail of colleagues. Yet he could also be charming and generous, former colleagues said. His drive for power was noted very early on in school with these comments: 'High school politics wasn't a big deal at our school but it was a big deal to him,' said Mark Liss, a classmate at New Providence High who beat him in a race for class president. 'I remember how depressed he was; student government meant everything to him.' *The New York Times* Reporter had written.

3 Sheridan, T.A. 2011 A smartest guy in the room about to be released. Available at http://www.executivefraudsters.com (Accessed 1 February 2013)

4 David Barboza, 2002. Enron's many strands: Fallen Star;From Enron Fast Track to total derailment. Available at: http://www.nytimes.com/2002/10/03/business/enron-s-many-strands-fallen-star-from-enron-fast-track-to-total-derailment.html. (accessed 8 November 2011)

A year later, Andy Fastow was elected president of the student council, and his English teacher, described Andy Fastow as a 'wheeler-dealer'.[5] He married an heiress to a large fortune in 1985, which gave him a platform to meet wealthy and influential individuals, and was headhunted by an executive recruiter (nameless unfortunately), as one of Jeff Skilling's first recruits. He became the mastermind behind the schemes that defrauded millions of dollars out of Enron into the pockets of Enron executives, including his own. Apparently he was able to plea bargain and show convincing signs of remorse to the trial judge and this assisted in his lower sentence.

From the findings of the Arrogant Fraudster type there are indeed some parallels with corporate psychopathy. Lack of remorse is seen as one of those characteristics, however I found in my research that they tended to use remorse at trial to reduce their sentences. In most cases the judge would see through the mitigation attempts by the fraudster and it would be remarked upon in their judgments that the ploy did not work.

Arrogant Fraudsters do not change, their unrelenting behaviour is meant to be able to be harnessed[6] with their immense energy put into side projects. This may happen to Andy Fastow upon his release, he may undertake projects that he feels will be satisfying. However, generally such satisfaction is grounded in their own needs being fulfilled and with a psychopath it is the need of power over others. Certainly the Arrogant Fraudsters in my research went on to repeat their offending behaviour even while on bail, convincing new employers that they were much maligned.

The outlook for Fastow would seem to be the same pathway as before, set in his early days of seeking power, perhaps it will be moderated to some degree, but it is more likely that we will be hearing more about Andy Fastow after his release. As they say in the media, 'Watch this space…'. It will be very interesting to see how this Arrogant Fraudster develops after his stint in prison.

I wrote this piece in 2011 and it was posted on my website, www.executivefraudsters.com. Since then Andy Fastow has re-entered the world working as a document clerk at the law firm who represented him. He has also requested speaking to business school students and has since spoken publicly about his experience with Enron. He is convincingly remorseful to his business school audiences, although when asked by a student how much money he

5 Ibid.

6 Babiak, Paul, and Robert D. Hare. 2007. *Snakes in suits*. New York: Harper Collins.

has he was told it was none of his business. Being rude is not the mark of a Likeable Fraudster.

Doing the rounds at business schools and corporate audiences is a popular activity of Arrogant Fraudsters post-imprisonment. Nick Leeson is still doing this at time of writing, and according to one website www.celebritynetworth.com he is worth US$9 million. Apparently Mr Fastow is now able to charge US$8,000 per presentation, which is a not bad return for extramural activities to his document clerk income.

A LIKEABLE FRAUDSTER-IN-THE MAKING

The next case is very different from the Enron debacle and demonstrates the possible application to others in the workplace. Jerome Kerviel was a rogue trader who lost US$ 6 billion and nearly brought down one of the most prominent financial institutions in Europe. He was actually a Likeable Fraudster but without managerial responsibilities. I have used this case as an extension of the Executive Impression Management to occupations other than purely managing budgets and human resources. Traders are given responsibility for making more money for their customers through judicious investing; buying when stock is low and selling the same stock when it is fetching high value. They are managing customer assets and even without the actual management of staff are still prone in my view to the types of impression management that exudes from the managers in my research.

Losing US$6 billion dollars is somewhat extreme, but as he used fictitious emails and fake trades, he lied to his senior managers about his losses. But was he a managerial fraudster? The counter accusations are: that there is scepticism in the banking community that he did this on his own (therefore must be in cahoots with other fraudsters); that he was a scapegoat for the bank's own losses of the previous quarter (attributed the fraudster tag unfairly) and that he has received cult status for having to put his career on the line as he was only doing his job of making money in the markets (in fact a non-fraudster).

From the information that is freely available on the Internet, I have come to the conclusion that most likely Kerviel was a Likeable Fraudster-in-the-making. This conclusion is based on information given in the media:[7]

7 Ben Martin, Nick Allen, Peter Allen and Henry Samuel, 2008, Rogue trader in police custody in France, *The Daily Telegraph*. Available at: http://www.telegraph.co.uk/news/uknews/1576621/Rogue-trader-in-police-custody-in-France.html (Accessed 13 October 2010).

- Kerviel was doing rogue trading out of a sense of trying to impress his superiors.
- He was quiet and introverted, and it is reported that he was liked by neighbours.
- 'His father, who taught apprentices boilermaking in a local training centre, died less than a year ago'[8]
- He lost the woman he was going to marry at about the same time.
- These two losses coincide with the beginning of his fictitious emails covering the trades.
- He lived in a fantasy world where he existed as the Master Trader, duplicating massive amount of trades every three days, as the losses grew.
- It takes a fair amount of time for this type of fraudster to develop; Kerviel's activity was cut short after one year. If the losses had not been uncovered one is led to believe that he would have carried on until the money ran out.

Although Kerviel did not profit directly from the trading at the point he was discovered, it is my belief that he fits the profile of what respondents called in their interviews the 'Likeable Fraudster'. This type is quiet, friendly and liked by many. However, it takes a deep family or personal crisis to erupt to spur them into the fraudulent activity: they see the only way out as gambling using their company's money to feed their image of being successful. His only solution was gaining money in trades to offset his extremely low self-esteem, and he used the bank's money to do so. Almost all of the Likeable Fraudsters liked and needed to gamble to make more money for themselves. Many have suggested that investment trading is a refined form of gambling and do not see it as a legitimate job. However, this is the reality of the stock market and the basis of capitalism and there are many who trade who become addicted to the high-pressure gamble making returns for their clients.

8 Ibid.

As a shocked neighbour who had known Kerviel since he was a baby reported: 'The two things happening at the same time must have been why everything went wrong.'[9]

The double losses were replicated in his trading, but this was *not* his intention, he wanted to *impress* his bosses with large earnings. He came from a different and lower echelon of French society – possibly his managers were seen as father figures to him. That of course is up to the psychologists to say and not my area of expertise. Likeable Fraudsters are also noted in my research for becoming suicidal upon discovery, which is exactly what happened to young Jerome Kerviel.

It was with considerable luck that Societe Generale discovered the losses when they did, as he was unstoppable and would have continued literally until there was no money left in the bank but earning on the way very large bonuses. It is quite clear that the emotive profiling[10] would have picked up Kerviel before any major loss. The bank should have completed some pre-employment screening, however he came straight from university and had no work history. These applicants are typical of ones that slip through the normal background screening checks, and Kerviel's case demonstrates clearly that thorough screening must take place on an annual basis with key personnel, such as traders and financiers, in fact anyone who has contact with the organisation's money. It is now up to other banks to heed the lesson that Societe Generale learnt so painfully: they nearly went broke in the process of Kerviel's frenzied activity.

BORN AGAIN FRAUDSTERS

I happen to know of two Managerial Fraudsters who found God after their frauds. It is interesting to note the differences that reflect their different Executive Impression Management. One fraudster was jailed for several years for stealing A$4 million from his organisation. He was already a practicing Christian and highly active in his family's church. He quickly became a youth leader as he enjoyed working with teenagers. By the time I knew about him, he had completed his jail term and was again active in the church community. He had already been on television to tell his story of what he did.

9 Ibid.

10 Sheridan, T.A. 2008. Emotive profiling. Vol3 75-88 In *Aviation Security Management*, 3 vols. Edited by Andrew R. Thomas. Westport, CT: Praeger Security International.

He comes across as a very convincing man. He says that his moment of truth was during the trial when the judge asked him directly if what he had done was a good thing or not. At this point he was said to have been overcome by God and changed his plea from not guilty (previously showing no remorse because he blamed the financial system) to guilty. He was then sentenced to several years in jail. He was noted in jail of being a model prisoner and used his time to proselytise to other inmates. Upon release he quickly became a speaker at church events and became a minor celebrity in his region after writing a book and subsequent TV appearances. In recognition of this work, he has been given a minor position in the church and has access to its funds. His previous co-workers data led to him being typed as an Arrogant Fraudster.

Another manager was jailed for a longer term than the example above for stealing less than a quarter of a million dollars from his organisation. Prior to the fraud he was noted as a successful man enjoying the good life and he was a good executive in his organisation. Finally the fraud was discovered and after a subsequent and genuine suicide attempt he was sent to jail in disgrace.

During his time there he had a spiritual moment where he was guided into the prison chapel and joined in the service. From then on he slowly pieced back his life. He was extremely remorseful at trial but the judge took no notice and certainly did not see his suicide attempt beyond a farce to mitigate his sentence. It is my view that the judge was biased from the outset and was not about to take any factors into mitigation. While in prison he began working with other inmates as a friendly but unqualified counsellor. After his sentence was completed he then tried to re-enter the community to gain work but found it impossible, because employers would not hire an ex-convict. He joined and became an active member of a church and has set up organisations to assist prisoners overseas. He willingly tells his story as testament to the power of conversion if asked, but does not use it as a means of being valued. In recognition of his contrition and his ongoing and considerable charitable works with prisoners, as well as his managerial skills, he is now an elder in the church. This man is a Likeable Fraudster and should have been given a much lighter sentence or even a fine with community work. However the event brought about his work overseas to help others, so there was a silver lining to the excessive sentence.

The similarities of the above accounts is striking, however there are subtle differences that point to the different type of Executive Impression Management used. The first account refers to an Arrogant Fraudster, the second to a Likeable Fraudster. The Arrogant Fraudster argued that it was the system's fault that he took and squandered the A$4 million. Whereas the testimony of the Likeable Fraudster is that of total remorse, blaming only himself for doing the crime, stemming from a moment of extreme foolishness. This moment is still perplexing him even as I write. The foolishness is the key here, the Trickster is working and hides the explanation from our conscious mind. When we feel foolish like the clown slipping on a banana skin, it is the Trickster part of us that is at work.

However, his childhood points to the trauma including domestic violence that he and his siblings endured. All of the children have exhibited signs of severe stress; but only one became a fraudster. We do know that children exposed to domestic violence choose from the two role models of perpetrator or victim. From my unqualified standpoint I would say that he followed the role of his mother, as did another brother who turned to alcohol at an early age, while the other child followed his father's footsteps and has broken off any relationship with his siblings.

As the Likeable Fraudster is intelligent and has good managerial skills he found himself in a position with access to money. It took a life crisis for him to be precipitated into the fraud and the rest is history. The life crisis was the death of his father and a subsequent inheritance and the prospect of his romantic relationship breaking up. The inheritance was actually much smaller than he thought he was getting and meanwhile he had played the successful business man role with his peers and the woman in his life. The crisis point came when he put down the phone after being told the low amount he was to receive from the executor of his father's estate. He was asked by staff how much he had received – pointing to how much he had told people of his forthcoming change of circumstances, and he indicated to all in the office that it was millions. As it was far less he resorted to using the organisation's money when the inheritance ran out some time later. Only skilled therapeutic intervention could have saved him from defrauding at that point. It was inevitable that he was to steal the funds. As Cressey had described earlier, the insurmountable pressure within becomes the driving force for fraud. However, what was not known until now is that this will only affect the managers who feel inferior to others. And this is most likely due to early childhood trauma.

One point that needs to be stated is that just because an individual finds God, or undergoes a spiritual experience and is an overtly model citizen, it does not mean that the individual's character has been reformed. One has to look at the co-workers, or if not working, his peers to see what type of Executive Impression Management is being given off. The Likeable Fraudster is the least harmful, but even he will use other's funds if exposed to strong enough pressure, unless there is effective therapeutic intervention.

Finally, Arrogant Fraudsters are attracted to non-profit organisations just as much as businesses. They may use the guise of the expert to gain entry and after that immediately start to defraud. It is no different to them to steal from deserving recipients of the non-profit organisations or business owners and shareholders. The venue may be different but vulnerable organisations are the main focus of their activities to gain entry. For the Likeable Fraudster, they are not immune to their potential life crisis to steal from non-profits either.

Chapter 10
Prevention

No organisation, including governments, is exempt from a determined managerial fraudster, no matter how good the systems to prevent fraud may be. As one fraud investigator told me, if an organisation is a target, then it can still happen. It is a bit like a house that is built to be burglar-proof. No matter the extent of the security, a motivated Arrogant Fraudster can nonetheless get inside. What can be done instead is to put in place a more sophisticated multi-edge strategy to protect and defend against fraud.

Prevention Systems

Here I am referring to prevention systems that are low cost and provide a barrier to managerial fraud. Furthermore, these are the best prevention systems that could be devised in the light of the new information from my research.

HOTLINE

Considering that tip-offs by staff or customers create the highest fraud detection rate according to the ACFE,[1] feedback is very important. It is far more effective than auditing controls. Over half of the reported tips come from employees. To increase the number of tips for managerial fraud it is imperative that the hotline is anonymous and safe from reprisals. Pressure is brought upon the reporting individual to give details and preferably evidence. What some senior managers do not understand is that evidence-collecting increases the chances of a co-worker being identified. Once the identity is known among management retaliation can take place. The co-workers in my research spoke of staff being laid off by the fraudster manager because they could easily blow the whistle on their clandestine activities. Firing staff who threaten the fraudster's activities leaves lives and careers wrecked: usually no good reason is given

1 Association of Certified Fraud Examiners. 2008. *Fraud check up*. Austin, TX: Association of Certified Fraud Examiners.

(for instance that the position is now redundant), neither will there be a good reference. There has to be a safe way that the information is given. It is far better to reward staff who are courageous enough to stand up and protect the organisation with something other than a wrecked career. In many jurisdictions there is protective legislation towards whistle-blowers. However, the process still leaves the worker with a sense of violation when their own behaviour is measured against the perpetrator's.

I remember one such event when I took the step of whistle-blowing in an organisation that was actively and determinedly not operating on equality issues as deemed by public consensus and law. As I am a woman and was whistle-blowing on gender issues, I soon became painted as an ambitious bitch who was not toeing the line to the organisation's values. Plus I imagine, many other insults made behind my back. I was leaving the organisation anyway, and I decided to go public as it made no difference to me. Little did I know that the public took great interest, and the next morning I was assailed by camera crews and reporters who wanted to publicise my complaint. Unfortunately public pressure did not change the organisation as they hid behind an exemption in the law. As the people involved had made that exemption it is no wonder that it continued in place. Many years later the organisation is still without women or racial minority representation and the white males hold fast under continual criticism.

Normally however, things are different. As more pressure is applied to the whistle-blower to produce details and evidence for an allegation, fewer people will use the hotline. Evidence collection is for the fraud investigator to do, not the whistle-blower. The latter will usually do so when the report is not believed.

Gathering evidence makes the individual at more risk of being fired by the fraudster as this activity will be beyond normal job duties. If the fraudster manager is also in charge of IT and information systems, it is even harder for a report to be made as emails can always be traced. Sherron Watkins, the whistle-blower at Enron, was not believed and after amassing factual evidence put herself at risk of being fired. It was only the collapse of Enron that saved her from being forcibly removed by the chairman, Kenneth Lay.

It may be fairly easy for larger organisations to install a dedicated hotline. Usually it is a number in HR. In my experience human resources departments have a very high leakage rate. They are also prone to dismiss accounts from those they deem gossip-mongers. Ideally the hotline should be off site with an independent and honest organisation.

For small businesses, whistle-blowing is particularly difficult. Staff are fewer and their position will give their identity away. Bearing in mind that tip-offs are the most effective tool against managerial fraud, it is far cheaper than sophisticated computer systems and audit controls. Small business associations, such as a Chamber of Commerce or trade associations, could and should provide a hotline to their member businesses. Again, the strictest confidence must be applied. The business owner can then be contacted by their association without any knowledge of the fraudster manager.

KEEPING UPWARD LINES OF INFORMATION CLEAR

Keeping communication lines open is a variation of whistle-blowing and can be internalised within the organisation so that management does not shoot the messenger. Strategic conversation is a valuable tool in any management consultant's range of solutions to prevent vital information becoming stuck at lower levels. Once information is flowing upwards, management can make more informed decisions.

Essentially it is the organisational suggestion box. Staff can put in ideas and information without fear, in fact the opposite is true, suggestions are often rewarded. One example of this is that in 1967 Jim Delligatti, an early franchisee in the McDonald's burger chain, suggested a double burger because he saw that men needed a more substantial meal than the traditional one-patty burger. The Big Mac was born and has become a mainstay of McDonald's offerings ever since.

If staff are used to being listened to, then they will start to tell the bad news as well as the good. Abolishing fear of reprisals is extremely important when dealing with bad news. This information is taken out of the tacit knowledge sphere into the public and any Respectful manager will appreciate the information no matter how bad it may seem. Taking into account the emotional content of giving such information is imperative and must be respected by upper management.[2]

We now know that Arrogant Fraudsters use superiority to control people, and self-promotion to upper management. Any business owner has to know if these issues are present because they will be blinded by the intensity of the

2 Feng Lui, Sally Maitlis 2014. Emotional dynamics and strategizing processes: a study of strategic conversations in top team meetings. *Journal of Management Studies* Special Issue: Strategy as Discourse: Its Significance, Challenges and Future Directions 51 (2): 202-234.

authenticity of the Executive Impression Management emanating from the Fraudster. Similarly, Likeable Fraudsters will use ingratiation upwards and manipulation with subtle bullying methods of exclusion to control others. Having open communication on such behaviour is therefore paramount.

FRAUD EDUCATION OF STAFF

One key finding of the investigation is that co-workers noticed little oddities, but could not connect the dots as fraudulent behaviour. This is totally understandable considering that the impression management is so strong. However, there was one case in a large institution that used fraud awareness training. The co-workers saw this and still did not understand that they had a fraudster manager. Nonetheless it forced the Likeable Fraudster to own up, as he thought that his behaviour would become blatantly obvious. It is a bit like if I think of something hard enough that you will become aware of it, even this goes against our rational sides of our brain which tell us not to be so ridiculous. It seems to me that if staff were aware of the Arrogant and Likeable Fraudster typology awareness would set in earlier and management could intervene.

Other Preventative Methods

From the study there are other prevention strategies that become apparent, the least of which is to disseminate the study's findings.

FINANCIAL EDUCATION OF BUSINESS OWNERS

Financial training of small business owners was mentioned earlier and deserves attention. For any small business association, a short course after hours would educate owners to understand basic financial statements and computer controls. If the owner is instructed before they set up business, even better. Intending business owners are often forced to produce business plans to raise finance from banks. Why don't the same banks provide an advice session or two for those who are selected to receive funding to know about basic financial information and fraud prevention procedures? I think they will once they realise that lower rates of fraud protect their investment. However, banks do not seem to care as they always hold valuable assets against loans. For instance, most often a small business owner can only raise money through the equity of his home. If the banks have to foreclose due to non-payment they are in the privileged position, usually above all other creditors, to regain their investment.

SPOT AUDITS

Many organisations overlook the very easy preventative measure against fraud. I suspect it is to do with a skewed value of trust. This would be on the lines of 'If you trust me you would not have to look'. I have listened to the uproar of departmental and unit managers riling against internal auditors just doing their job. The value of trust, the core value, is revealed in this way: 'I know I can be trusted, you are welcome to look.' Some more enlightened department managers use it as an open day like parents reviewing work at their children's school, which encourages transparency and the real core value of trust.

Small businesses do not have internal audits, but almost all have an accountant or bookkeeper to produce their financial statements. Having quarterly or semi-annual reports is not going to scare a fraudster, but looking at their computer does. A smart small business operator should bring in his accountant on a random basis and have them go through data held on that computer. If the manager is using his own laptop, then disallow it immediately. That was exactly how one fraudster got away with stealing over a million dollars, by putting the data on his own machine. He then left the business to conduct his illegal transactions after hours. Computers these days are comparatively cheap, there is no need for a state of the art computer to chunk through a small business's information. If the accountant is not computer savvy, then find one who is: not being current with technology is a death knell of any accountant. Find one who can process the data quickly and efficiently, that is all that is required.

PRE-EMPLOYMENT SCREENING

This screening process takes place before entry into an organisation. Usually basic reference checking is done with at best a further check or two with people who know the candidate but are not listed as referees. In some jurisdictions pre-employment screening is mandatory for those joining financial services. Screening usually includes checks for criminal conviction, civil courts, two last employers (if not already done), education and present and previous residence checks.

For managers, basic screening should also include directorships, media checks for adverse reports, bankruptcy records, criminal convictions in other jurisdictions and so on. Some pre-employment screening companies can also look at financial probity, civil and criminal court cases, international terrorist and other watch lists, driving convictions, previous employments, identity verification, residential status, right to work status, residency, professional memberships and licences, corporate shareholdings and so on.

However, as good as this list is, it will still not catch the potential fraudster. Arrogant Fraudsters can build up their profiles with different names and bogus employments. One case that was studied in this investigation was a managerial fraudster who came to the business straight from prison. It is very easy these days to cook up Internet material about oneself, including fictitious information that looks authentic. Remember how good these people are at appearing more authentic than normal? Well, this will apply to their fictional self, the impression management that they want you to believe.

Fraudster Screening

Screening out fraudsters has to be taken one step further for the organisation that is serious about fraud prevention.

THE LIKEABLE FRAUDSTER

To weed out Likeable Fraudsters, a thorough examination of their past has to be undertaken. Examine all previous employments and check the real reasons for their exits. This will prevent taking in a wounded fraudster who is so nice that you would have to be heartless in not taking them on. A thorough review of life events, especially in their childhood, must be undertaken to see if there is trauma. As we have seen from this research, previous trauma is likely to detonate the potential for fraud. If say there is reason to suspect that there is potential for the manager to defraud, the organisation should consider making available therapeutic counselling. The caveat here is that the individual has to have the motivation to deal with past history in order for this to be effective. This can be criticised as being intrusive, but self-awareness is an important prerequisite for a Respectful Manager and as we have already seen, we tend to be blind to our dark side. Also a more ethical argument has to be raised: who else is going to assist the candidate to become not just a mediocre manager but a star? Training and team-building is just as intrusive and more than acceptable in most organisations, so why not preventative counselling?

There are horror stories of personal information being divulged in team-building exercises only to be abused later by other members and secrets become office gossip. The proposed counselling carries the protection of confidentiality so that others in the organisation would not obtain this information. And if the counselling meetings are after hours it is none of anyone's business, it is purely part of that individual's personal development. The organisation has to recognise its responsibility to their staff, after all they give one-third of their lives to their work and sometimes a good deal more. Likeable Fraudsters are indeed likeable and the organisation will find that they have a good hard working manager if, and only if, the issue of their trauma is dealt with effectively. In the meantime, use the candidate's skills to assist the business but there must be no access to funds until the all clear is given. If the potential Likeable Fraudster has access to individual therapeutic counselling, he knows that he has future access at any time. What is needed here is the avoidance of the build up of pressure for the individual. Good counselling provides a trusting relationship and if it is available at all times during the career path, a very good manager can excel.

Likeable Fraudsters have a penchant for gambling, and any whisper of betting should be taken seriously. The nay-sayers will frown upon the organisation being so paternalistic and intruding on personal lives. However, it is far better to quietly investigate the level of gambling. Alcoholics are extremely good at hiding their addiction and appear high-functioning: so it is with gamblers, so a soft approach is better than a confrontation. In fact, any manager with an addiction must have therapeutic support with no access to funds.

PREVENTING ARROGANT FRAUDSTERS

A different group to avoid hiring is of course the Arrogant Fraudster. A curious oddity about the managerial fraudsters who were in the study is that all circumvented the employment interview. If the organisation is under pressure to accept an incoming manager, he must be refused point blank. All managerial appointments must be made with the normal hiring process of written application to the duty statement, interview, reference checking, and if it is still part of the hiring process self-reporting psychological testing. All this can be overcome with a determined Arrogant Fraudster as they will lie their way through.

Sometimes a regulator of the industry, an administrator to avoid bankruptcy, or someone else with power over the organisation will pressure for a quick appointment. Stand firm and call an open competition with other candidates. If the desired manager decides to withdraw from a competitive hiring, take heart as the organisation may have saved itself from a huge fraud.

Remember that the Arrogant Fraudster is not going to appear flaky to anyone he has set his eyes on, and therein lies the danger. There are no warning signs – apart from what has been found in this investigation – and the organisation will be submitted to the gentle art of persuasion, self-promotion, lies and later outright bullying.

Ideally the best means to prevent an Arrogant Fraudster is to use a service that provides thorough evidence-based investigation into the person's past. This includes examining every past employment and reason for exit – the real reason, that is. Professional memberships and education are often overlooked for double-checking. I even investigate primary schools, the candidate's family and childhood to see if all the information given by the candidate is correct.

It is vital that this is undertaken. Skimping with this vital step is asking for trouble, particularly for access to finance functions. Key appointments have to have this type of investigation into every facet of that person's life. Many jurisdictions rely on a free press to vet public officials, for instance Presidents, Prime Ministers and so on. However, it is often too late after the individual is appointed.

Take that lesson and apply it to organisations and there will be seen to be many an inappropriate selection of CEO, chairman of the board, CFOs who lead organisations under their stewardship into disaster. At hiring, the Arrogant Fraudster and other undesirables are prevented from entry once an independent examination of their past reveals their lies.

Confronting a liar is hard work at the best of times and the only way is with irrefutable evidence. The Arrogant Fraudsters feel superior to all and will bully their way in if not stopped. That is why a solid hiring process is necessary, so that the more suitable applicant is hired. In a field of one the organisation can be cornered into accepting the brazen candidate in order to avoid lawsuits in public airspace among other bullying tactics.

PROMOTION AND PERFORMANCE REVIEWS

It is my belief that many Likeable Fraudsters who are working in financial institutions in particular should have a yearly audit on life events such as a death in the family and so on. A telling case about the effect of such events is that a judge remarked about a woman who stole A$20 million from her employer when events got on top of her. Apparently she had marriage problems, two autistic children and a stressful job.[3]

Installing a 360-degree survey on the manager in question is another tool to gather information that otherwise would elude the performance reviewer. These are so common these days that most managers will know about them and not be alarmed. Again it is imperative that staff must be free from identification and reprisal for this to work properly to evaluate the impression management that is being used. Any sign that the manager in question may be a fraudster must be checked immediately. Using promotion and annual performance reviews are excellent methods to ensure that fraudsters have not unwittingly been hired into the organisation. Prevention is far better than cure, having effective systems in place will prevent entry of predatory Arrogant Fraudsters and the unlucky Likeable Fraudsters who undergo unbearable emotional pressure to steal.

3 Sheridan, T.A., 2010. 'Delusional' Senior Accountant Causer stole $20M. Available at: http://executivefraudsters.com/category/likeable-fraudster/page/4/ (accessed 28 August 2010)

Chapter 11
Conclusion

Now we have come full circle to the question that I was originally confronted with: 'How can I trust that this manager is not going to harm an organisation?' The investigation has given a working methodology to analyse and identify the impression management that is being used by the manager in question. Once that is understood preventive measures can be put in place to avoid harm to the organisation.

Earlier I described two candidates at the beginning of the book. I had a choice between the eager character as opposed to the sleek film star. If I had the knowledge then of what I know now I could have confidently made a recommendation for hiring. The anxious applicant may have been using the Likeable Fraudster impression management and the handsome manager using impression management of the Arrogant Fraudster or they were neither and actually Respectful types. It is only on further and detailed investigation that the information can be elicited to make an informed decision.

Background Details

We now know that early trauma and maternal attachment profiles can cause severe stress that later explodes and turns a conscientious manager into a Likeable Fraudster. In addition what seems to be light-headed conceit from an expert with access to finance could actually be a serious warning signal.

Observing behaviour through previous co-workers can give the clues to the inconsistency of their behaviour with their little oddities, as well as their need to control through their arrogance. Different impression management strategies that are used to upper management, such as ingratiation and self-promotion, rather than those strategies used for subordinates, is another telling characteristic. Putting all these factors together we can say which manager is likely to defraud and which one is not.

Inconsistencies

As hard as they try, the fraudster managers are forced over time to use inconsistent impression management. They adopt a camouflage of Respectful (Consistent Benign) executive impression management to their co-workers. In addition it was the perceived power relationship from the fraudsters' disguised impression management which enabled the development of the two fraudster types. That is the Superior 'power over' used by the Arrogant Fraudsters and the Inferior 'power under' (for instance manipulation) used by the Likeable Fraudster

It was found that for recipients of fraudster impression management, it was the small lapses in consistency demanded by the long-term usage of the fraudsters' disguise as a manager exuding Respectful (consistent and benign,) impression management were the only indicator of an executive fraudster at work. These slip-ups were never seen as possible fraud indicators because they appeared only odd or idiosyncratic and were accepted as part of that manager's behaviour. However, an inconsistency is one of the key variables in understanding that this could be highly dangerous to the organisation. A manager who is known for telling a lie or two is not one to trust: it is only a Respectful manager who will avoid lying at all costs.

Abuse of Power

The workplace distorts the normal impression management process as described by Goffman, through invested power conferred upon managers by their status in the organisation. Therefore fraudster managers were able to hold power over their subordinates. Similarly they held power upwards too over their line management and boards of directors, by using expert power and the impression management strategies of self-promotion and sometimes ingratiation.

Morality and Authenticity

Attributions of morality and authenticity were studied and it was found that fraudsters in particular traded in trust – the foundation of authenticity. The disguised impression management engendered trust so well that it lasted for many years in some cases, resulting in shock and disbelief by the co-workers when the disguise was shattered at the moment of discovery of the fraud.

Goffman's prediction of the individual's true character being revealed in a moment of crisis was borne out by the witnessing of the moment of discovery of the fraud where flashes of fear were apparent, indicating the fraudsters' weak characters. However, for the co-workers the unfolding of the fraud left them with emotional harm, which resulted in most staff leaving the workplace and sometimes even changing careers.

The prominent fraud theories were also investigated by using a semi-structured interview and there was some indication that the fraudsters traded on authenticity more than the non-fraudsters. The fraudster managers were also difficult to detect in their impression management, particularly as the Red Flags seemed relevant for other managers using inconsistent malevolent impression management, not just fraudsters. Hence the difficulty in detection as non-fraudsters triggered these indicators as well as fraudster managers.

Theory Does Count

This new bit of theory only came about through asking the manager's co-workers to tell their stories. Incredibly no-one has done this before, yet this is intuitive to me as most fraudsters will lie to convince others of their innocence. Also I used qualitative methods to analyse and coalesce data. Few crime researchers use qualitative methods, even now with the advent of acceptance of this type of research. However, with my past education in social science, I had come to realise the limitations of quantitative methodology and I had confidence that the method would work. Having a management background in small business as well as large organisations and non-profits was able to put me into a good position to take a macro view of a micro process which is part and parcel of social interaction in the workplace.

Sociologists have long taken the lead creating theory for white-collar crime in general, and for fraud in particular, notably Sutherland and Cressey. In this investigation Goffman's impression management theory was used to explore the different behaviours that are committed by managerial fraudsters by understanding the illusory mechanism that was layered over the real managerial behaviour. It was found that there were two types of impression management: the Arrogant and the Likeable Fraudster. The honest Respectful impression management was accepted and reciprocated by a happy staff willing to work with a manager who was consistent, egalitarian and open. However, those 'Respectful' managers, who were meeting their own financial needs and not organisational goals with lapses in their impression management, are not to be trusted. Co-workers reported damage to their self-esteem and lack of trust after working with managerial fraudsters. Self-serving managers are difficult enough to deal with, but stealing coupled with an impression management illusion of honesty from the fraudsters has far worse consequences for the business itself, the business owners, board members and individual staff.

This new piece of the jigsaw regarding managerial fraud is due solely to Goffman's insights and intuition by inspecting exceptions to his theory of impression management. If this study had not focused on impression management and the collective voice of the co-workers, the findings of consistency and power as the basis of Executive Impression Management would have not been found as quickly or indeed at all. It must be said that any value of this study to our collective understanding is directly attributable to Erving Goffman and his awe-inspiring work, without which the study could not have occurred.

We now have a powerful new typology to identify managerial fraudsters based on the robust, effective and predictive impression management theory. It unifies previous paradoxical information from the Red Flag personal characteristics and other traits generated from the psychological literature. This makes it far easier to spot the fraudsters in an organisation and has improved pre-employment screening considerably. A firm closed door is the best and only way to prevent fraudsters entering the organisation.

Bibliography

Agnew, Robert. 1994. The techniques of neutralization and violence. *Criminology* 32 (4): 555–606.

Akers, Ronald L. 1990. Rational choice, deterrence and social learning theory in criminology: the path not taken. *The Journal of Criminal Law and Criminology* 81 (3): 653–676.

Albanese, J. S. 2008. White collar crimes and casino gambling: looking for empirical links to forgery, embezzlement, and fraud. *Crime Law and Social Change* 49 (5): 333–347.

Albrecht, W. Steve, Conan C. Albrecht, and Chad O. Albrecht. 2004. Fraud and corporate executives: agency, stewardship and broken trust. *Journal of Forensic Accounting* 5 (1): 109–124.

Albrecht, C. C., W. S. Albrecht, and J. G. Dunn. 2001. Can auditors detect fraud: a review of the research evidence. *Journal of Forensic Accounting* 2 (1): 1–12.

American Institute of Certified Public Accountants Inc. 2002. *Appendix to SAS No. 99, fraud risk factors*. American Institute of Certified Public Accountants, Inc. http://fvs.aicpa.org.

American Psychiatric Association. 2013. *Diagnostic and statistical manual of mental disorders*, 5th edn. Arlington, VA: American Psychiatric Publishing.

Anon. 1990. Wassendorf, Ida obituary *Cedar Rapids Gazette*, 25 July 1990.

Apostolou, Nicholas, and Larry D. Crumbley. 2008. Auditors' responsibilities with respect to fraud: a possible shift? *The CPA Journal* 78 (2): 32–37.

Ashforth, B. E., and V. Anand. 2003. The normalization of corruption in organizations. *Research in Organizational Behavior* 25: 1–52.

Association of Certified Fraud Examiners. 2006. *Report to the nation on occupational fraud and abuse*. Austin, TX: Association of Certified Fraud Examiners Inc.

Association of Certified Fraud Examiners. 2008. *Fraud check up*. Austin, TX: Association of Certified Fraud Examiners.

Association of Certified Fraud Examiners. 2010. *Report to the nations on occupational fraud and abuse*. Austin TX: Association of Certified Fraud Examiners Inc.

Argyris, C., and D. A. Schon. 1974. *Theory in practice: increasing professional effectiveness*. San Francisco, CA: Jossey-Bass.

Argyris, C. 1980. Making the undiscussable and its' undiscussability discussable. *Public Administration Review* 40 (3): 205–213.

Australian Institute of Criminology and PriceWaterhouseCoopers. 2003. *Serious fraud in Australia and New Zealand.* Canberra: Australian Institute of Criminology.

Australian Institute of Criminology. 2004. *Crimes against business: a review of victimisation, predictors and prevention*. Canberra: Australian Institute of Criminology.

Australian Institute of Criminology. 2008. Gambling motivated fraud in Australia: who, why and how. In *AIC Crime Reduction Matters*, No. 72, 19 September 2008. Canberra: Australian Institute of Criminology.

Avolio, B. J., and B. M. Bass. 1999. Re-examining the components of transformational and transactional leadership using the Multifactor Leadership Questionnaire. *Journal of Occupational & Organizational Psychology* 72 (4): 441–462.

Avolio, B. J., W. L. Gardner, F. O. Walumbwa, F. Luthans, and D. R. May. 2004. Unlocking the mask: a look at the process by which authentic leaders impact follower attitudes and behaviors. *The Leadership Quarterly* 15 (6): 801–823.

Babiak, Paul, and Robert D. Hare. 2007. *Snakes in suits*. New York: Harper Collins.

Bandura, Albert. 2002. Selective moral disengagement in the exercise of moral agency. *Journal of Moral Education* 31 (2): 101–119.

Bandura, Albert, Gian Vittorio Caprara, Claudio Barbaranelli, Concetta Pastorelli, and Camillo Regalia. 2001. Sociocognitive self-regulatory mechanisms governing transgressive behavior. *Journal of Personality and Social Psychology* 80 (1): 125–135.

Barboza, David. 2002. *Enron's many strands: Fallen Star;From Enron Fast Track to total derailment*. Available at: http://www.nytimes.com/2002/10/03/business/enron-s-many-strands-fallen-star-from-enron-fast-track-to-total-derailment.html. (accessed 8 November 2011)

Bartram, D. 2004. Assessment in organizations. *Applied Psychology: An International Review* 53 (2): 237–259.

Bass, B. M., and P. Steidmeier. 1999. Ethics, character, and authentic transformational leadership behaviour. *The Leadership Quarterly* 10 (2): 181–217.

Baucus, Melissa S. 1994. Pressure, opportunity and predisposition: a multivariate model of corporate of corporate illegality. *Journal of Management* 20 (4): 699–721.

Baumeister, R. F. 1982. A self-presentational view of social phenomena. *Psychological Bulletin* 91 (1): 3–26.

Baumeister, R. F., E. Bratslavsky, C. Finkenauer, and K. Vohs. 2001. Bad is stronger than good. *Review of General Psychology* 5 (4): 323–370.

BBC. World News. Sunday 27 January, 2002. Enron's J. Clifford Baxter: A profile. http: //news.bbc.co.uk/2/hi/business/1784945.stm (accessed 22 December 2013).

BDO International. 2008. *BDO not-for-profit fraud survey 2008*. http://www.bdo.com.au/services/forensic-accounting/resources/not-for-profit_fraud_survey_2008 (accessed 18 March 2009).

Becker, D'Arcy, Janice Connolly, Paula Lentz, and Joline Morrison. 2006. Using the business fraud triangle to predict academic dishonesty among business students. *Academy of Educational Leadership* 10 (1): 37–54.

Block, L. 2003. The leadership–culture connection: an exploratory investigation. *Leadership and Organization Development Journal* 24 (5/6): 318–335.

Bok, Sissela. 1978. *Lying: moral choice in public and private life*. New York: Vintage Books.

Boslego, J. 2005. Engineering social trust. *Harvard International Review* 27 (1): 28–32.

Bowlby, J. 1979. *The making and breaking of affectional bonds*. London: Tavistock.

Brinkmann, Johannes. 2001. On business ethics and moralism. *Business Ethics: A European Review* 10 (4): 311–319.

Brottman, Mikita. 2009. The company man: a case of white-collar crime. *American Journal of Psychoanalysis* 69 (2): 121–135.

Broughton, T. A. 1995. Some notes on the art of lying. In *The best writing on writing*, ed. J. Heffron, 1–14. New York: Story Press.

Brown, D. K. 2003. Goffman's dramaturgical sociology: developing a meaningful theoretical context and exercise involving 'embarrassment and social organization'. *Teaching Sociology* 31 (3): 288–299.

Brown, M. E., L. K. Treviño, and D. A. Harrison. 2005. Ethical leadership: a social learning perspective for construct development and testing. *Organizational Behavior and Human Decision Processes* 97 (2): 117–134.

Bucy, P. H., E. P. Formby, M. S. Raspanti, and K. E. Rooney. 2008. Why do they do it? *St John's Law Review* 82 (2): 401–571.

Burger, Jerry M., and Harris M. Cooper. 1979. The desirability of control. *Motivation and Emotion* 3 (4): 381–393.

Burns, J. M. 1978. *Leadership*. New York: Harper and Row.

Bytestart Ltd. 2005. *Small company fraud – how to spot a fraudster!* http://www.bytestart.co.uk/content/news/1_12/small-company-fraud.shtml (accessed 16 November 2009).

Calhoun, G. M. 1924. The jurisprudence of the Greek city. *Columbia Law Review* 24 (2): 154–171.

Cannell, C. F., and R. L. Kahn. 1953. The collection of data by interviewing. In *Research methods in the behavioral sciences*, ed. L. Festinger and D. Katz, 327–380. New York: Dryden Press.

Carr, A. Z. 1968. Is business bluffing unethical? *Harvard Business Review* 46 (1): 143–153.

Chang, Howard, and David S. Evans. 2008. Has the pendulum swung too far? *Regulation* 30 (4): 48–53.

Chang, J. J. S. 2008. An analysis of advance fee fraud on the internet. *Journal of Financial Crime* 15 (1): 71–81. 10.1108/13590790810841716

Chartered Institute of Personnel and Development, and Credit Industry Fraud Avoidance System CIFAS. 2007. *Tackling staff fraud and dishonesty: managing and mitigating the risks.* London: Chartered Institute of Personnel and Development.

Childers, D. 2009. Tapping into tips. *The Internal Auditor* 66 (6): 29–32.

Chriss, J. J. 1995. Habermas, Goffman, and communicative action: implications for professional practice. *American Sociological Review* 60 (4): 545–566.

Clark, T., and G. Salaman. 1998. Creating the 'right' impression: towards a dramaturgy of management consultancy. *The Service Industries Journal* 18 (1): 18–38.

Clarke, John. 2005. *Working with monsters: how to identify and protect yourself from the workplace psychopath.* Sydney: Random House.

Clegg, S. R., M. Kornberger, C. Carter, and C. Rhodes. 2006. For management? *Management Learning* 37 (1): 7–27.

Choo, Freddie, and Kim Tan. 2007. An 'American Dream' theory of corporate executive fraud. *Accounting Forum (Adelaide)* 31 (2): 203–215.

Cohen, J. R., Y. Ding, C. Lesage, and H. Stolowy. 2008. The role of manager's behaviour in corporate fraud. *Social Science Research Network,* http://www.knowledgeleader.com/KnowledgeLeader/Content.nsf/Web+Content/ChecklistsGuidesFraudRedFlags!OpenDocument#Understanding (accessed 29 March 2009).

Coleman, James William. 1987. Toward an integrated theory of white-collar crime. *The American Journal of Sociology* 93 (2): 406–439.

Collins, Judith M., and Frank L. Schmidt. 1993. Personality, integrity, and white collar crime: a construct validity study. *Personnel Psychology* 46 (2): 295–311.

Collins, R. 1986. The passing of intellectual generations: reflections on the death of Erving Goffman. *Sociological Theory* 4 (1): 106–113.

Collinson, D. 2006. Rethinking followership: a post-structuralist analysis of follower identities. *The Leadership Quarterly* 17 (2): 179–189.

Conger, J. A. 1990. The dark side of leadership. *Organizational Dynamics* 19 (2): 44–56.

Cooper, Kathie, and Henmant Deo. 2005. Recurring cycle of Australian corporate reforms: 'a never ending story'. *Journal of American Academy of Business, Cambridge* 7 (2): 156–163.

Coram, P., C. Ferguson, and R. Moroney. 2008. Internal audit, alternative internal audit structures and the level of misappropriation of assets fraud. *Accounting & Finance* 48 (4): 543–559.

Credit Industry Fraud Avoidance System (CIFAS). *Employee fraud – the enemy within*. Credit Industry Fraud Avoidance System, 2004, cited 23 February 2009. Available from http: //www.cifas.org.uk/default.asp?edit_id=579-57.

Cressey, D. 1973. *Other people's money: a study in the social psychology of embezzlement*. Montclair, NJ: Patterson-Smith.

Cullen, Francis T., Jennifer L. Hartman, and Cheryl Lero Jonson. 2009. Bad guys: why the public supports punishing white-collar offenders. *Crime Law and Social Change* 51 (1): 31–44.

Dasborough, M. T., N. M. Ashkanasy, E. Y. J. Tee, and H. H. M. Tse. 2009. What goes around comes around: how meso-level negative emotional contagion can ultimately determine organizational attitudes toward leaders. *The Leadership Quarterly* 20 (4): 571–585.

Davis, Stephen Harvard. 2005. Should a 60 per cent success rate be acceptable? *Industrial and Commercial Training* 37 (6/7): 331–336.

De Hoogh, A. H. B., and D. N. D. Hartog. 2008. Ethical and despotic leadership, relationships with leader's social responsibility, top management team effectiveness and subordinates' optimism: a multi-method study. *The Leadership Quarterly* 19 (3): 297–311.

Delgado-García, J. B., J. M. d. l. Fuente-Sabaté, and E. d. Quevedo-Puente. 2010. Too negative to take risks? The effect of the CEO's emotional traits on firm risk. *British Journal of Management* 21 (2): 313–326.

Dodge, M., and G. Geis. 2009. Social and political transformations in white-collar crime scholarship: introductory notes. *Crime Law and Social Change* 51 (1): 1–3.

Doidge, Norman. 2007. *The brain that changes itself*. New York: Viking/Penguin Group (USA) Inc.

Dozier, J. B., and M. P. Miceli. 1985. Potential predictors of whistle-blowing: a prosocial behaviour perspective. *Academy of Management Review* 10 (4): 823–836.

Drucker, P. F. 1999. *Management challenges for the 21st century*. Oxford: Butterworth-Heinemann.

Duffield, Grace, and Peter Grabosky. 2001. The psychology of fraud. In *Trends and issues in crime and criminal justice*. Canberra: Australian Government, Australian Institute of Criminology.

Einarsen, S. 1999. The nature and causes of bullying at work. *International Journal of Manpower* 20 (1–2): 16– 28.

Einarsen, S., M. S. Aasland, and A. Skogstad. 2007. Destructive leadership behaviour: a definition and conceptual model. *The Leadership Quarterly* 18 (3): 207–216.

Elangovan, A. R., and J. L. Xie. 2000. Effects of perceived power of supervisor on subordinate work attitudes. *Leadership & Organization Development Journal* 21 (6): 319–328.

Elias, S. 2008. Fifty years of influence in the workplace: the evolution of the French and Raven power taxonomy. *Journal of Management History* 14 (3): 267–283.

Emerson, R. M. 1976. Social exchange theory. *Annual Review of Sociology* 2: 335–363.

Ernst and Young. 2003. *Fraud, the unmanaged risk, 8th global survey*, edited by M. Savage. Ernst and Young South Africa.

Etzioni, A. 1968. Basic human needs, alienation and inauthenticity. *American Sociological Review* 33 (4): 870–885.

Feng Lui, Sally Maitlis 2014. Emotional dynamics and strategizing processes: a study of strategic conversations in top team meetings. *Journal of Management Studies* Special Issue: Strategy as Discourse: Its Significance, Challenges and Future Directions 51 (2): 202–234.

Fisher, J. E. 1977. Playing favorites in large organizations. *Business Horizons* 20 (3): 68–74.

Fleming, P., and S. Zyglidopoulos. 2008. The escalation of deception in organizations. *Journal of Business Ethics* 81 (4): 837–850.

Flesher, D. L. 1999. Attitudes toward whistle-blowing hotlines. *National Forum* 79 (2): 5–7.

French, J. R. P., and B. H. Raven. 1960. The bases of social power. In *Group dynamics: research and theory*, ed. D. Cartwright and A. Zander, 607–623. Evanston IL: Harper and Row.

Friedrichs, D. 2004. Enron et al.: paradigmatic white collar crime cases for the new century. *Critical Criminology* 12 (2): 113–132.

Gardner, W. L. 1992. Lessons in organizational dramaturgy: the art of impression management. *Organizational Dynamics* 21 (1): 33–46.

Gardner, W. L., and B. J. Avolio. 1998. The charismatic relationship: a dramaturgical perspective. *Academy of Management Review* 23 (1): 32–58.

Gardner, W. L., and M. J. Martinko. 1988. Impression management: an observational study linking audience characteristics with verbal self-presentations. *Academy of Management Journal* 31 (1): 42–65.

Geis, Gilbert. 2000. On the absence of self-control as the basis for a general theory of crime: a critique. *Theoretical Criminology* 4 (1): 35–53.

Geller, E. S. 1999. Interpersonal trust. *Professional Safety* 44 (4): 16–20.

Ghosh, D. 2008. Corporate values, workplace decisions and ethical standards of employees. *Journal of Management Issues* 20 (1): 68–87.

Ghoshal, Sumantra. 2005. Bad management theories are destroying good management practices. *Academy of Management Learning and Education* 4 (1): 75–91.

Giacalone, Robert A., and Paul Rosenfeld, eds. 1991. *Applied impression management: how image-making affects managerial decisions*. Newbury Park, CA: Sage.

Gibeaut, J. 2007. Mortgage fund mess. *ABA Journal* 93: 50–57.

Giddens, Anthony. 1972. *Emile Durkheim: selected writings*. London: Cambridge University Press.

Gilmore, D. C., and G. R. Ferris. 1989. The effects of applicant impression management tactics on interviewer judgments. *Journal of Management* 15 (4): 557–564.

Gini, A. 1997. Moral leadership: an overview. *Journal of Business Ethics* 16 (3): 323–336.

Ginzel, L. E., R. M. Kramer, and R. I. Sutton. 1992. Organizational impression management as a reciprocal influence process: the neglected role of the organizational audience. *Research in Organizational Behaviour* 15: 227–266.

Gioia, D. 1983. Perceptions of managerial power as a consequence of managerial behavior and reputation. *Journal of Management* 9 (1): 7–27.

Glaser, B. G., and A. Strauss. 1967. *The discovery of grounded theory*. Chicago, IL: Aldine Publishing Co.

Goffee, R., and G. Jones. 2005. Managing authenticity. *Harvard Business Review* 83 (12): 86–94.

Goffman, E. 1952. On cooling the mark out. *Psychiatry: Journal of Interpersonal Relations* 15 (4): 451–463. http://www.ncbi.nlm.nih.gov/pubmed/13014214 (accessed 4 February 2011).

Goffman, E. 1959. *The presentation of self in everyday life*. New York: Anchor Books, Doubleday.

Goffman, E. 1962. *Asylums : Essays on the social situation of mental patients and other inmates*. Chicago, IL: Aldine.

Goffman, E. 1967. *Interaction ritual: essays on face-to-face behavior*. New York: Pantheon Books. Original edition, 1967.

Goffman, E. 1974. *Frame analysis, an essay on the organization of experience*. Boston, MA: University Press of New England. Original edition, 1974.

Goleman, Daniel. 1995. *Emotional intelligence: why it can matter more than IQ*. New York: Bantam Books.

Grabosky, P., and G. Duffield. 2001. *Red flags of fraud*. Canberra: Australian Government, Australian Institute of Criminology.

Graycar, Adam, and Russell Smith. 2002. *Identifying and responding to corporate fraud*. Canberra: Australian Institute of Criminology.

Greenberg, J., C. E. Ashton-James, and N. M. Ashkanasy. 2007. Social comparison processes in organizations. *Organizational Behavior and Human Decision Processes* 102 (1): 22–41.

Greener, I. 2006. Nick Leeson and the collapse of Barings Bank: socio-technical networks and the 'rogue trader'. *Organization* 13 (3): 421–442.

Grover, S. L. 1993. Lying, deceit, and subterfuge: a model of dishonesty in the workplace. *Organization Science* 4 (3): 478–495.

Guadagno, R., and R. Cialdini. 2007. Gender differences in impression management in organizations: a qualitative review. *Sex Roles* 56 (7–8): 483–494.

Guy, C. William. 2001. Eroding ethics of executive search. *Consulting to Management* 12 (3): 51–57.

Hansen, Laura L. 2009. Corporate financial crime: social diagnosis and treatment. *Journal of Financial Crime* 16 (1): 28–40.

Harrell, W. Andrew, and Timothy Hartnagel. 1976. The impact of Machiavellianism and the trustfulness of the victim on laboratory theft. *Sociometry* 39 (2): 157–165.

Hayes, H., and T. Prenzler. 2003. *Profiling fraudsters: a Queensland case study in fraudster crime: final report to Crime Prevention Queensland.* Brisbane: Griffith University.

Heath, Joseph. 2008. Business ethics and moral motivation: a criminological perspective. *Journal of Business Ethics* 83 (4): 595–614.

Heaven, Patrick C. L., and Michael Virgen. 2001. Personality, perceptions of family and peer influences, and males' self-reported delinquency. *Personality and Individual Differences* 30 (2): 321–331.

Higgs, Malcolm. 2009. The good, the bad and the ugly: leadership and narcissism. *Journal of Change Management* 9 (2): 165.

Higson, A. 2002. *Indications of fraud in SMEs.* London: Fraud Advisory Panel. http://www.fraudadvisorypanel.org/newsite/Publications/Publications_research.htm (accessed 31 August 2009).

Hirschi, Travis, and Michael R. Gottfredson. 2000. In defense of self-control. *Theoretical Criminology* 4 (1): 55–69.

Hochhauser, Mark. 2004. Smart executives, dumb decisions. *Risk Management* 51 (9): 64–65.

Hooks, K. L., S. E. Kaplan, J. J. Schultz, and L. A. Ponemon. 1994. Enhancing communication to assist in fraud prevention and detection. Comment: whistle-blowing as an internal control mechanism: Individual and organizational considerations. *Auditing* 13 (2): 86–131.

Horowitz, I. L. 1962. Consensus, conflict and cooperation: a sociological inventory. *Social Forces* 41 (2): 177–188.

House, Robert J. , and Jane M. Howell. 1992. Personality and charismatic leadership. *The Leadership Quarterly* 3 (2): 81–108.

Huffstutter, P.J., Ann Saphir, Tom Polansek and David Sheppard, 24 September 2012, Special Report: Iowa broker built empire on a lie concealed in a postal box Reuters. Available at http://uk.reuters.com/article/2012/09/24/us-wasendorf-life-one-idUSBRE88N0EJ20120924 (accessed 1 February 2013).

Ilies, R., F. P. Morgeson, and J. D. Nahrgang. 2005. Authentic leadership and eudaemonic well-being: understanding leader–follower outcomes. *The Leadership Quarterly* 16 (3): 373–394.

Jayakody, J. A. S. K. 2008. Charisma as a cognitive-affective phenomenon: a follower-centric approach. *Management Decision* 46 (6): 832–845.

Jernigan III, I. E., and J. M. Beggs. 2005. An examination of satisfaction with my supervisor and organizational commitment. *Journal of Applied Social Psychology* 35 (10): 2171–2192.

Johnson, A. 1995. *The Blackwell dictionary of sociology: a user's guide to sociological language.* Cambridge, MA: Blackwell.

Johnson, L. R., and H. R. Rudolph. 2008. Prevent large cash losses from small business fraud. *Journal of Corporate Accounting & Finance* 20 (1): 37–44.

Johnstone, P. 1998. Serious white collar fraud: historical and contemporary perspectives. *Crime Law and Social Change* 30 (2): 107–130.

Jones, E. E., and T. S. Pittman. 1982. Toward a general theory of strategic self-presentation. In *Psychological Perspectives on the Self*, ed. J. Suls, 231–262. Hillsdale, NJ: Lawrence Erlbaum Associates.

Jung, Carl Gustav. 2009. *Liber Novus (The New Book)*. Translated by J. P. Mark Kyburz and Sonu Shamdasani. Philemon Foundation and W.W. Norton & Co.

Kernis, M. H. 2003. Optimal self-esteem and authenticity: separating fantasy from reality. *Psychological Inquiry* 14 (1): 83–89.

Kets de Vries, Manfred F. R. 1989. Leaders who self-destruct: the causes and cures. *Organizational Dynamics* 17 (4): 5–17.

Khatri, N., and E. W. K. Tsang. 2003. Antecedents and consequences of cronyism in organizations. *Journal of Business Ethics* 43 (4): 289–303.

Konovsky, M. A., and F. Jaster. 1989. 'Blaming the victim' and other ways business men and women account for questionable behaviour. *Journal of Business Ethics* 8 (5): 391–398.

KPMG Forensic. 2007. *Profile of a fraudster survey*. London: KPMG Forensic. www.kpmg.co.uk/pubs/ProfileofaFraudsterSurvey(web).pdf

KPMG Forensic. 2009. *Fraud survey 2008*. Sydney: KPMG. www.kpmg.com.au (accessed 18 March 2009).

Krambia-Kapardis, Maria. 2002. A fraud detection model: a must for auditors. *Journal of Financial Regulation and Compliance* 10 (3): 266–279.

Lacroix, W. L. 1976. *Principles for ethics in business*. Lanham, Maryland: University Press of America.

LaSalle, Randall E. 2007. Effects of the fraud triangle on students' risk assessments. *Journal of Accounting Education* 25 (1–2): 74–87.

Leary, M. R., and R. M. Kowalski. 1990. Impression management: a literature review and two-component model. *Psychological Bulletin* 107 (1): 34–47.

Lee, R. M., and C. M. Renzetti. 1990. The problems of researching sensitive topics: AN overview and introduction. *American Behavioral Scientist* 33 (5): 510–528.

Levi, Michael. 1988. The prevention of fraud. In *Crime Prevention Unit: Paper 17*, edited by K. Heal. London: Home Office Crime Prevention Unit. Available online at: http://collection.europarchive.org/tna/20080205132101/homeoffice.gov.uk/rds/prgpdfs/fcpu17.pdf (Accessed 14 July 2009).

Levi, M. 2006. The media construction of financial white-collar crimes. *The British Journal of Criminology* 46 (6): 1037–1057.

Levi, M., J. Burrows, M. H. Fleming, and K. Matthews. 2007. *The nature, extent and economic impact of fraud in the UK*. London: Association of Chief Police Officers.

Levi, Michael, and John Burrows. 2008. Measuring the impact of fraud in the UK. *The British Journal of Criminology* 48 (3): 293–318.

Livingstone Smith, D. 2007. *Why we lie: the evolutionary roots of deception and the unconscious mind*. New York: St Martin's Griffin.

Liu Feng, and Sally Maitlis 2013. Emotional dynamics and strategizing processes: a study of strategic conversations in top team meetings. *Journal of Management Studies* Forthcoming in *Journal of Management Studies* Special Issue on Discourse and Strategizing.

Locke, Edwin A. 2005. Why emotional intelligence is an invalid concept. *Journal of Organizational Behavior* 26 (4): 425–431.

Locke, E. A., and J. Woiceshyn. 1995. Why businessmen should be honest: the argument from rational egoism. *Journal of Organizational Behavior* 16 (5): 405–414.

Ben Martin, Nick Allen, Peter Allen and Henry Samuel, 2008, Rogue trader in police custody in France, *The Daily Telegraph*. Available at: http://www.telegraph.co.uk/news/uknews/1576621/Rogue-trader-in-police-custody-in-France.html (accessed 13 October 2010).

McCarthy, D., S. M. Puffer, R. C. May, D. E. Ledgerwood, and W. H. Stewart. 2008. Overcoming resistance to change in Russian organizations: the legacy of transactional leadership. *Organizational Dynamics* 37 (3): 221–235.

McHoskey, J. W. 2001. Machiavellianism and personality dysfunction. *Personality and Individual Differences* 31 (5): 791–798.

McKay, P. F., D. R. Avery, and M. A. Morris. 2009. A tale of two climates: diversity climate from subordinates' and managers' perspectives and role performance in store unit sales performance. *Personnel Psychology* 62 (4): 767–791.

Mangham, I. 1990. Managing as a performing art. *British Journal of Management* 1 (2): 105–115.

Manning, P. 1992. *Erving Goffman and modern sociology*. Stanford, CA: Stanford University Press.

Mayo Clinic. 2013. *Post traumatic stress disorder*. Mayo Clinic 2013, cited October. Available from http://www.mayoclinic.com/health/post-traumatic-stress-disorder/DS00246.

Merton, Robert K. 1938. Social structure and anomie. *American Sociological Review* 3 (5): 672–682.

Merton, R. K. 1968. *Social theory and social structure*, enlarged edn. New York: Free Press.

Mills, Charles Wright. 1959. *The power elite*. New York: Oxford University Press.

Mintzberg, H. 2004. *Managers not MBAs: a hard look at the soft practice of managing and management development*. San Francisco, CA: Berrett-Koehler.

Morse, Gardiner. 2004. Executive psychopaths. *Harvard Business Review* 82 (10): 20–22.

Murphy, Daniel S., and Mathew B. Robinson. 2008. The maximiser: clarifying Merton's theories of anomie and strain. *Theoretical Criminology* 12 (4): 501–521.

Myers, Isabel Briggs with Peter B. Myers. 1980, 1995. *Gifts differing: understanding personality type.* Mountain View, CA: Davies-Black Publishing.

Norman, S. M., B. J. Avolio, and F. Luthans. 2010. The impact of positivity and transparency on trust in leaders and their perceived effectiveness. *The Leadership Quarterly* 21 (3): 350–364.

Norris, D. B. 2001. The unreasonable and arbitrary manager. *Consulting to Management* 12 (3): 35–36.

O'Connor, P. 2006. Young people's constructions of the self: late modern elements and gender differences. *Sociology* 40 (1): 107–124.

Parry, K. W. 1998. Grounded theory and social process: a new direction for leadership research. *The Leadership Quarterly* 9 (1): 85–105.

Paulhus, Delroy L., and Kevin M. WIlliams. 2002. The dark triad of personality: narcissism, Machiavllianism and psychopathy. *Journal of Research in Personality* 36 (6): 556–563.

Pelletier, K., and M. Bligh. 2008. The aftermath of organizational corruption: employee attributions and emotional reactions. *Journal of Business Ethics* 80 (4): 823–844.

Peltier-Rivest, Dominic. 2009. An analysis of the victims of occupational fraud: a Canadian perspective. *Journal of Financial Crime: A Canadian perspective* 16 (1): 60–67.

Peterson, B. K., and T. H. Gibson. 2003. Student health services: a case of employee fraud. *Journal of Accounting Education* 21 (1): 61–73.

Perrone, Santina. 2000. Crimes against small business in Australia: a preliminary analysis, 184. In *Trends & Issues in Crime and Criminal Justice*. Canberra: Australian Institute of Criminology.

Peterson, B. K., and T. H. Gibson. 2003. Student health services: a case of employee fraud. *Journal of Accounting Education* 21 (1): 61–73.

Peeters, H., and F. Lievens. 2006. Verbal and nonverbal impression management tactics in behavior description and situational interviews. *International Journal of Selection and Assessment* 14 (3): 206–222.

Pincus, K. 1989. The efficacy of a red flags questionnaire for assessing the possibility of fraud. *Accounting, Organizations and Society* 14 (1/2): 153–163.

Piquero, Nicole Leeper, and Alex Piquero. 2006. Control balance theory and exploitative crime. *Criminology* 44 (2): 397–430.

Prama, Gede. 2013. *Songs of Compassion,* cited 30 July 2013. Available from http: //gedepramascompassion.com/author/gedepramacompassion/.

Protiviti. 2000. *Fraud detection: red flags*. http://www.knowledgeleader.com/KnowledgeLeader/Content.nsf/Web+Content/ChecklistsGuidesFraudRedFlags!OpenDocument#Understanding (accessed 29 March 2009).

Ramamoorti, S. 2008. The psychology and sociology of fraud: integrating the behavioral sciences component into fraud and forensic accounting curricula. *Issues in Accounting Education* 23 (4): 521–533.

Rand, A. 1957. *Atlas shrugged*. New York: Random House.

Raven, B. H. 1993. The bases of power: origins and recent developments. *Journal of Social Issues* 49 (4): 227–251.

Richards, Lori. 2008. Why does fraud occur and what can deter or prevent it? In *Southwest Securities Enforcement Conference*. Fort Worth, Tx: U.S. Securities and Exchange Commission. Available online at http://www.sec.gov/news/speech/2008/spch090908lar.htm (Accessed 10 March 2009).

Riordan, Catherine A., Marsha K. James, and Michael J. Runzi. 1989. Explaining failures at work: an accounter's dilemma. *Journal of General Psychology* 116 (2): 197–205.

Romney, M. B., W. S. Albrecht, and D. J. Cherrington. 1980a. Auditors and the detection of fraud. *Journal of Accountancy* 149 (5): 63–69.

Romney, M. B., W. S. Albrecht, and D. J. Cherrington. 1980b. Red-flagging the white collar criminal; potential fraud situations have common characteristics, according to a survey of published cases, which can be used as early warning signals to prevent actual acts. *Management Accounting* 61 (9): 51–56.

Rosenfeld, P., and R. A. Giacalone. 1991. From extreme to mainstream: applied impression management in organizations. In *Applied impression management*, ed. R. A. Giacalone and P. Rosenfeld, Newbury Park, CA: Sage.

Rozell, E. J., and D. E. Gundersen. 2003. The effects of leader impression management on group perceptions of cohesion, consensus, and communication. *Small Group Research* 34 (2): 197–223.

Russell, Stuart. 2002. The continuing relevance of Marxism to critical criminology. *Critical Criminology* 11 (2): 113–135.

Russell, Roger. 2002. Small businesses still see CPA as most trusted advisor. *Accounting Today* 16 (12): 5–7.

Ryan, L. V. 2000. Moral aspects of executive leadership. *International Journal of Value-Based Management* 13: 109–122.

Sakurai, Yuka, and Russell G. Smith. 2003. Gambling as a motivation for the commission of financial crime. In *Trends and issues in crime and criminal justice, no. 256*. Canberra: Australian Institute of Criminology.

Sanders, K., L. Dorenbosch, and R. De Reuver. 2008. The impact of individual and shared employee perceptions of HRM on affective commitment: considering climate strength. *Personnel Review* 37 (4): 412–425.

Sayles, Leonard R. 2006. The tipping point: how good executives go bad. *Corporate Finance Review* 11 (1): 18–26.

Schlenker, B. R., and M. F. Weigold. 1992. Interpersonal processes involving impression regulation and management. *Annual Review of Psychology* 43: 133–168.

Shapiro, Susan. 1990. Collaring the crime, not the criminal: reconsidering the concept of white-collar crime. *American Sociological Review* 55 (3): 346–365.

Sheridan, T.A. 2005. *Voicing women managers' unemployment experience in Australia: the hidden toll*. Perth: Women Chiefs of Enterprises International (Australia), August.

Sheridan, T.A. 2008. Emotive profiling. Vol. 1, 74–88. In *Aviation security management*, 3 vols, edited by Andrew R. Thomas. Westport, CT: Praeger Security International.

Sheridan, T.A. 2010. *'Delusional' Senior Accountant Causer stole $20M*. Available at: http://executivefraudsters.com/category/likeable-fraudster/page/4/ (accessed 28 August 2010)

Sheridan, T.A. 2011. A smartest guy in the room about to be released. Available at http: //executivefraudsters.com (accessed 1 February 2013)

Sherman, Lawrence W., and Heather Strang 2007. *Restoratve justice: the evidence*. London: The Smith Institute. http://www.restorativejustice.org/10fulltext/restorative-justice-the-evidence (accessed 3 April 2009).

Shichor, David. 2009. 'Scholarly influence' and white-collar crime scholarship. *Crime, Law and Social Change* 51 (1): 175–187.

Shover, Neal, and Francis T. Cullen. 2008. Studying and teaching white collar crime: populist and patrician perspectives. *Journal of Criminal Justice Education* 19 (2): 155–174.

Silvester, J., F. M. Anderson-Gough, N. R. Anderson, and A. R. Mohamed. 2002. Locus of control, attributions and impression management in the selection interview. *Journal of Occupational and Organizational Psychology* 75 (1): 59–77.

Simmel, G. 1904. The sociology of conflict. I. *The American Journal of Sociology* 9 (4): 490–525.

Sinha, P. N., and B. Jackson. 2006. A Burkean inquiry into leader–follower identification motives. *Culture and Organization* 12 (3): 233–247.

Smith, Russell G. 1997. Measuring the extent of fraud in Australia. In *Trends and issues in crime and criminal justice*, No. 74. Canberra: Australian Institute of Criminology. Available online at: http://aic.gov.au/documents/2/F/9/%7B2F915E58-E75E-4E30-A428-0215B2AFA36E%7Dti74.pdf (Accessed 27 November 2009).

Smith, Russell. 1999. *Organisations as victims of fraud, and how they deal with it*. Canberra: Australian Institute of Criminology.

Smith, T. 2003. The metaphysical case for honesty. *Journal of Value Inquiry* 37 (4): 517–531.

Smith, Tony R. 2004. Low self-control, staged opportunity, and subsequent fraudulent behavior. *Criminal Justice and Behaviour* 31 (5): 542–565.

Snell, R. S., and Y. L. Wong. 2007. Differentiating good soldiers from good actors. *Journal of Management Studies* 44 (6): 883–909.

Soltani, E., P.-C. Lai, R. Van Der Meer, and T. M. Williams. 2008. Managerial approaches towards service quality: the case of three service organisations. *Service Industries Journal* 28 (10): 1399–1414.

Stevens, C. K., and A. L. Kristof. 1995. Making the right impression: a field study of applicant impression management during job interviews. *Journal of Applied Psychology* 80 (5): 587–607.

Sutherland, E. H. 1940. White collar criminality. *American Sociological Review* 5 (1): 1–12.

Sykes, Gresham M., and David Matza. 1957. Techniques of neutralization: a theory of delinquency. *American Sociological Review* 22 (6): 664–670.

Takala, T., and J. Urpilainen. 1999. Managerial work and lying: a conceptual framework and an explorative case study. *Journal of Business Ethics* 20 (3): 181–195.

Tamayo, Alvaro, and Felix Raymond. 1977. Self-concept of psychopaths. *Journal of Psychology* 97 (1): 71–78.

Tanure, B., and R. Gonzalez-Duarte. 2007. Managing people in radical changes (M&As). *International Journal of Manpower* 5: 369–383.

Tinsley, Ross, and Paul A. Lynch. 2008. Differentiation and tourism destination development: Small business success in a close-knit community. *Tourism and Hospitality Research* 8 (3): 161–177.

Tittle, Charles R. 1995. *Control balance: toward a general theory of deviance.* Boulder, CO: Westview.

Tittle, Charles R. 2004. Refining control balance theory. *Theoretical Criminology* 8 (4): 395–428.

Tittle, Charles R., Mary J. Burke, Elton F. Jackson. 1986. Modeling Sutherland's theory of differential association: towards an empirical clarification. *Social Forces* 65 (2): 405–432.

Tombs, S., and D. Whyte. 2002. Unmasking the crimes of the powerful. *Critical Criminology* 11 (3): 217–236.

Tourish, D., and N. Vatcha. 2005. Charismatic leadership and corporate cultism at Enron: the elimination of dissent, the promotion of conformity and organizational collapse *Leadership* 1 (4): 455–480.

Travers, A. 1997. 'Erving Goffman and modern sociology' by Philip Manning (a review). *Reviewing Sociology* (1) (electronic article) http://www.rdg.ac.uk/RevSoc/archive/volume10/number1/10–1e.htm (accessed 28 June 2010).

Trevino, L. K., and S. A. Youngblood. 1990. Bad apples in bad barrels: a causal analysis in ethical decision-making behaviour. *Journal of Applied Psychology* 75 (4): 378–385.

Tseelon, E. 1992. Is the presented self sincere? Goffman, impression management and the postmodern self. *Theory Culture & Society* 9 (2): 115–128.

Tucker, S., N. Turner, J. Barling, E. M. Reid, and C. Elving. 2006. Apologies and transformational leadership. *Journal of Business Ethics* 63 (2): 195–207.

Turner, N., J. Barling, O. Epitropaki, V. Butcher, and C. Milner. 2002. Transformational leadership and moral reasoning. *Journal of Applied Psychology* 87 (2): 304–311.

Varma, A., S. M. Toh, and S. Pichler. 2006. Ingratiation in job applications: impact on selection decisions. *Journal of Managerial Psychology* 21 (3): 200–210.

Verrier, Nancy Newton. 1993. *The primal wound: understanding the adopted child.* Louisville, KY: Gateway Press.

Vredenburgh, D., and Y. Brender. 1998. The hierarchical abuse of power in work organizations. *Journal of Business Ethics* 17 (12): 1337–1347.

Walters, Glen D., Chad A. Brinkley, Philip R. Magaletta, and Pamela M. Diamond. 2008. Taxometric analysis of the Levenson Self-Report Psychopathy Scale. *Journal of Personality Assessment* 90 (5): 491–498.

Wareing, R., and J. Stockdale. 1989. Decision making in the promotion interview. *Management Decision* 27 (3): 22–28.

Watkins, Sherron, and Jone L. Pearce. 2003. Former Enron vice president Sherron Watkins on the Enron collapse: address to the Academy. *Academy of Management Executive* 17 (4): 119–125.

Watson, C. 1982. The presentation of self and the new institutional inmate: an analysis of prisoners' responses to assessment for release. *Symbolic Interaction* 5 (2): 243–259.

Weinstein, E. A., and L. S. Beckhouse. 1969. Audience and personality factors in presentation of self. *Sociological Quarterly* 10 (4): 527–537.

Weisenborn, D., and D. M. Norris. 1997. Red flags of management fraud. *The National Public Accountant* 42 (2): 29–35.

Weymes, E. 2004. Management theory: balancing individual freedom with organizational needs. *The Journal of Corporate Citizenship* Winter (16): 85–99.

White, R., and D. Hanson. 2002. Corporate self, corporate reputation and corporate annual reports: re-enrolling Goffman. *Scandinavian Journal of Management* 18 (3): 285–301.

Williams, K. C., E. H. Hernandez, A. R. Petrosky, and R. A. Page. 2009. The business of lying. *Journal of Leadership, Accountability and Ethics* Winter: 1–20.

Williams, Kevin M., Alicia Spidel, and Delroy L. Paulhus. 2005. Sex, lies, and more lies: exploring the intimate relationships of subclinical psychopaths. In *First Conference of the Society for the Scientific Study of Pscyhopathy*. Vancouver, BC: University of British Columbia. Available from: www2.psych.ubc.ca (accessed 23 March 2010).

Wood, R. E., and T. R. Mitchell. 1981. Manager behavior in a social context: the impact of impression management on attributions and disciplinary actions. *Organizational Behavior and Human Performance* 28 (3): 356–378.

Woods, P., and B. Jeffrey. 2002. The reconstruction of primary teachers' identities. *British Journal of Sociology of Education* 23 (1): 89–106.

Wozniak, J. F. 2001. Assessing contemporary white collar crime textbooks: a review of common themes and prospects for teaching. *Journal of Criminal Justice Education* 12 (2): 455–475.

Wozniak, John F. 2009. C. Wright Mills and higher immorality: implications for corporate crime, ethics and peacemaking criminology. *Crime Law and Social Change* 51 (1): 189–203.

Yeager, P. C. 2009. Science, values and politics: an insider's reflections on corporate crime research. *Crime Law and Social Change* 51 (1): 5–30.

Young, T. R. 1990. *The drama of social life: essays in critical dramaturgy*. Piscataway, NJ: Transaction Publishers.

Yukl, G. 1992. Consequences of influence tactics used with subordinates, peers, and the boss. *Journal of Applied Psychology* 77 (4): 525–535.

Zahra, S. A., R. L. Priem, and A. A. Rasheed. 2005. The antecedents and consequences of top management fraud. *Journal of Management* 31 (6): 803–828.

Zahra, S. A., R. L. Priem, and A. A. Rasheed. 2007. Understanding the effects of top management fraud. *Organizational Dynamics* 36 (2): 122–139.

Zimmerli, W. C., and M. S. Asslander. 2007. Business ethics as applied ethics. In *Corporate ethics and corporate governance*, ed. W. C. Zimmerli, K. Richter and M. Holzinger, 37–54. Berlin and New York: Springer.

Index

For Product Safety Concerns and Information please contact our EU representative GPSR@taylorandfrancis.com Taylor & Francis Verlag GmbH, Kaufingerstraße 24, 80331 München, Germany

Batch number: 10726294

Printed by Printforce, the Netherlands